Course Booklet

Connecting Networks

Version 6

CISCO

ciscopress.com

Cisco | Networking Academy
Mind Wide Open

Connecting Networks Version 6 Course Booklet

Copyright © 2018 Cisco Systems, Inc.

Published by:

Cisco Press

800 East 96th Street

Indianapolis, IN 46240 USA

Printed in the United States of America

1   17

Library of Congress Control Number: 2017946332

ISBN-13: 978-1-58713-431-9

ISBN-10: 1-58713-431-4

Editor-in-Chief
Mark Taub

**Alliances Manager,
Cisco Press**
Ron Fligge

Executive Editor
Mary Beth Ray

Managing Editor
Sandra Schroeder

Senior Project Editor
Tonya Simpson

Editorial Assistant
Vanessa Evans

Cover Designer
Chuti Prasertsith

Composition
codeMantra

Indexer
Cheryl Lenser

Warning and Disclaimer

This book is designed to provide information about Cisco Networking Academy Connecting Networks course. Every effort has been made to make this book as complete and as accurate as possible, but no warranty or fitness is implied.

The information is provided on an "as is" basis. The authors, Cisco Press, and Cisco Systems, Inc. shall have neither liability nor responsibility to any person or entity with respect to any loss or damages arising from the information contained in this book or from the use of the discs or programs that may accompany it.

The opinions expressed in this book belong to the author and are not necessarily those of Cisco Systems, Inc.

Trademark Acknowledgments

All terms mentioned in this book that are known to be trademarks or service marks have been appropriately capitalized. Cisco Press or Cisco Systems, Inc., cannot attest to the accuracy of this information. Use of a term in this book should not be regarded as affecting the validity of any trademark or service mark.

Feedback Information

At Cisco Press, our goal is to create in-depth technical books of the highest quality and value. Each book is crafted with care and precision, undergoing rigorous development that involves the unique expertise of members from the professional technical community.

Readers' feedback is a natural continuation of this process. If you have any comments regarding how we could improve the quality of this book, or otherwise alter it to better suit your needs, you can contact us through email at feedback@ciscopress.com. Please make sure to include the book title and ISBN in your message.

We greatly appreciate your assistance.

Reader Services

Register your copy at www.ciscopress.com/title/9781587134319 for convenient access to downloads, updates, and corrections as they become available. To start the registration process, go to www.ciscopress.com/register and log in or create an account*. Enter the product ISBN 9781587134319 and click Submit. When the process is complete, you will find any available bonus content under Registered Products.

*Be sure to check the box that you would like to hear from us to receive exclusive discounts on future editions of this product.

CISCO.

Americas Headquarters	Asia Pacific Headquarters	Europe Headquarters
Cisco Systems, Inc.	Cisco Systems (USA) Pte. Ltd.	Cisco Systems International BV Amsterdam,
San Jose, CA	Singapore	The Netherlands

Cisco has more than 200 offices worldwide. Addresses, phone numbers, and fax numbers are listed on the Cisco Website at **www.cisco.com/go/offices.**

Cisco and the Cisco logo are trademarks or registered trademarks of Cisco and/or its affiliates in the U.S. and other countries. To view a list of Cisco trademarks, go to this URL: www.cisco.com/go/trademarks. Third party trademarks mentioned are the property of their respective owners. The use of the word partner does not imply a partnership relationship between Cisco and any other company. (1110R)

Contents at a Glance

Contents

Command Syntax Conventions

The conventions used to present command syntax in this book are the same conventions used in the IOS Command Reference. The Command Reference describes these conventions as follows:

- **Boldface** indicates commands and keywords that are entered literally as shown. In actual configuration examples and output (not general command syntax), boldface indicates commands that are manually input by the user (such as a **show** command).

- *Italic* indicates arguments for which you supply actual values.

- Vertical bars (|) separate alternative, mutually exclusive elements.

- Square brackets ([ ]) indicate an optional element.

- Braces ({ }) indicate a required choice.

- Braces within brackets ([{ }]) indicate a required choice within an optional element.

About This Course Booklet

Your Cisco Networking Academy Course Booklet is designed as a study resource you can easily read, highlight, and review on the go, wherever the Internet is not available or practical:

- The text is extracted directly, word-for-word, from the online course so you can highlight important points and take notes in the "Your Chapter Notes" section.

- Headings with the exact page correlations provide a quick reference to the online course for your classroom discussions and exam preparation.

- An icon system directs you to the online curriculum to take full advantage of the images embedded within the Networking Academy online course interface and reminds you to perform the labs, Class activities, Interactive activities, Packet Tracer activities, watch videos, and take the chapter quizzes and exams.

The Course Booklet is a basic, economical paper-based resource to help you succeed with the Cisco Networking Academy online course.

Companion Guide

Looking for more than the online curriculum? The Companion Guide is fully aligned with Networking Academy's online course chapters and offers additional book-based pedagogy to reinforce key concepts, enhance student comprehension, and promote retention. Using this full-fledged textbook, students can focus scarce study time, organize review for quizzes and exams, and get the day-to-day reference answers they're looking for.

The Companion Guide also offers instructors additional opportunities to assign take-home reading or vocabulary homework, helping students prepare more for in-class lab work and discussions.

Available in print and all major eBook formats (book: 9781587134326; eBook: 9780134760889).

Course Introduction

0.0 Connecting Networks

0.0.1 Message to the Student

Refer to
Online Course
for Illustration

0.0.1.1 Welcome

Welcome to the CCNA R&S Connecting Networks course. The goal of this course is to introduce you to fundamental networking concepts and technologies. These online course materials will assist you in developing the skills necessary to plan and implement small networks across a range of applications.

You can use your smart phone, tablet, laptop, or desktop to access your course, participate in discussions with your instructor, view your grades, read or review text, and practice using interactive media. However, some media are complex and must be viewed on a PC, as well as Packet Tracer activities, quizzes, and exams.

Refer to
Online Course
for Illustration

0.0.1.2 A Global Community

When you participate in the Networking Academy, you are joining a global community linked by common goals and technologies. Schools, colleges, universities, and other entities in over 160 countries participate in the program. A visualization of the global Networking Academy community is available at http://www.netacad.com.

Look for the Cisco Networking Academy official site on Facebook and LinkedIn. The Facebook site is where you can meet and engage with other Networking Academy students from around the world. The Cisco Networking Academy LinkedIn site connects you with job postings, and you can see how others are effectively communicating their skills.

Refer to
Online Course
for Illustration

0.0.1.3 More Than Just Information

The NetAcad learning environment is an important part of the overall course experience for students and instructors in the Networking Academy. These online course materials include course text and related interactive media, Packet Tracer simulation activities, real equipment labs, remote access labs, and many different types of quizzes. All of these materials provide important feedback to help you assess your progress throughout the course.

The material in this course encompasses a broad range of technologies that facilitate how people work, live, play, and learn by communicating with voice, video, and other data. Networking and the internet affect people differently in different parts of the world. Although we have worked with instructors from around the world to create these materials, it is important that you work with your instructor and fellow students to make the material in this course applicable to your local situation.

Refer to
Online Course
for Illustration

0.0.1.4 How We Teach

E doing is a design philosophy that applies the principle that people learn best by doing. The curriculum includes embedded, highly interactive E doing activities to help stimulate learning, increase knowledge retention, and make the whole learning experience much richer - and that makes understanding the content much easier.

Refer to
Online Course
for Illustration

0.0.1.5 Practice Leads to Mastery

In a typical lesson, after learning about a topic for the first time, you will check your understanding with some interactive media items. If there are new commands to learn, you will practice them with the Syntax Checker before using the commands to configure or troubleshoot a network in Packet Tracer, the Networking Academy network simulation tool. Next, you will do practice activities on real equipment in your classroom or accessed remotely over the internet.

Packet Tracer can also provide additional practice any time by creating your own activities or you may want to competitively test your skills with classmates in multi-user games. Packet Tracer skills assessments and skills integration labs give you rich feedback on the skills you are able to demonstrate and are great practice for chapter, checkpoint, and final exams.

Refer to
Online Course
for Illustration

0.0.1.6 Mind Wide Open

An important goal in education is to enrich you, the student, by expanding what you know and can do. It is important to realize, however, that the instructional materials and the instructor can only facilitate the process. You must make the commitment yourself to learn new skills. The following pages share a few suggestions to help you learn and prepare for transitioning your new skills to the workplace.

Refer to
Online Course
for Illustration

0.0.1.7 Engineering Journals

Professionals in the networking field often keep Engineering Journals in which they write down the things they observe and learn such as how to use protocols and commands. Keeping an Engineering Journal creates a reference you can use at work in your ICT job. Writing is one way to reinforce your learning – along with Reading, Seeing, and Practicing.

A sample entry for implementing a technology could include the necessary software commands, the purpose of the commands, command variables, and a topology diagram indicating the context for using the commands to configure the technology.

Refer to
Online Course
for Illustration

0.0.1.8 Explore the World of Networking

Packet Tracer is a networking learning tool that supports a wide range of physical and logical simulations. It also provides visualization tools to help you understand the internal workings of a network.

The pre-made Packet Tracer activities consist of network simulations, games, activities, and challenges that provide a broad range of learning experiences. These tools will help you develop an understanding of how data flows in a network.

Refer to
Online Course
for Illustration

0.0.1.9 Create Your Own Worlds

You can also use Packet Tracer to create your own experiments and networking scenarios. We hope that, over time, you consider using Packet Tracer - not only for experiencing the pre-built activities, but also to become an author, explorer, and experimenter.

The online course materials have embedded Packet Tracer activities that will launch on computers running Windows operating systems, if Packet Tracer is installed. This integration may also work on other operating systems using Windows emulation.

Refer to
Online Course
for Illustration

0.0.1.10 How Packet Tracer Helps Master Concepts

Educational Games

Packet Tracer Multi-User games enable you or a team to compete with other students to see who can accurately complete a series of networking tasks the fastest. It is an excellent way to practice the skills you are learning in Packet Tracer activities and hands-on labs.

Cisco Aspire is a single-player, standalone strategic simulation game. Players test their networking skills by completing contracts in a virtual city. The Networking Academy Edition is specifically designed to help you prepare for the CCENT certification exam. It also incorporates business and communication skills ICT employers seek in job candidates.

Performance-Based Assessments

The Networking Academy performance-based assessments have you do Packet Tracer activities like you have been doing all along, only now integrated with an online assessment engine that will automatically score your results and provide you with immediate feedback. This feedback helps you to more accurately identify the knowledge and skills you have mastered and where you need more practice. There are also questions on chapter quizzes and exams that use Packet Tracer activities to give you additional feedback on your progress.

Refer to
Online Course
for Illustration

0.0.1.11 Course Overview

As the course title states, the focus of this course is on the WAN technologies and network services required by converged applications in a complex network. In this course, you will learn the selection criteria of network devices and WAN technologies to meet network requirements. You will do the following:

- Describe different WAN technologies and their benefits

- Configure and troubleshoot PPP

- Configure PPPoE, GRE, and single-homed eBGP

- Configure and troubleshoot extended IPv4 and IPv6 ACLs

- Explain how to mitigate common LAN security attacks

- Describe QoS operation

- Describe evolving networks including cloud, virtualization, SDN, and the Internet of Things

- Troubleshoot end-to-end connectivity in a small to medium-sized business network, using a systematic approach

WAN Concepts

1.0 Introduction

Refer to
Online Course
for Illustration

1.0.1.1 Chapter 1: WAN Concepts

Businesses must connect LANs to provide communications between them, even when these LANs are far apart. Wide-area networks (WANs) are used to connect remote LANs. A WAN may cover a city, country, or global region. A WAN is owned by a service provider, and a business pays a fee to use the provider's WAN network services.

Different technologies are used for WANs than for LANs. This chapter introduces WAN standards, technologies, and purposes. It covers selecting the appropriate WAN technologies, services, and devices to meet the changing business requirements of an evolving enterprise.

Refer to
Online Course
for Illustration

1.0.1.2 Class Activity – Branching Out

Branching Out

Your medium-sized company is opening a new branch office to serve a wider, client-based network. This branch will focus on regular, day-to-day network operations, but will also provide TelePresence, web conferencing, IP telephony, video on demand, and wireless services.

Although you know that an ISP can provide WAN routers and switches to accommodate the branch office connectivity for the network, you prefer to use your own customer premises equipment (CPE). To ensure interoperability, Cisco devices have been used in all other branch-office WANs.

As the branch-office network administrator, it is your responsibility to research possible network devices for purchase and use over the WAN.

1.1 WAN Technologies Overview

1.1.1 Purpose of WANs

Refer to
Online Course
for Illustration

1.1.1.1 Why a WAN?

A WAN operates beyond the geographic scope of a LAN. As shown in the figure, WANs are used to interconnect the enterprise LAN to remote LANs in branch sites and telecommuter sites.

A WAN is owned by a service provider. An organization must pay a fee to use the provider's network services to connect remote sites. WAN service providers include carriers, such as a telephone network, cable company, or satellite service. Service providers provide links to interconnect remote sites for the purpose of transporting data, voice, and video.

In contrast, LANs are typically owned by an organization and used to connect local computers, peripherals, and other devices within a single building or other small geographic area.

Refer to
Online Course
for Illustration

1.1.1.2   Are WANs Necessary?

Without WANs, LANs would be a series of isolated networks. LANs provide both speed and cost-efficiency for transmitting data over relatively small geographic areas. However, as organizations expand, businesses require communication among geographically separated sites. The following are some examples:

- Regional or branch offices of an organization need to be able to communicate and share data with the central site.

- Organizations need to share information with other customer organizations. For example, software manufacturers routinely communicate product and promotional information to distributors that sell their products to end users.

- Employees who travel on company business frequently need to access information that resides on their corporate networks.

Home computer users also need to send and receive data across increasingly larger distances. Here are some examples:

- Consumers now commonly communicate over the Internet with banks, stores, and a variety of providers of goods and services.

- Students do research for classes by accessing library indexes and publications located in other parts of their country and in other parts of the world.

It is not feasible to connect computers across a country, or around the world, with physical cables. Therefore, different technologies have evolved to support this communication requirement. Increasingly, the Internet is being used as an inexpensive alternative to enterprise WANs. New technologies are available to businesses to provide security and privacy for their Internet communications and transactions. WANs used by themselves, or in concert with the Internet, allow organizations and individuals to meet their wide-area communication needs.

Refer to
Interactive Graphic
in online course

1.1.1.3   WAN Topologies

Interconnecting multiple sites across WANs can involve a variety of service provider technologies and WAN topologies. Common WAN topologies are:

- Point-to-Point

- Hub-and-Spoke

- Full Mesh

- Dual-Homed

Point-to-Point

A point-to-point topology, as shown in Figure 1, employs a point-to-point circuit between two endpoints. Typically involving dedicated leased-line connections like T1/E1 lines, a point-to-point connection involves a Layer 2 transport service through the service provider network. Packets sent from one site are delivered to the other site and vice versa. A point-to-point connection is transparent to the customer network, as if there was a direct physical link between two endpoints.

Hub-and-Spoke

If a private network connection between multiple sites is required, then a point-to-point topology with multiple point-to-point circuits is one option. Each point-to-point circuit requires its own dedicated hardware interface which will require multiple routers with multiple WAN interface cards. This can be expensive. A less expensive option is a point-to-multipoint topology, also known as a hub and spoke topology.

With a hub-and-spoke topology a single interface to the hub can be shared by all spoke circuits. For example, spoke sites can be interconnected through the hub site using virtual circuits and routed subinterfaces at the hub. A hub-and-spoke topology is also an example of a single-homed topology. Figure 2 displays a sample hub-and-spoke topology consisting of four routers with one router as hub connected to the other three spoke routers across a WAN cloud.

Full Mesh

One of the disadvantages of hub-and-spoke topologies is that all communication has to go through the hub. With a full mesh topology using virtual circuits, any site can communicate directly with any other site. The disadvantage here is the large number of virtual circuits that need to be configured and maintained. Figure 3 displays a sample full mesh topology consisting of four routers connected to each other across a WAN cloud.

Dual-homed Topology

A dual-homed topology provides redundancy. As shown in Figure 4, two hub routers are dual-homed and redundantly attached to three spoke routers across a WAN cloud. The disadvantage to dual-homed topologies is that they are more expensive to implement than single-homed topologies. This is because they require additional networking hardware, like additional routers and switches. Dual-homed topologies are also more difficult to implement because they require additional, and more complex, configurations. However, the advantage of dual-homed topologies is that they offer enhanced network redundancy, load balancing, distributed computing or processing, and the ability to implement backup service provider connections.

1.1.1.4 Evolving Networks

Refer to Online Course for Illustration

Every business is unique and how an organization grows depends on many factors. These factors include the type of products or service the business sells, the management philosophy of the owners, and the economic climate of the country in which the business operates.

In slow economic times, many businesses focus on increasing their profitability by improving the efficiency of their existing operations, increasing employee productivity, and lowering operating costs. Establishing and managing networks can represent significant installation and operating expenses. To justify such a large expense, companies expect their networks to perform optimally and to be able to deliver an ever increasing array of services and applications to support productivity and profitability.

The example used in this chapter is of a fictitious company called SPAN Engineering. This topic will illustrate how SPAN's network requirements change as the company grows from a small, local, business into a global enterprise.

Refer to **Online Course** for Illustration

1.1.1.5 Small Office

SPAN Engineering, an environmental consulting firm, has developed a special process for converting household waste into electricity and is developing a small pilot project for a municipal government in its local area. The company, which has been in business for four years, has grown to include 15 employees: six engineers, four computer-aided drawing (CAD) designers, a receptionist, two senior partners, and two office assistants.

SPAN Engineering's management is working to win full-scale contracts after the pilot project successfully demonstrates the feasibility of their process. Until then, the company must manage its costs carefully.

For their small office, SPAN Engineering uses a single LAN to share information between computers, and to share peripherals, such as a printer, a large-scale plotter (to print engineering drawings), and fax equipment. They have recently upgraded their LAN to provide inexpensive Voice over IP (VoIP) service to save on the costs of separate phone lines for their employees.

Connection to the Internet is through a common broadband service called Digital Subscriber Line (DSL), which is supplied by their local telephone service provider. With so few employees, bandwidth is not a significant problem.

The company cannot afford in-house IT support staff, and uses support services purchased from the DSL provider. The company also uses a hosting service rather than purchasing and operating its own FTP and email servers.

The figure shows an example of a small office and its network.

Refer to **Online Course** for Illustration

1.1.1.6 Campus Network

Five years later, SPAN Engineering has grown rapidly. The company was contracted to design and implement a full-sized waste conversion facility soon after the successful implementation of their first pilot plant. Since then, SPAN has won other projects in neighboring municipalities, and in other parts of the country.

To handle the additional workload, the business has hired more staff and leased more office space. It is now a small- to medium-sized business with several hundred employees. Many projects are being developed at the same time, and each requires a project manager and support staff. The company has organized itself into functional departments, with each department having its own organizational team. To meet its growing needs, the company has moved into several floors of a larger office building.

As the business has expanded, the network has also grown. Instead of a single small LAN, the network now consists of several subnetworks, each devoted to a different department. For example, all the engineering staff is on one LAN, while the marketing staff is on another LAN. These multiple LANs are joined to create a company-wide network, or campus, which spans several floors of the building.

The business now has in-house IT staff to support and maintain the network. The network includes dedicated servers for email, data transfer, and file storage, and web-based productivity tools and applications. There is also a company intranet to provide in-house documents and information to employees. An extranet provides project information to designated customers.

The figure shows an example of SPAN's campus network.

Refer to
Online Course
for Illustration

1.1.1.7   Branch Networks

Another six years later, SPAN Engineering has been so successful with its patented process that demand for its services has skyrocketed. New projects are underway in multiple cities. To manage those projects, the company has opened small branch offices closer to the project sites.

This situation presents new challenges to the IT team. To manage the delivery of information and services throughout the company, SPAN Engineering now has a data center, which houses the various databases and servers of the company. To ensure that all parts of the business are able to access the same services and applications regardless of where the offices are located, the company must now implement a WAN.

For its branch offices that are in nearby cities, the company decides to use private dedicated lines through their local service provider. However, for those offices that are located in other countries, the Internet is an attractive WAN connection option. Although connecting offices through the Internet is economical, it introduces security and privacy issues that the IT team must address.

Refer to
Interactive Graphic
in online course

1.1.1.8   Distributed Network

SPAN Engineering has now been in business for 20 years and has grown to thousands of employees distributed in offices worldwide, as shown in Figure 1. The cost of the network and its related services is a significant expense. The company is looking to provide its employees with the best network services at the lowest cost. Optimized network services would allow each employee to work at a high rate of efficiency.

To increase profitability, SPAN Engineering must reduce its operating expenses. It has relocated some of its office facilities to less expensive areas. The company is also encouraging teleworking and virtual teams. Web-based applications, including web-conferencing, e-learning, and online collaboration tools, are being used to increase productivity and reduce costs. Site-to-site and remote access Virtual Private Networks (VPNs) enable the company to use the Internet to connect easily and securely with employees and facilities around the world. To meet these requirements, the network must provide the necessary converged services and secure Internet WAN connectivity to remote offices and individuals, as shown in Figure 2.

As seen in this example, network requirements of a company can change dramatically as the company grows over time. Distributing employees saves costs in many ways, but it puts increased demands on the network. Not only must a network meet the day-to-day operational needs of the business, but it must be able to adapt and grow as the company changes. Network designers and administrators meet these challenges by carefully choosing network technologies, protocols, and service providers. They must also optimize their networks by using many of the network design techniques and architectures described in this course.

Refer to
Interactive Graphic
in online course

1.1.1.9   Activity - Identify WAN Topologies

1.1.2   WAN Operations

Refer to
Online Course
for Illustration

1.1.2.1   WANs in the OSI Model

WAN operations focus primarily on the physical layer (OSI Layer 1) and the data link layer (OSI Layer 2). WAN access standards typically describe both physical layer delivery methods and data link layer requirements. The data link layer requirements include physical addressing, flow control, and encapsulation.

WAN access standards are defined and managed by a number of recognized authorities:

- Telecommunications Industry Association and the Electronic Industries Alliance (TIA/EIA)

- International Organization for Standardization (ISO)

- Institute of Electrical and Electronics Engineers (IEEE)

Layer 1 protocols describe how to provide electrical, mechanical, operational, and functional connections to the services of a communications service provider.

Layer 2 protocols define how data is encapsulated for transmission toward a remote location, and the mechanisms for transferring the resulting frames. A variety of different technologies are used, such as the Point-to-Point Protocol (PPP), Frame Relay, and ATM. Some of these protocols use the same basic framing or a subset of the High-Level Data Link Control (HDLC) mechanism.

Most WAN links are point-to-point. For this reason, the address field in the Layer 2 frame is usually not used.

Refer to
Online Course
for Illustration

1.1.2.2   Common WAN Terminology

One primary difference between a WAN and a LAN is that a company or organization must subscribe to an outside WAN service provider to use WAN carrier network services. A WAN uses data links provided by carrier services to access the Internet and connect different locations of an organization to each other. These data links also connect to locations of other organizations, to external services, and to remote users.

The physical layer of a WAN describes the physical connections between the company network and the service provider network. The figure illustrates the terminology commonly used to describe WAN connections:

- **Customer Premises Equipment (CPE)** - The CPE consists of the devices and inside wiring located on the enterprise edge connecting to a carrier link. The subscriber either owns the CPE or leases the CPE from the service provider. A subscriber, in this context, is a company that arranges for WAN services from a service provider.

- **Data Communications Equipment (DCE)** - Also called data circuit-terminating equipment, the DCE consists of devices that put data on the local loop. The DCE primarily provides an interface to connect subscribers to a communication link on the WAN cloud.

- **Data Terminal Equipment (DTE)** - The customer devices that pass the data from a customer network or host computer for transmission over the WAN. The DTE connects to the local loop through the DCE.

- **Demarcation Point** - This is a point established in a building or complex to separate customer equipment from service provider equipment. Physically, the demarcation point is the cabling junction box, located on the customer premises, that connects the CPE wiring to the local loop. It is usually placed for easy access by a technician. The demarcation point is the place where the responsibility for the connection changes from the user to the service provider. When problems arise, it is necessary to determine whether the user or the service provider is responsible for troubleshooting or repair.

- **Local Loop** - The actual copper or fiber cable that connects the CPE to the CO of the service provider. The local loop is also sometimes called the "last-mile".

- **Central Office (CO)** - The CO is the local service provider facility or building that connects the CPE to the provider network.

- **Toll network** - This consists of the long-haul, all-digital, fiber-optic communications lines, switches, routers, and other equipment inside the WAN provider network.

Refer to
Online Course
for Illustration

1.1.2.3   WAN Devices

There are many types of devices that are specific to WAN environments:

- **Dialup modem** - Voiceband modems are considered to be a legacy WAN technology. A voiceband modem converts (i.e., modulates) the digital signals produced by a computer into voice frequencies. These frequencies are then transmitted over the analog lines of the public telephone network. On the other side of the connection, another modem converts the sounds back into a digital signal (i.e., demodulates) for input to a computer or network connection.

- **Access server** - This server controls and coordinates dialup modem, dial-in and dial-out user communications. Considered to be a legacy technology, an access server may have a mixture of analog and digital interfaces and support hundreds of simultaneous users.

- **Broadband modem** - A type of digital modem used with high-speed DSL or cable Internet service. Both operate in a similar manner to the voiceband modem, but use higher broadband frequencies and transmission speeds.

- **CSU/DSU** - Digital-leased lines require a CSU and a DSU. A CSU/DSU can be a separate device like a modem or it can be an interface on a router. The CSU provides termination for the digital signal and ensures connection integrity through error correction and line monitoring. The DSU converts the line frames into frames that the LAN can interpret and vice versa.

- **WAN switch** - A multiport internetworking device used in service provider networks. These devices typically switch traffic, such as Frame Relay or ATM, and operate at Layer 2.

- **Router** - Provides internetworking and WAN access interface ports that are used to connect to the service provider network. These interfaces may be serial connections, Ethernet, or other WAN interfaces. With some types of WAN interfaces, an external device, such as a DSU/CSU or modem (analog, cable, or DSL), is required to connect the router to the local service provider.

- **Core router/Multilayer switch** - A router or multilayer switch that resides within the middle or backbone of the WAN, rather than at its periphery. To fulfill this role, a router or multilayer switch must be able to support multiple telecommunications interfaces of the highest speed used in the WAN core. It must also be able to forward IP packets at full speed on all of those interfaces. The router or multilayer switch must also support the routing protocols being used in the core.

Note The preceding list is not exhaustive and other devices may be required, depending on the WAN access technology chosen.

WAN technologies are either circuit-switched or packet-switched. The type of devices used depends on the WAN technology implemented.

1.1.2.4 Circuit Switching

Refer to **Video** in online course

A circuit-switched network is one that establishes a dedicated circuit (or channel) between nodes and terminals before the users may communicate. Specifically, circuit switching dynamically establishes a dedicated virtual connection for voice or data between a sender and a receiver. Before communication can start, it is necessary to establish the connection through the network of the service provider.

As an example, when a subscriber makes a telephone call, the dialed number is used to set switches in the exchanges along the route of the call so that there is a continuous circuit from the caller to the called party. Because of the switching operation used to establish the circuit, the telephone system is called a circuit-switched network. If the telephones are replaced with modems, then the switched circuit is able to carry computer data.

If the circuit carries computer data, the usage of this fixed capacity may not be efficient. For example, if the circuit is used to access the Internet, there is a burst of activity on the circuit while a web page is transferred. This could be followed by no activity while the user reads the page, and then another burst of activity while the next page is transferred. This variation in usage between none and maximum is typical of computer network traffic. Because the subscriber has sole use of the fixed capacity allocation, switched circuits are generally an expensive way of moving data.

The two most common types of circuit-switched WAN technologies are the public switched telephone network (PSTN) and the Integrated Services Digital Network (ISDN).

Click Play in the figure to see how circuit switching works.

1.1.2.5 Packet Switching

Refer to **Video** in online course

In contrast to circuit switching, packet switching splits traffic data into packets that are routed over a shared network. Packet-switching networks do not require a circuit to be established, and they allow many pairs of nodes to communicate over the same channel.

The switches in a packet-switched network (PSN) determine the links that packets must be sent over based on the addressing information in each packet. The following are two approaches to this link determination:

- **Connectionless systems** - Full addressing information must be carried in each packet. Each switch must evaluate the address to determine where to send the packet. An example of a connectionless system is the Internet.

- **Connection-oriented systems** - The network predetermines the route for a packet, and each packet only has to carry an identifier. The switch determines the onward route by looking up the identifier in tables held in memory. The set of entries in the tables identifies a particular route or circuit through the system. When the circuit is established temporarily while a packet is traveling through it, and then breaks down again, it is called a virtual circuit (VC). An example of a connection-oriented system is Frame Relay. In the case of Frame Relay, the identifiers used are called data-link connection identifiers (DLCIs).

Because the internal links between the switches are shared between many users, the cost of packet switching is lower than that of circuit switching. However, delays (latency) and variability of delay (jitter) are greater in packet-switched networks than in circuit-switched networks. This is because the links are shared, and packets must be entirely received at one switch before moving to the next. Despite the latency and jitter inherent in shared networks, modern technology allows satisfactory transport of voice and video communications on these networks.

Click Play in the figure to see a packet-switching example. In the animation, SRV1 is sending data to SRV2. As the packet traverses the provider network, it arrives at the first provider switch. The packet is added to the queue and forwarded after the other packets in the queue have been forwarded. Eventually, the packet reaches SRV2.

> Refer to
> **Interactive Graphic**
> in online course

1.1.2.6   Activity - Identify WAN Terminology

1.2   Selecting a WAN Technology

1.2.1   WAN Services

> Refer to
> **Interactive Graphic**
> in online course

1.2.1.1   WAN Link Connection Options

There are several WAN access connection options that ISPs can use to connect the local loop to the enterprise edge. These WAN access options differ in technology, speed, and cost. Each has distinct advantages and disadvantages. Familiarity with these technologies is an important part of network design.

As shown in Figure 1, there are two way that an enterprise can get WAN access:

- **Private WAN infrastructure** - Service providers may offer dedicated point-to-point leased lines, circuit-switched links, such as PSTN or ISDN, and packet-switched links, such as Ethernet WAN, ATM, or Frame Relay.

- **Public WAN infrastructure** - Service providers may offer broadband Internet access using digital subscriber line (DSL), cable, and satellite access. Broadband connection options are typically used to connect small offices and telecommuting employees to a corporate site over the Internet. Data travelling between corporate sites over the public WAN infrastructure should be protected using VPNs.

The topology in Figure 2 illustrates some of these WAN access technologies.

Refer to
Interactive Graphic
in online course

1.2.1.2   Service Provider Network Infrastructure

When a WAN service provider receives data from a client at a site, it must forward the data to the remote site for final delivery to the recipient. In some cases, the remote site may be connected to the same service provider as the originating site. In other cases, the remote site may be connected to a different ISP, and the originating ISP must pass the data to the connecting ISP.

Long-range communications are usually those connections between ISPs, or between branch offices in very large companies.

Service provider networks are complex. They consist mostly of high-bandwidth fiber-optic media, using either the Synchronous Optical Networking (SONET) or Synchronous Digital Hierarchy (SDH) standard. These standards define how to transfer multiple data, voice, and video traffic over optical fiber using lasers or light-emitting diodes (LEDs) over great distances.

Note   SONET is an American-based ANSI standard, while SDH is a European-based ETSI and ITU standard. Both are essentially the same and, therefore, often listed as SONET/SDH.

A newer fiber-optic media development for long-range communications is called dense wavelength division multiplexing (DWDM). DWDM multiplies the amount of bandwidth that a single strand of fiber can support, as shown in Figure 1.

There are several ways that DWDM enables long-range communication:

- Enables bidirectional communications over one strand of fiber.
- Can multiplex more than 80 different channels of data (i.e., wavelengths) onto a single fiber.
- Each channel is capable of carrying a 10 Gb/s multiplexed signal.
- Assigns incoming optical signals to specific wavelengths of light (i.e., frequencies).
- Can amplify these wavelengths to boost the signal strength.
- Supports SONET and SDH standards.

DWDM circuits are used in all modern submarine communications cable systems and other long-haul circuits, as shown in Figure 2.

Refer to
Interactive Graphic
in online course

1.2.1.3   Activity - Classify WAN Access Options

1.2.2   Private WAN Infrastructures

Refer to
Online Course
for Illustration

1.2.2.1   Leased Lines

When permanent dedicated connections are required, a point-to-point link is used to provide a pre-established WAN communications path from the customer premises to the provider network. Point-to-point lines are usually leased from a service provider and are called leased lines.

Leased lines have existed since the early 1950s and for this reason, are referred to by different names such as leased circuits, serial link, serial line, point-to-point link, and T1/E1 or T3/E3 lines. The term leased line refers to the fact that the organization pays a monthly lease fee to a service provider to use the line. Leased lines are available in different capacities and are generally priced based on the bandwidth required and the distance between the two connected points.

In North America, service providers use the T-carrier system to define the digital transmission capability of a serial copper media link, while Europe uses the E-carrier system, as shown in the figure. For instance, a T1 link supports 1.544 Mb/s, an E1 supports 2.048 Mb/s, a T3 supports 43.7 Mb/s, and an E3 connection supports 34.368 Mb/s. Optical Carrier (OC) transmission rates are used to define the digital transmitting capacity of a fiber-optic network.

There are advantages to the use of leased lines:

- **Simplicity** - Point-to-point communication links require minimal expertise to install and maintain.

- **Quality** - Point-to-point communication links usually offer high service quality, if they have adequate bandwidth. The dedicated capacity removes latency or jitter between the endpoints.

- **Availability** - Constant availability is essential for some applications, such as e-commerce. Point-to-point communication links provide permanent, dedicated capacity which is required for VoIP or Video over IP.

There are also disadvantages to the use of leased lines:

- **Cost** - Point-to-point links are generally the most expensive type of WAN access. The cost of leased line solutions can become significant when they are used to connect many sites over increasing distances. In addition, each endpoint requires an interface on the router, which increases equipment costs.

- **Limited flexibility** - WAN traffic is often variable, and leased lines have a fixed capacity, so that the bandwidth of the line seldom matches the need exactly. Any change to the leased line generally requires a site visit by ISP personnel to adjust capacity.

The Layer 2 protocol is usually HDLC or PPP.

1.2.2.2   Dialup

Refer to **Online Course** for Illustration

Dialup WAN access may be required when no other WAN technology is available. For example, a remote location could use modems and analog dialed telephone lines to provide low capacity and dedicated switched connections. Dialup access is suitable when intermittent, low-volume data transfers are needed.

Traditional telephony uses a copper cable, called the local loop, to connect the telephone handset in the subscriber premises to the CO. The signal on the local loop during a call is a continuously varying electronic signal that is a translation of the subscriber voice into an analog signal.

Traditional local loops can transport binary computer data through the voice telephone network using a modem. The modem modulates the binary data into an analog signal at the source and demodulates the analog signal to binary data at the destination. The physical characteristics of the local loop and its connection to the PSTN limit the rate of the signal to less than 56 kb/s.

For small businesses, these relatively low-speed dialup connections are adequate for the exchange of sales figures, prices, routine reports, and email. Using automatic dialup at night or on weekends for large file transfers and data backup can take advantage of lower off-peak tariffs (toll charges). Tariffs are based on the distance between the endpoints, time of day, and the duration of the call.

The advantages of modem and analog lines are simplicity, availability, and low implementation cost. The disadvantages are the low data rates and a relatively long connection time. The dedicated circuit has little delay or jitter for point-to-point traffic, but voice or video traffic does not operate adequately at these low bit rates.

Note   Although very few enterprises support dialup access, it is still a viable solution for remote areas with limited WAN access options.

Refer to
Interactive Graphic
in online course

1.2.2.3   ISDN

Integrated Services Digital Network (ISDN) is a circuit-switching technology that enables the local loop of a PSTN to carry digital signals, resulting in higher capacity switched connections.

ISDN changes the internal connections of the PSTN from carrying analog signals to time-division multiplexed (TDM) digital signals. TDM allows two or more signals, or bit streams, to be transferred as subchannels in one communication channel. The signals appear to transfer simultaneously; but physically, the signals are taking turns on the channel.

Figure 1 displays a sample ISDN topology. The ISDN connection may require a terminal adapter (TA) which is a device used to connect ISDN Basic Rate Interface (BRI) connections to a router.

There are two types of ISDN interfaces:

■ **Basic Rate Interface (BRI)** - ISDN BRI is intended for the home and small enterprise and provides two 64 kb/s bearer channels (B) for carrying voice and data and a 16 kb/s delta channel (D) for signaling, call setup and other purposes. The BRI D channel is often underused, because it has only two B channels to control (Figure 2).

■ **Primary Rate Interface (PRI)** — ISDN is also available for larger installations. In North America, PRI delivers 23 B channels with 64 kb/s and one D channel with 64 kb/s for a total bit rate of up to 1.544 Mb/s. This includes some additional overhead for synchronization. In Europe, Australia, and other parts of the world, ISDN PRI provides 30 B channels and one D channel, for a total bit rate of up to 2.048 Mb/s, including synchronization overhead (Figure 3).

BRI has a call setup time that is less than a second, and the 64 kb/s B channel provides greater capacity than an analog modem link. If greater capacity is required, a second B channel can be activated to provide a total of 128 kb/s. This permits several simultaneous voice conversations, a voice conversation and data transfer, or a video conference using one channel for voice and the other for video.

Another common application of ISDN is to provide additional capacity as needed on a leased line connection. The leased line is sized to carry average traffic loads while ISDN is added during peak demand periods. ISDN is also used as a backup if the leased line fails.

ISDN tariffs are based on a per-B channel basis and are similar to those of analog voice connections.

With PRI ISDN, multiple B channels can be connected between two endpoints. This allows for videoconferencing and high-bandwidth data connections with no latency or jitter. However, multiple connections can be very expensive over long distances.

Note   Although ISDN is still an important technology for telephone service provider networks, it has declined in popularity as an Internet connection option with the introduction of high-speed DSL and other broadband services.

Refer to
Online Course
for Illustration

1.2.2.4   Frame Relay

Frame Relay is a simple Layer 2 non-broadcast multi-access (NBMA) WAN technology used to interconnect enterprise LANs. A single router interface can be used to connect to multiple sites using PVCs. PVCs are used to carry both voice and data traffic between a source and destination, and support data rates up to 4 Mb/s, with some providers offering even higher rates.

An edge router only requires a single interface, even when multiple virtual circuits (VCs) are used. The leased line to the Frame Relay network edge allows cost-effective connections between widely scattered LANs.

Frame Relay creates PVCs which are uniquely identified by a data-link connection identifier (DLCI). The PVCs and DLCIs ensure bidirectional communication from one DTE device to another.

For instance, in the figure, R1 will use DLCI 102 to reach R2 while R2 will use DLCI 201 to reach R1.

Refer to
Online Course
for Illustration

1.2.2.5   ATM

Asynchronous Transfer Mode (ATM) technology is capable of transferring voice, video, and data through private and public networks. It is built on a cell-based architecture rather than on a frame-based architecture. ATM cells are always a fixed length of 53 bytes. The ATM cell contains a 5-byte ATM header followed by 48 bytes of ATM payload. Small, fixed-length cells are well-suited for carrying voice and video traffic because this traffic is intolerant of delay. Video and voice traffic do not have to wait for larger data packets to be transmitted.

The 53-byte ATM cell is less efficient than the bigger frames and packets of Frame Relay. Furthermore, the ATM cell has at least 5 bytes of overhead for each 48-byte payload. When the cell is carrying segmented network layer packets, the overhead is higher because the ATM switch must be able to reassemble the packets at the destination. A typical ATM line needs almost 20 percent greater bandwidth than Frame Relay to carry the same volume of network layer data.

ATM was designed to be extremely scalable and to support link speeds of T1/E1 to OC-12 (622 Mb/s) and faster.

ATM offers both PVCs and SVCs, although PVCs are more common with WANs. As with other shared technologies, ATM allows multiple VCs on a single leased-line connection to the network edge.

Refer to
Online Course
for Illustration

1.2.2.6   Ethernet WAN

Ethernet was originally developed to be a LAN access technology. Originally Ethernet was not suitable as a WAN access technology because at that time, the maximum cable length was one kilometer. However, newer Ethernet standards using fiber-optic cables have made Ethernet a reasonable WAN access option. For instance, the IEEE 1000BASE-LX standard supports fiber-optic cable lengths of 5 km, while the IEEE 1000BASE-ZX standard supports cable lengths up to 70 km.

Service providers now offer Ethernet WAN service using fiber-optic cabling. The Ethernet WAN service can go by many names, including Metropolitan Ethernet (MetroE), Ethernet over MPLS (EoMPLS), and Virtual Private LAN Service (VPLS).

There are several benefits to an Ethernet WAN:

- **Reduced expenses and administration** - Ethernet WAN provides a switched, high-bandwidth Layer 2 network capable of managing data, voice, and video all on the same infrastructure. This characteristic increases bandwidth and eliminates expensive conversions to other WAN technologies. The technology enables businesses to inexpensively connect numerous sites in a metropolitan area, to each other, and to the Internet.

- **Easy integration with existing networks** - Ethernet WAN connects easily to existing Ethernet LANs, reducing installation costs and time.

- **Enhanced business productivity** - Ethernet WAN enables businesses to take advantage of productivity-enhancing IP applications that are difficult to implement on TDM or Frame Relay networks, such as hosted IP communications, VoIP, and streaming and broadcast video.

Note   Ethernet WANs have gained in popularity and are now commonly being used to replace the traditional Frame Relay and ATM WAN links.

Refer to
Online Course
for Illustration

1.2.2.7   MPLS

Multiprotocol Label Switching (MPLS) is a multiprotocol high-performance WAN technology that directs data from one router to the next. MPLS is based on short path labels rather than IP network addresses.

MPLS has several defining characteristics. It is multiprotocol, meaning it has the ability to carry any payload including IPv4, IPv6, Ethernet, ATM, DSL, and Frame Relay traffic. It uses labels which tell a router what to do with a packet. The labels identify paths between distant routers rather than endpoints, and while MPLS actually routes IPv4 and IPv6 packets, everything else is switched.

MPLS is a service provider technology. Leased lines deliver bits between sites, and Frame Relay and Ethernet WAN deliver frames between sites. However, MPLS can deliver any type of packet between sites. MPLS can encapsulate packets of various network protocols. It supports a wide range of WAN technologies including T-carrier / E-carrier links, Carrier Ethernet, ATM, Frame Relay, and DSL.

The sample topology in the figure illustrates how MPLS is used. Notice that the different sites can connect to the MPLS cloud using different access technologies. In the figure, CE refers to the customer edge, PE is the provider edge router which adds and removes labels, while P is an internal provider router which switches MPLS labeled packets.

Note   MPLS is primarily a service provider WAN technology.

Refer to
Online Course
for Illustration

1.2.2.8   VSAT

All private WAN technologies discussed so far used either copper or fiber-optic media. What if an organization needed connectivity in a remote location where there are no service providers that offer WAN service?

Very small aperture terminal (VSAT) is a solution that creates a private WAN using satellite communications. A VSAT is a small satellite dish similar to those used for home Internet and TV. VSATs create a private WAN while providing connectivity to remote locations.

Specifically, a router connects to a satellite dish which is pointed to a service provider's satellite. This satellite is in geosynchronous orbit in space. The signals must travel approximately 35,786 kilometers (22,236 miles) to the satellite and back.

The example in the figure displays a VSAT dish on the roofs of the buildings communicating with a satellite thousands of kilometers away in space.

Refer to
Interactive Graphic
in online course

1.2.2.9   Activity - Identify Private WAN Infrastructure Terminology

1.2.3   Public WAN Infrastructure

Refer to
Online Course
for Illustration

1.2.3.1   DSL

DSL technology is an always-on connection technology that uses existing twisted-pair telephone lines to transport high-bandwidth data, and provides IP services to subscribers. A DSL modem converts an Ethernet signal from the user device to a DSL signal, which is transmitted to the central office.

Multiple DSL subscriber lines are multiplexed into a single, high-capacity link using a DSL access multiplexer (DSLAM) at the provider location. DSLAMs incorporate TDM technology to aggregate many subscriber lines into a single medium, generally a T3 (DS3) connection. Current DSL technologies use sophisticated coding and modulation techniques to achieve fast data rates.

There is a wide variety of DSL types, standards, and emerging standards. DSL is now a popular choice for enterprise IT departments to support home workers. Generally, a subscriber cannot choose to connect to an enterprise network directly, but must first connect to an ISP, and then an IP connection is made through the Internet to the enterprise. Security risks are incurred in this process, but can be mediated with security measures.

The topology in the figure displays a sample DSL WAN connection.

Refer to
Online Course
for Illustration

1.2.3.2   Cable

Coaxial cable is widely used in urban areas to distribute television signals. Network access is available from many cable television providers. This allows for greater bandwidth than the conventional telephone local loop.

Cable modems provide an always-on connection and a simple installation. A subscriber connects a computer or LAN router to the cable modem, which translates the digital signals into the broadband frequencies used for transmitting on a cable television network. The local cable TV office, which is called the cable headend, contains the computer system and databases needed to provide Internet access. The most important component located at the headend is the cable modem termination system (CMTS), which sends and receives digital cable modem signals on a cable network and is necessary for providing Internet services to cable subscribers.

Cable modem subscribers must use the ISP associated with the service provider. All the local subscribers share the same cable bandwidth. As more users join the service, available bandwidth may drop below the expected rate.

The topology in the figure displays a sample cable WAN connection.

1.2.3.3   Wireless

Refer to **Online Course** for Illustration

Wireless technology uses the unlicensed radio spectrum to send and receive data. The unlicensed spectrum is accessible to anyone who has a wireless router and wireless technology in the device they are using.

Until recently, one limitation of wireless access has been the need to be within the local transmission range (typically less than 100 feet) of a wireless router or a wireless modem that has a wired connection to the Internet. The following new developments in broadband wireless technology are changing this situation:

- **Municipal Wi-Fi** - Many cities have begun setting up municipal wireless networks. Some of these networks provide high-speed Internet access for free or for substantially less than the price of other broadband services. Others are for city use only, allowing police and fire departments and other city employees to do certain aspects of their jobs remotely. To connect to a municipal Wi-Fi, a subscriber typically needs a wireless modem, which provides a stronger radio and directional antenna than conventional wireless adapters. Most service providers provide the necessary equipment for free or for a fee, much like they do with DSL or cable modems.

- **WiMAX** - Worldwide Interoperability for Microwave Access (WiMAX) is a new technology that is just beginning to come into use. It is described in the IEEE standard 802.16. WiMAX provides high-speed broadband service with wireless access and provides broad coverage like a cell phone network rather than through small Wi-Fi hotspots. WiMAX operates in a similar way to Wi-Fi, but at higher speeds, over greater distances, and for a greater number of users. It uses a network of WiMAX towers that are similar to cell phone towers. To access a WiMAX network, subscribers must subscribe to an ISP with a WiMAX tower within 30 miles of their location. They also need some type of WiMAX receiver and a special encryption code to get access to the base station.

- **Satellite Internet** - Typically used by rural users where cable and DSL are not available. A VSAT provides two-way (upload and download) data communications. The upload speed is about one-tenth of the 500 kb/s download speed. Cable and DSL have higher download speeds, but satellite systems are about 10 times faster than an analog modem. To access satellite Internet services, subscribers need a satellite dish, two modems (uplink and downlink), and coaxial cables between the dish and the modem.

The figure displays an example of a WiMAX network.

Refer to
Online Course
for Illustration

1.2.3.4   3G/4G Cellular

Increasingly, cellular service is another wireless WAN technology being used to connect users and remote locations where no other WAN access technology is available. Many users with smart phones and tablets can use cellular data to email, surf the web, download apps, and watch videos.

Phones, tablet computers, laptops, and even some routers can communicate through to the Internet using cellular technology. These devices use radio waves to communicate through a nearby mobile phone tower. The device has a small radio antenna, and the provider has a much larger antenna sitting at the top of a tower somewhere within miles of the phone.

These are two common cellular industry terms:

- **3G/4G Wireless** - Abbreviation for 3rd generation and 4th generation cellular access. These technologies support wireless Internet access.

- **Long-Term Evolution (LTE)** - Refers to a newer and faster technology and is considered to be part of fourth generation (4G) technology.

Refer to
Interactive Graphic
in online course

1.2.3.5   VPN Technology

Security risks are incurred when a teleworker or a remote office worker uses a broadband service to access the corporate WAN over the Internet. To address security concerns, broadband services provide capabilities for using VPN connections to a network device that accepts VPN connections, which is typically located at the corporate site.

A VPN is an encrypted connection between private networks over a public network, such as the Internet. Instead of using a dedicated Layer 2 connection, such as a leased line, a VPN uses virtual connections called VPN tunnels, which are routed through the Internet from the private network of the company to the remote site or employee host.

There are several benefits to using VPN:

- **Cost savings** - VPNs enable organizations to use the global Internet to connect remote offices, and to connect remote users to the main corporate site. This eliminates expensive, dedicated WAN links and modem banks.

- **Security** - VPNs provide the highest level of security by using advanced encryption and authentication protocols that protect data from unauthorized access.

- **Scalability** - Because VPNs use the Internet infrastructure within ISPs and devices, it is easy to add new users. Corporations are able to add large amounts of capacity without adding significant infrastructure.

- **Compatibility with broadband technology** - VPN technology is supported by broadband service providers such as DSL and cable. VPNs allow mobile workers and telecommuters to take advantage of their home high-speed Internet service to access their corporate networks. Business-grade, high-speed broadband connections can also provide a cost-effective solution for connecting remote offices.

There are two types of VPN access:

- **Site-to-site VPNs** - Site-to-site VPNs connect entire networks to each other; for example, they can connect a branch office network to a company headquarters network, as shown in Figure 1. Each site is equipped with a VPN gateway, such as a router, firewall,

VPN concentrator, or security appliance. In the figure, a remote branch office uses a site-to-site-VPN to connect with the corporate head office.

- **Remote-access VPNs** - Remote-access VPNs enable individual hosts, such as telecommuters, mobile users, and extranet consumers, to access a company network securely over the Internet. Each host (Teleworker 1 and Teleworker 2) typically has VPN client software loaded or uses a web-based client, as shown in Figure 2.

Refer to **Interactive Graphic** in online course

1.2.3.6   Activity - Identify Public WAN Infrastructure Terminology

1.2.4   Selecting WAN Services

Refer to **Online Course** for Illustration

1.2.4.1   Choosing a WAN Link Connection

There are many important factors to consider when choosing an appropriate WAN connection. For a network administrator to decide which WAN technology best meets the requirements of their specific business, they must answer the following questions:

What is the purpose of the WAN?

There are a few issues to consider:

- Will the enterprise connect local branches in the same city area, connect remote branches, or connect to a single branch?

- Will the WAN be used to connect internal employees, or external business partners and customers, or all three?

- Will the enterprise connect to customers, connect to business partners, connect to employees, or some combination of these?

- Will the WAN provide authorized users limited or full access to the company intranet?

What is the geographic scope?

There are a few issues to consider:

- Is the WAN local, regional, or global?

- Is the WAN one-to-one (single branch), one-to-many branches, or many-to-many (distributed)?

What are the traffic requirements?

There are a few issues to consider:

- What type of traffic must be supported (data only, VoIP, video, large files, streaming files)? This determines the quality and performance requirements.

- What volume of traffic type (voice, video, or data) must be supported for each destination? This determines the bandwidth capacity required for the WAN connection to the ISP.

- What Quality of Service is required? This may limit the choices. If the traffic is highly sensitive to latency and jitter, eliminate any WAN connection options that cannot provide the required quality.

- What are the security requirements (data integrity, confidentiality, and security)? These are important factors if the traffic is of a highly confidential nature, or if it provides essential services, such as emergency response.

Refer to **Online Course** for Illustration

1.2.4.2   Choosing a WAN Link Connection (Cont.)

In addition to gathering information about the scope of the WAN, the administrator must also determine:

- **Should the WAN use a private or public infrastructure?** - A private infrastructure offers the best security and confidentiality, whereas the public Internet infrastructure offers the most flexibility and lowest ongoing expense. The choice depends on the purpose of the WAN, the types of traffic it carries, and available operating budget. For example, if the purpose is to provide a nearby branch with high-speed secure services, a private dedicated or switched connection may be best. If the purpose is to connect many remote offices, a public WAN using the Internet may be the best choice. For distributed operations, a combination of options may be the solution.

- **For a private WAN, should it be dedicated or switched?** - Real-time, high-volume transactions have special requirements that could favor a dedicated line, such as traffic flowing between the data center and the corporate head office. If the enterprise is connecting to a local single branch, a dedicated leased line could be used. However, that option would become very expensive for a WAN connecting multiple offices. In that case, a switched connection might be better.

- **For a public WAN, what type of VPN access is required?** - If the purpose of the WAN is to connect a remote office, a site-to-site VPN may be the best choice. To connect teleworkers or customers, remote-access VPNs are a better option. If the WAN is serving a mixture of remote offices, teleworkers, and authorized customers, such as a global company with distributed operations, a combination of VPN options may be required.

- **Which connection options are available locally?** - In some areas, not all WAN connection options are available. In this case, the selection process is simplified, although the resulting WAN may provide less than optimal performance. For example, in a rural or remote area, the only option may be VSAT or cellular access.

- **What is the cost of the available connection options?** - Depending on the option chosen, the WAN can be a significant ongoing expense. The cost of a particular option must be weighed against how well it meets the other requirements. For example, a dedicated leased line is the most expensive option, but the expense may be justified if it is critical to ensure secure transmission of high volumes of real-time data. For less demanding applications, a less expensive switched or Internet connection option may be more suitable.

Using the guidelines described above, as well as those described by the Cisco Enterprise Architecture, a network administrator should be able to choose an appropriate WAN connection to meet the requirements of different business scenarios.

Refer to
Lab Activity
for this chapter

1.2.4.3   Lab - Researching WAN Technologies

In this lab, you will complete the following objectives:

■ Part 1: Investigate Dedicated WAN Technologies and Providers

■ Part 2: Investigate a Dedicated Leased Line Service Provider in Your Area

1.3   Summary

Refer to
Online Course
for Illustration

1.3.1.1   Class Activity - WAN Device Modules

WAN Device Modules

Your medium-sized company is upgrading its network. To make the most of the equipment currently in use, you decide to purchase WAN modules instead of new equipment.

All branch offices use either Cisco 1900 or 2911 series ISRs. You will be updating these routers in several locations. Each branch has its own ISP requirements to consider.

To update the devices, focus on the following WAN modules access types:

■ Ethernet

■ Broadband

■ T1/E1 and ISDN PRI

■ BRI

■ Serial

■ T1 and E1 Trunk Voice and WAN

■ Wireless LANs and WANs

Refer to
Online Course
for Illustration

1.3.1.2   Chapter 1: WAN Concepts

A business can use private lines or the public network infrastructure for WAN connections. A public infrastructure connection can be a cost-effective alternative to a private connection between LANs, as long as security is also planned.

WAN access standards operate at Layers 1 and 2 of the OSI model, and are defined and managed by the TIA/EIA, ISO, and IEEE. A WAN may be circuit-switched or packet-switched.

There is common terminology used to identify the physical components of WAN connections and who, the service provider or the customer, is responsible for which components.

Service provider networks are complex and the service provider's backbone networks consist primarily of high-bandwidth fiber-optic media. The device used for interconnection to a customer is specific to the WAN technology that is implemented.

Permanent, dedicated point-to-point connections are provided by using leased lines. Dialup access, although slow, is still viable for remote areas with limited WAN options. Other private connection options include ISDN, Frame Relay, ATM, Ethernet WAN, MPLS, and VSAT.

Public infrastructure connections include DSL, cable, wireless, and 3G/4G cellular. Security over public infrastructure connections can be provided by using remote-access or site-to-site Virtual Private Networks (VPNs).

Go to the online course to take the quiz and exam.

Chapter 1 Quiz

This quiz is designed to provide an additional opportunity to practice the skills and knowledge presented in the chapter and to prepare for the chapter exam. You will be allowed multiple attempts and the grade does not appear in the gradebook.

Chapter 1 Exam

The chapter exam assesses your knowledge of the chapter content.

Your Chapter Notes

Point-to-Point Connections

2.0 Introduction

Refer to **Online Course** for Illustration

2.0.1.1 Chapter 2: Point-to-Point Connections

One of the most common types of WAN connections, especially in long-distance communications, is a point-to-point connection, also called a serial or leased-line connection. Because these connections are typically provided by a carrier, such as a telephone company, boundaries between what is managed by the carrier and what is managed by the customer must be clearly established.

This chapter covers the terms, technology, and protocols used in serial connections. The HDLC and Point-to-Point Protocols (PPP) are introduced. HDLC is the default protocol on a Cisco router serial interface. PPP is a protocol that is able to handle authentication, compression, error detection, monitor link quality, and logically bundle multiple serial connections together to share the load.

Refer to **Online Course** for Illustration

2.0.1.2 Class Activity - PPP Persuasion

PPP Persuasion

Your network engineering supervisor recently attended a networking conference where Layer 2 protocols were discussed. He knows that you have Cisco equipment on the premises, but he would also like to offer security and advanced TCP/IP options and controls on that same equipment by using the Point-to-Point Protocol (PPP).

After researching the PPP protocol, you find it offers some advantages over the HDLC protocol, currently used on your network.

Create a matrix listing the advantages and disadvantages of using the HDLC vs. PPP protocols. When comparing the two protocols, include:

- Ease of configuration
- Adaptability to non-proprietary network equipment
- Security options
- Bandwidth usage and compression
- Bandwidth consolidation

Share your chart with another student or class. Justify whether or not you would suggest sharing the matrix with the network engineering supervisor to justify a change being made from HDLC to PPP for Layer 2 network connectivity.

2.1   Serial Point-to-Point Overview

2.1.1   Serial Communications

Refer to
Interactive Graphic
in online course

2.1.1.1   Serial and Parallel Ports

A common type of WAN connections is the point-to-point connection. As shown in Figure 1, point-to-point connections are used to connect LANs to service provider WANs, and to connect LAN segments within an enterprise network.

A LAN-to-WAN point-to-point connection is also referred to as a serial connection or leased-line connection. This is because the lines are leased from a carrier (usually a telephone company) and are dedicated for use by the company leasing the lines. Companies pay for a continuous connection between two remote sites, and the line is continuously active and available. Leased lines are a frequently used type of WAN access, and they are generally priced based on the bandwidth required and the distance between the two connected points.

Understanding how point-to-point serial communication across a leased line works is important to an overall understanding of how WANs function.

Communications across a serial connection is a method of data transmissions in which the bits are transmitted sequentially over a single channel. This is equivalent to a pipe only wide enough to fit one ball at a time. Multiple balls can go into the pipe, but only one at a time, and they only have one exit point, the other end of the pipe. A serial port is bidirectional, and often referred to as a bidirectional port or a communications port.

This is in contrast to parallel communications in which bits can be transmitted simultaneously over multiple wires. Click Play in Figure 2 to see an illustration of the difference between serial and parallel connections. A parallel connection theoretically transfers data eight times faster than a serial connection. Based on this theory, a parallel connection sends a byte (eight bits) in the time that a serial connection sends a single bit. However, parallel communications do have issues with crosstalk across wires, especially as the wire length increases. Clock skew is also an issue with parallel communications. Clock skew occurs when data across the various wires does not arrive at the same time, creating synchronization issues. Finally, many parallel communications support only one-direction, outbound only communication, but some support half-duplex communication (two-way communication, but only one way at a time).

At one time, most PCs included both serial and parallel ports. Parallel ports were used to connect printers, computers, and other devices that required relatively high bandwidth. Parallel ports were also used between internal components. For external communications, a serial bus was primarily used to connect to phone lines and devices that could potentially be further distance than a parallel transfer would allow. Because serial communications are less complex and require simpler circuitry, serial communications are considerably less expensive to implement. Serial communications use fewer wires, cheaper cables, and fewer connector pins.

On most PCs, parallel ports and RS-232 serial ports have been replaced by the higher speed serial Universal Serial Bus (USB) interfaces. For long-distance communication, many WANs also use serial transmission.

Refer to
Online Course
for Illustration

2.1.1.2   Point-to-Point Communication Links

When permanent dedicated connections are required, a point-to-point link is used to provide a single, pre-established WAN communications path. This path goes from the customer premises, through the provider network, to a remote destination, as shown in the figure.

A point-to-point link can connect two geographically distant sites, such as a corporate office in New York and a regional office in London. For a point-to-point line, the carrier dedicates specific resources for a line that is leased by the customer (leased line).

Note   Point-to-point connections are not limited to connections that cross land. There are hundreds of thousands of miles of undersea fiber-optic cables that connect countries and continents worldwide. An Internet search of "undersea Internet cable map" produces several cable maps of these undersea connections.

Point-to-point links are usually more expensive than shared services. The cost of leased-line solutions can become significant when used to connect many sites over increasing distances. However, there are times when the benefits outweigh the cost of the leased line. The dedicated capacity removes latency or jitter between the endpoints. Constant availability is essential for some applications such as VoIP or video over IP.

Refer to
Online Course
for Illustration

2.1.1.3   Serial Bandwidth

Bandwidth refers to the rate at which data is transferred over the communication link. The underlying carrier technology will dictate how much bandwidth is available. There is a difference in bandwidth points between the North American (T-carrier) specification and the European (E-carrier) system. Optical networks also use a different bandwidth hierarchy, which again differs between North America and Europe. In the U.S., Optical Carrier (OC) defines the bandwidth points.

In North America, the bandwidth is usually expressed as a digital signal level number (DS0, DS1, etc.), which refers to the rate and format of the signal. The most fundamental line speed is 64 kb/s, or DS0, which is the bandwidth required for an uncompressed, digitized phone call. Serial connection bandwidths can be incrementally increased to accommodate the need for faster transmission. For example, 24 DS0s can be bundled to get a DS1 line (also called a T1 line) with a speed of 1.544 Mb/s. Also, 28 DS1s can be bundled to get a DS3 line (also called a T3 line) with a speed of 44.736 Mb/s. Leased lines are available in different capacities and are generally priced based on the bandwidth required and the distance between the two connected points.

OC transmission rates are a set of standardized specifications for the transmission of digital signals carried on SONET fiber-optic networks. The designation uses OC, followed by an integer value representing the base transmission rate of 51.84 Mb/s. For example, OC-1 has a transmission capacity of 51.84 Mb/s, whereas an OC-3 transmission medium would be three times 51.84 Mb/s, or 155.52 Mb/s.

The figure lists the most common line types and the associated bit rate capacity of each.

Note   E1 (2.048 Mb/s) and E3 (34.368 Mb/s) are European standards like T1 and T3, but with different bandwidths and frame structures.

2.1.2   HDLC Encapsulation

Refer to
Online Course
for Illustration

2.1.2.1   WAN Encapsulation Protocols

On each WAN connection, data is encapsulated into frames before crossing the WAN link. To ensure that the correct protocol is used, the appropriate Layer 2 encapsulation type must be configured. The choice of protocol depends on the WAN technology and the communicating equipment. The figure displays the more common WAN protocols and where they are used. The following are short descriptions of each type of WAN protocol:

- **HDLC** - The default encapsulation type on point-to-point connections, dedicated links, and circuit-switched connections when the link uses two Cisco devices. HDLC is now the basis for synchronous PPP used by many servers to connect to a WAN, most commonly the Internet.

- **PPP** - Provides router-to-router and host-to-network connections over synchronous and asynchronous circuits. PPP works with several network layer protocols, such as IPv4 and IPv6. PPP is based on the HDLC encapsulation protocol, but also has built-in security mechanisms such as PAP and CHAP.

- **Serial Line Internet Protocol (SLIP)** - A standard protocol for point-to-point serial connections using TCP/IP. SLIP has been largely displaced by PPP.

- **X.25/Link Access Procedure, Balanced (LAPB)** - An ITU-T standard that defines how connections between a DTE and DCE are maintained for remote terminal access and computer communications in public data networks. X.25 specifies LAPB, a data link layer protocol. X.25 is a predecessor to Frame Relay.

- **Frame Relay** - An industry standard, switched, data link layer protocol that handles multiple virtual circuits. Frame Relay is a next generation protocol after X.25. Frame Relay eliminates some of the time-consuming processes (such as error correction and flow control) employed in X.25.

- **ATM** - The international standard for cell relay in which devices send multiple service types, such as voice, video, or data, in fixed-length (53-byte) cells. Fixed-length cells allow processing to occur in hardware; thereby, reducing transit delays. ATM takes advantage of high-speed transmission media such as E3, SONET, and T3.

HDLC and PPP are the focus of this course. The other WAN protocols listed are considered either legacy technologies or beyond the scope of this course.

Refer to
Online Course
for Illustration

2.1.2.2   HDLC Encapsulation

HDLC is a bit-oriented synchronous data link layer protocol developed by the International Organization for Standardization (ISO). The current standard for HDLC is ISO 13239. HDLC was developed from the Synchronous Data Link Control (SDLC) standard proposed in the 1970s. HDLC provides both connection-oriented and connectionless service.

HDLC uses synchronous serial transmission to provide error-free communication between two points. HDLC defines a Layer 2 framing structure that allows for flow control and error control through the use of acknowledgments. Each frame has the same format, whether it is a data frame or a control frame.

When frames are transmitted over synchronous or asynchronous links, those links have no mechanism to mark the beginning or end of frames. For this reason, HDLC uses a frame delimiter, or flag, to mark the beginning and the end of each frame.

Cisco has developed an extension to the HLDC protocol to solve the inability to provide multiprotocol support. Although Cisco HLDC (also referred to as cHDLC) is proprietary, Cisco has allowed many other network equipment vendors to implement it. Cisco HDLC frames contain a field for identifying the network protocol being encapsulated. The figure compares standard HLDC to Cisco HLDC.

2.1.2.3   Configuring HDLC Encapsulation

Refer to
Online Course
for Illustration

Cisco HDLC is the default encapsulation method used by Cisco devices on synchronous serial lines.

Use Cisco HDLC as a point-to-point protocol on leased lines between two Cisco devices. If connecting non-Cisco devices, use synchronous PPP.

If the default encapsulation method has been changed, use the **encapsulation hdlc** command in privileged EXEC mode to re-enable HDLC.

As shown in the figure, there are two steps to re-enable HDLC encapsulation:

Step 1.   Enter the interface configuration mode of the serial interface.

Step 2.   Enter the **encapsulation hdlc** command to specify the encapsulation protocol on the interface.

2.1.2.4   Troubleshooting a Serial Interface

Refer to
Interactive Graphic
in online course

The output of the **show interfaces serial** command displays information specific to serial interfaces. Add the specific interface number you wish to investigate, such as **show interface serial 0/0/0**. When HDLC is configured, "encapsulation HDLC" should be reflected in the output, as highlighted in Figure 1. "Serial 0/0/0 is up, line protocol is up", indicates that the line is up and functioning; "encapsulation HDLC", indicates that the default serial encapsulation (HDLC) is enabled.

The **show interfaces serial** command returns one of six possible states:

- Serial x is up, line protocol is up

- Serial x is down, line protocol is down

- Serial x is up, line protocol is down

- Serial x is up, line protocol is up (looped)

- Serial x is up, line protocol is down (disabled)

- Serial x is administratively down, line protocol is down

Of the six possible states, there are five problem states. Figure 2 lists the five problem states, the issues associated with that state, and how to troubleshoot the issue.

The **show controllers** command is another important diagnostic tool when troubleshooting serial lines, as shown in Figure 3. The output indicates the state of the interface channels and whether a cable is attached to the interface. In the figure, interface serial 0/0/0 has a V.35 DCE cable attached. The command syntax varies, depending on the platform. Cisco 7000 series routers use a cBus controller card for connecting serial links. With these routers, use the **show controllers cbus** command.

If the electrical interface output displays as "UNKNOWN" instead of "V.35", "EIA/TIA-449", or some other electrical interface type, the likely problem is an improperly connected cable. A problem with the internal wiring of the card is also possible. If the electrical interface is unknown, the corresponding display for the **show interfaces serial** command shows that the interface and line protocol are down.

Use the Syntax Checker in Figure 4 to practice troubleshooting a serial interface.

Refer to **Packet Tracer Activity** for this chapter

2.1.2.5   Packet Tracer - Troubleshooting Serial Interfaces

Background/Scenario

You have been asked to troubleshoot WAN connections for a local telephone company (Telco). The Telco router is supposed to communicate with four remote sites, but none of them are working. Use your knowledge of the OSI model and a few general rules to identify and repair the errors in the network.

2.2   PPP Operation

2.2.1   Benefits of PPP

Refer to **Online Course** for Illustration

2.2.1.1   Introducing PPP

HDLC is the default serial encapsulation method when connecting two Cisco routers. With an added protocol type field, the Cisco version of HDLC is proprietary. Thus, Cisco HDLC can only work with other Cisco devices. However, when there is a need to connect to a non-Cisco router, PPP encapsulation should be used, as shown in the figure.

PPP encapsulation has been carefully designed to retain compatibility with most commonly used supporting hardware. PPP encapsulates data frames for transmission over Layer 2 physical links. PPP establishes a direct connection using serial cables, phone lines, trunk lines, cellular telephones, specialized radio links, or fiber-optic links.

PPP contains three main components:

- HDLC-like framing for transporting multiprotocol packets over point-to-point links.

- Extensible Link Control Protocol (LCP) for establishing, configuring, and testing the data-link connection.

- Family of Network Control Protocols (NCPs) for establishing and configuring different network layer protocols. PPP allows the simultaneous use of multiple network layer protocols. The most common NCPs are IPv4 Control Protocol and IPv6 Control Protocol.

Note   Other NCPs include AppleTalk Control Protocol, Novell IPX Control Protocol, Cisco Systems Control Protocol, SNA Control Protocol, and Compression Control Protocol.

Refer to
Online Course
for Illustration

2.2.1.2   Advantages of PPP

PPP originally emerged as an encapsulation protocol for transporting IPv4 traffic over point-to-point links. PPP provides a standard method for transporting multiprotocol packets over point-to-point links.

There are many advantages to using PPP, including the fact that it is not proprietary. PPP includes many features not available in HDLC:

- The link quality management feature (LQM) monitors the quality of the link. LQM can be configured with the interface command **ppp quality** *percentage*. If the error percentage falls below the configured threshold, the link is taken down and packets are rerouted or dropped.

- PPP supports PAP and CHAP authentication. This feature is explained and practiced in a later section.

2.2.2   LCP and NCP

Refer to
Online Course
for Illustration

2.2.2.1   PPP Layered Architecture

A layered architecture is a logical model, design, or blueprint that aids in communication between interconnecting layers. The figure maps the layered architecture of PPP against the Open System Interconnection (OSI) model. PPP and OSI share the same physical layer, but PPP distributes the functions of LCP and NCP differently.

At the physical layer, you can configure PPP on a range of interfaces. The only absolute requirement imposed by PPP is a full-duplex circuit, either dedicated or switched, that can operate in an asynchronous or synchronous bit-serial mode. The physical layer standards are transparent to PPP link layer frames. PPP does not impose any restrictions regarding transmission rate.

Most of the work done by PPP happens at the data link and network layers, by LCP and NCPs.

Refer to
Online Course
for Illustration

2.2.2.2   PPP – Link Control Protocol (LCP)

LCP functions within the data link layer and has a role in establishing, configuring, and testing the data-link connection. LCP establishes the point-to-point link. LCP also negotiates and sets up control options on the WAN data link, which are handled by the NCPs.

LCP provides automatic configuration of the interfaces at each end:

- Handling varying limits on packet size

- Detecting common misconfiguration errors

- Terminating the link

- Determining when a link is functioning properly or when it is failing

After the link is established, PPP also uses LCP to agree automatically on encapsulation formats such as authentication, compression, and error detection.

Refer to
Interactive Graphic
in online course

2.2.2.3   PPP – Network Control Protocol (NCP)

PPP permits multiple network layer protocols to operate on the same communications link. For every network layer protocol used, PPP uses a separate NCP, as shown in Figure 1. For example, IPv4 uses IP Control Protocol (IPCP) and IPv6 uses IPv6 Control Protocol (IPv6CP).

NCPs include functional fields containing standardized codes to indicate the network layer protocol that PPP encapsulates. Figure 2 lists the PPP protocol field numbers. Each NCP manages the specific needs required by its respective network layer protocols. The various NCP components encapsulate and negotiate options for multiple network layer protocols.

Refer to
Online Course
for Illustration

2.2.2.4   PPP Frame Structure

A PPP frame consists of six fields. The following descriptions summarize the PPP frame fields illustrated in the figure:

- **Flag** - A single byte that indicates the beginning or end of a frame. The Flag field consists of the binary sequence 01111110.

- **Address** - A single byte that contains the binary sequence 11111111, the standard broadcast address. PPP does not assign individual station addresses.

- **Control** - A single byte that contains the binary sequence 00000011, which calls for transmission of user data in an unsequenced frame.

- **Protocol** - Two bytes that identify the protocol encapsulated in the information field of the frame. The 2-byte Protocol field identifies the protocol of the PPP payload.

- **Data** - Zero or more bytes that contain the datagram for the protocol specified in the protocol field.

- **Frame Check Sequence (FCS)** - This is normally 16 bits (2 bytes). If the receiver's calculation of the FCS does not match the FCS in the PPP frame, the PPP frame is silently discarded.

LCPs can negotiate modifications to the standard PPP frame structure. Modified frames, however, are always distinguishable from standard frames.

Refer to
Interactive Graphic
in online course

2.2.2.5   Activity - Identify PPP Features and Operations

2.2.3   PPP Sessions

Refer to
Online Course
for Illustration

2.2.3.1   Establishing a PPP Session

There are three phases of establishing a PPP session, as shown in the figure:

- **Phase 1: Link establishment and configuration negotiation** - Before PPP exchanges any network layer datagrams, such as IP, the LCP must first open the connection and negotiate configuration options. This phase is complete when the receiving router sends a configuration-acknowledgment frame back to the router initiating the connection.

- **Phase 2: Link quality determination (optional)** - The LCP tests the link to determine whether the link quality is sufficient to bring up network layer protocols. The LCP can delay transmission of network layer protocol information until this phase is complete.

- **Phase 3: Network layer protocol configuration negotiation** - After the LCP has finished the link quality determination phase, the appropriate NCP can separately configure the network layer protocols, and bring them up and take them down at any time. If the LCP closes the link, it informs the network layer protocols so that they can take appropriate action.

The link remains configured for communications until explicit LCP or NCP frames close the link, or until some external event occurs such as an inactivity timer expiring, or an administrator intervening.

The LCP can terminate the link at any time. This is usually done when one of the routers requests termination, but can happen because of a physical event, such as the loss of a carrier or the expiration of an idle-period timer.

Refer to **Interactive Graphic** in online course

2.2.3.2   LCP Operation

LCP operation includes provisions for link establishment, link maintenance, and link termination. LCP operation uses three classes of LCP frames to accomplish the work of each of the LCP phases:

- Link-establishment frames establish and configure a link (Configure-Request, Configure-Ack, Configure-Nak, and Configure-Reject).

- Link-maintenance frames manage and debug a link (Code-Reject, Protocol-Reject, Echo-Request, Echo-Reply, and Discard-Request).

- Link-termination frames terminate a link (Terminate-Request and Terminate-Ack).

Link Establishment

Link establishment is the first phase of LCP operation, as seen in Figure 1. This phase must complete successfully, before any network layer packets can be exchanged. During link establishment, the LCP opens the connection and negotiates the configuration parameters. The link establishment process starts with the initiating device sending a Configure-Request frame to the responder. The Configure-Request frame includes a variable number of configuration options needed to set up on the link.

The initiator includes the options for how it wants the link created, including protocol or authentication parameters. The responder processes the request:

- If the options are not acceptable or not recognized, the responder sends a Configure-Nak or Configure-Reject message. If this occurs and the negotiation fails, the initiator must restart the process with new options.

- If the options are acceptable, the responder responds with a Configure-Ack message and the process moves on to the authentication stage. The operation of the link is handed over to the NCP.

When NCP has completed all necessary configurations, including validating authentication if configured, the line is available for data transfer. During the exchange of data, LCP transitions into link maintenance.

Link Maintenance

During link maintenance, LCP can use messages to provide feedback and test the link, as shown in Figure 2:

- **Echo-Request, Echo-Reply, and Discard-Request** - These frames can be used for testing the link.

- **Code-Reject and Protocol-Reject** - These frame types provide feedback when one device receives an invalid frame. The sending device will resend the packet.

Link Termination

After the transfer of data at the network layer completes, the LCP terminates the link, as shown in Figure 3. NCP only terminates the network layer and NCP link. The link remains open until the LCP terminates it. If the LCP terminates the link before NCP, the NCP session is also terminated.

PPP can terminate the link at any time. This might happen because of the loss of the carrier, authentication failure, link quality failure, the expiration of an idle-period timer, or the administrative closing of the link. The LCP closes the link by exchanging Terminate packets. The device initiating the shutdown sends a Terminate-Request message. The other device replies with a Terminate-Ack. A termination request indicates that the device sending it needs to close the link. When the link is closing, PPP informs the network layer protocols so that they may take appropriate action.

Refer to
Online Course
for Illustration

2.2.3.3   PPP Configuration Options

PPP can be configured to support various optional functions, as shown in the figure. There are three optional functions:

- Authentication using either PAP or CHAP

- Compression using either Stacker or Predictor

- Multilink that combines two or more channels to increase the WAN bandwidth

Refer to
Online Course
for Illustration

2.2.3.4   NCP Explained

After the LCP has configured and authenticated the basic link, the appropriate NCP is invoked to complete the specific configuration of the network layer protocol being used. When the NCP has successfully configured the network layer protocol, the network protocol is in the open state on the established LCP link. At this point, PPP can carry the corresponding network layer protocol packets.

IPCP Example

As an example of how the NCP layer works, the NCP configuration of IPv4 is shown in the figure. After LCP has established the link, the routers exchange IPCP messages, negotiating options specific to IPv4. IPCP is responsible for configuring, enabling, and disabling the IPv4 modules on both ends of the link.

IPCP negotiates two options:

- **Compression** - Allows devices to negotiate an algorithm to compress TCP and IP headers and save bandwidth. The Van Jacobson TCP/IP header compression reduces the size of the TCP/IP headers to as few as 3 bytes. This can be a significant improvement on slow serial lines, particularly for interactive traffic.

- **IPv4-Address** - Allows the initiating device to specify an IPv4 address to use for routing IP over the PPP link, or to request an IPv4 address for the responder. Prior to the advent of broadband technologies such as DSL and cable modem services, dialup network devices commonly used the IPv4 address option.

After the NCP process is complete, the link goes into the open state and LCP takes over again in a link maintenance phase. Link traffic consists of any possible combination of LCP, NCP, and network layer protocol packets. When data transfer is complete, NCP terminates the protocol link and LCP terminates the PPP connection.

Refer to
Interactive Graphic
in online course

2.2.3.5 Activity - Identify the Steps in the LCP Link Negotiation Process

2.3 PPP Implementation

2.3.1 Configure PPP

Refer to
Online Course
for Illustration

2.3.1.1 PPP Configuration Options

In the previous section, configurable LCP options were introduced to meet specific WAN connection requirements. PPP may include several LCP options:

- **Authentication** - Peer routers exchange authentication messages. Two authentication choices are Password Authentication Protocol (PAP) and Challenge Handshake Authentication Protocol (CHAP).

- **Compression** - Increases the effective throughput on PPP connections by reducing the amount of bits that must travel across the link. The protocol decompresses the frame at its destination. Two compression protocols available in Cisco routers are Stacker and Predictor. Click here to learn more about Stacker and Predictor.

- **Error detection** - Identifies fault conditions. The Quality and Magic Number options help ensure a reliable, loop-free data link. The Magic Number field helps in detecting links that are in a looped-back condition. Until the Magic-Number Configuration Option has been successfully negotiated, the Magic-Number must be transmitted as zero. Magic numbers are generated randomly at each end of the connection.

- **PPP Callback** - PPP callback is used to enhance security. With this LCP option, a Cisco router can act as a callback client or a callback server. The client makes the initial call, requests that the server call it back, and terminates its initial call. The callback router answers the initial call and makes the return call to the client based on its configuration statements.

■ **Multilink** - This alternative provides load balancing over the router interfaces that PPP uses. Multilink PPP, also referred to as MP, MPPP, MLP, or Multilink, provides a method for spreading traffic across multiple physical WAN links while providing packet fragmentation and reassembly, proper sequencing, multivendor interoperability, and load balancing on inbound and outbound traffic.

When options are configured, a corresponding field value is inserted into the LCP option field.

Refer to
Online Course
for Illustration

2.3.1.2   PPP Basic Configuration Command

To set PPP as the encapsulation method used by a serial interface, use the **encapsulation ppp** interface configuration command. The command has no arguments. Remember that if PPP is not configured on a Cisco router, the default encapsulation for serial interfaces is HDLC.

The figure shows that routers R1 and R2 have been configured with both an IPv4 and an IPv6 address on the serial interfaces. PPP is a Layer 2 encapsulation that supports various Layer 3 protocols including IPv4 and IPv6.

Refer to
Online Course
for Illustration

2.3.1.3   PPP Compression Commands

Point-to-point software compression on serial interfaces can be configured after PPP encapsulation is enabled. Because this option invokes a software compression process, it can affect system performance. If the traffic already consists of compressed files, such as .zip, .tar, or .mpeg, do not use this option. The figure shows the command syntax for the **compress** command.

Refer to
Interactive Graphic
in online course

2.3.1.4   PPP Link Quality Monitoring Command

LCP provides an optional link quality determination phase. In this phase, LCP tests the link to determine whether the link quality is sufficient to use Layer 3 protocols.

The **ppp quality** *percentage* command ensures that the link meets the quality requirement set; otherwise, the link closes down.

The percentages are calculated for both incoming and outgoing directions. The outgoing quality is calculated by comparing the total number of packets and bytes sent, to the total number of packets and bytes received by the destination node. The incoming quality is calculated by comparing the total number of packets and bytes received to the total number of packets and bytes sent by the destination node.

If the link quality percentage is not maintained and the configured threshold, the link is deemed to be of poor quality and is taken down. LQM implements a time lag so that the link does not bounce up and down.

The configuration **ppp quality 80**, shown in Figure 1, sets minimum quality to 80%.

Use the Syntax Checker in Figure 2 to configure PPP encapsulation, compression, and LQM on router R1's Serial 0/0/1 interface.

Refer to
Online Course
for Illustration

2.3.1.5   PPP Multilink Commands

Multilink PPP (also referred to as MP, MPPP, MLP, or Multilink) provides a method for spreading traffic across multiple physical WAN links. Multilink PPP also provides packet fragmentation and reassembly, proper sequencing, multivendor interoperability, and load balancing on inbound and outbound traffic.

MPPP allows packets to be fragmented and sends these fragments simultaneously over multiple point-to-point links to the same remote address. The multiple physical links come up in response to a user-defined load threshold. MPPP can measure the load on just inbound traffic, or on just outbound traffic, but not on the combined load of both inbound and outbound traffic.

Configuring MPPP requires two steps, as shown in the figure.

Step 1.   Create a multilink bundle.

- The **interface multilink** *number* command creates the multilink interface.

- In interface configuration mode, an IP address is assigned to the multilink interface. In this example, both IPv4 and IPv6 addresses are configured on routers R3 and R4.

- The interface is enabled for multilink PPP.

- The interface is assigned a multilink group number.

Step 2.   Assign interfaces to the multilink bundle.

Each interface that is part of the multilink group:

- Is enabled for PPP encapsulation.

- Is enabled for multilink PPP.

- Is bound to the multilink bundle using the PPP multilink group number configured in Step 1.

To disable PPP multilink, use the **no ppp multilink** command on each of the bundled interfaces. For example:

```
R3(config)# interface s0/0/0
R3(config-if)# no ppp multilink
R3(config-if)# interface s0/0/1
R3(config-if)# no ppp multilink
```

Refer to
Interactive Graphic
in online course

2.3.1.6   Verifying PPP Configuration

Use the **show interfaces serial** command to verify proper configuration of HDLC or PPP encapsulation. The command output in Figure 1 shows a PPP configuration.

When you configure HDLC, the output of the **show interfaces serial** command should display encapsulation HDLC. When PPP is configured, the LCP and NCP states also display. Notice that NCPs IPCP and IPV6CP are open for IPv4 and IPv6 because R1 and R2 were configured with both IPv4 and IPv6 addresses.

Figure 2 summarizes commands used when verifying PPP.

The **show ppp multilink** command verifies that PPP multilink is enabled on R3, as shown in Figure 3. The output indicates the interface Multilink 1, the hostnames of both the local and remote endpoints, and the serial interfaces assigned to the multilink bundle.

2.3.2   Configure PPP Authentication

Refer to
Online Course
for Illustration

2.3.2.1   PPP Authentication Protocols

PPP defines an LCP that allows negotiation of an authentication protocol for authenticating its peer before allowing network layer protocols to transmit over the link. RFC 1334, *PPP Authentication Protocols*, defines two protocols for authentication, PAP and CHAP, as shown in the figure.

PAP is a very basic two-way process. There is no encryption. The username and password are sent in plaintext. If it is accepted, the connection is allowed. CHAP is more secure than PAP. It involves a three-way exchange of a shared secret.

The authentication phase of a PPP session is optional. If used, the peer is authenticated after LCP establishes the link and chooses the authentication protocol. Authentication takes place before the network layer protocol configuration phase begins.

The authentication options require that the calling side of the link enter authentication information. This helps to ensure that the user has the permission of the network administrator to make the call. Peer routers exchange authentication messages.

Refer to
Interactive Graphic
in online course

2.3.2.2   Password Authentication Protocol (PAP)

PAP provides a simple method for a remote node to establish its identity using a two-way handshake. PAP is not interactive. When the **ppp authentication pap** command is used, the username and password are sent as one LCP data package as shown in Figure 1, rather than one PPP device sending a login prompt and waiting for a response as in some authentication mechanisms.

PAP Process

After PPP completes the link establishment phase, the remote node repeatedly sends a username-password pair across the link until the receiving node acknowledges it or terminates the connection.

At the receiving node, the username-password is checked by the device running PPP. This device either allows or denies the connection. An accept or reject message is returned to the requester, as shown in Figure 2.

PAP is not a strong authentication protocol. Using PAP, passwords are sent across the link in plaintext and there is no protection from playback or repeated trial-and-error attacks. The remote node is in control of the frequency and timing of the login attempts.

Nonetheless, there are times when using PAP can be justified. Despite its shortcomings, PAP may be used in the following environments:

- A large installed base of client applications that do not support CHAP

- Incompatibilities between different vendor implementations of CHAP

- Situations where a plaintext password must be available to simulate a login at the remote host

Refer to
Interactive Graphic
in online course

2.3.2.3   Challenge Handshake Authentication Protocol (CHAP)

After authentication is established with PAP, it does not re-authenticate. This leaves the network vulnerable to attack. Unlike PAP, which only authenticates once, CHAP conducts periodic challenges to make sure that the remote node still has a valid password value. The password value is variable and changes unpredictably while the link exists. CHAP uses the **ppp authentication chap** command.

CHAP Process

After the PPP link establishment phase is complete, the local router sends a challenge message to the remote node, as shown in Figure 1.

The remote node responds with a value that is calculated using a one-way hash function. This is typically Message Digest 5 (MD5) based on the password and challenge message, as shown in Figure 2.

The local router checks the response against its own calculation of the expected hash value. If the values match, the initiating node acknowledges the authentication, as shown in Figure 3. If the values do not match, the initiating node immediately terminates the connection.

CHAP provides protection against a playback attack by using a variable challenge value that is unique and unpredictable. Because the challenge is unique and random, the resulting hash value is also unique and random. The use of repeated challenges limits the time of exposure to any single attack. The local router, or a third-party authentication server, is in control of the frequency and timing of the challenges.

Refer to
Online Course
for Illustration

2.3.2.4   PPP Authentication Command

To specify the order in which the CHAP or PAP protocols are requested on the interface, use the **ppp authentication** interface configuration command, as shown in the figure. Use the **no** form of the command to disable this authentication.

PAP, CHAP, or both can be enabled. If both methods are enabled, the first method specified is requested during link negotiation. If the peer suggests using the second method or simply refuses the first method, the second method should be tried. Some remote devices support CHAP only and some PAP only. The order in which you specify the methods is based on your concerns about the ability of the remote device to correctly negotiate the appropriate method as well as your concern about data line security.

Refer to
Interactive Graphic
in online course

2.3.2.5   Configuring PPP with Authentication

The procedure outlined in the table describes how to configure PPP encapsulation and PAP/CHAP authentication protocols. Correct configuration is essential, because PAP and CHAP use these parameters to authenticate.

Configuring PAP Authentication

Figure 1 is an example of a two-way PAP authentication configuration. Both routers authenticate and are authenticated, so the PAP authentication commands mirror each other. The PAP username and password that each router sends must match those specified with the **username** *name* **password** *password* command of the other router.

PAP provides a simple method for a remote node to establish its identity using a two-way handshake. This is done only on initial link establishment. The hostname on one router must match the username the other router has configured for PPP. The passwords must also match. Specify the username and password parameters, use the following command: **ppp pap sent-username** *name* **password** *password*.

Use the Syntax Checker in Figure 2 to configure PAP authentication on router R1's serial 0/0/1 interface.

Configuring CHAP Authentication

CHAP periodically verifies the identity of the remote node using a three-way handshake. The hostname on one router must match the username the other router has configured. The passwords must also match. This occurs on initial link establishment and can be repeated any time after the link has been established. Figure 3 is an example of a CHAP configuration.

Use the Syntax Checker in Figure 4 to configure CHAP authentication on router R1's serial 0/0/1 interface.

*Refer to **Packet Tracer Activity** for this chapter*

2.3.2.6   Packet Tracer - Configuring PAP and CHAP Authentication

Background/Scenario

In this activity, you will practice configuring PPP encapsulation on serial links. You will also configure PPP PAP authentication and PPP CHAP authentication.

*Refer to **Lab Activity** for this chapter*

2.3.2.7 Lab - Configuring Basic PPP with Authentication

In this lab, you will complete the following objectives:

- Part 1: Configure Basic Device Settings
- Part 2: Configure PPP Encapsulation
- Part 3: Configure PPP CHAP Authentication

2.4   Troubleshoot WAN Connectivity

2.4.1   Troubleshoot PPP

*Refer to **Online Course** for Illustration*

2.4.1.1   Troubleshooting PPP Serial Encapsulation

The **debug** command is used for troubleshooting and is accessed from privileged EXEC mode of the command-line interface. A **debug** output displays information about various router operations, related traffic generated or received by the router, and any error messages. It can consume a significant amount of resources, and the router is forced to process-switch the packets being debugged. The **debug** command must not be used as a monitoring tool; rather, it is meant to be used for a short period of time for troubleshooting.

Use the **debug ppp** command to display information about the operation of PPP. The figure shows the command syntax. Use the **no** form of this command to disable debugging output.

Use the **debug ppp** command when trying to search the following:

- NCPs that are supported on either end of a PPP connection

- Any loops that might exist in a PPP internetwork

- Nodes that are (or are not) properly negotiating PPP connections

- Errors that have occurred over the PPP connection

- Causes for CHAP session failures

- Causes for PAP session failures

- Information specific to the exchange of PPP connections using the Callback Control Protocol (CBCP), used by Microsoft clients

- Incorrect packet sequence number information where MPPC compression is enabled

Refer to
Interactive Graphic
in online course

2.4.1.2   Debug PPP

In addition to the **debug ppp** command, there are other commands that are available for troubleshooting a PPP connection.

A good command to use when troubleshooting serial interface encapsulation is the **debug ppp packet** command, as shown in Figure 1. The figure example depicts packet exchanges under normal PPP operation, including LCP state, LQM procedures, and the LCP magic number.

Figure 2 displays the output of the **debug ppp negotiation** command in a normal negotiation, where both sides agree on NCP parameters. In this case, protocol types IPv4 and IPv6 are proposed and acknowledged. The **debug ppp negotiation** command enables the network administrator to view the PPP negotiation transactions, identify the problem or stage when the error occurs, and develop a resolution. The output includes the LCP negotiation, authentication, and NCP negotiation.

The **debug ppp error** command is used to display protocol errors and error statistics associated with PPP connection negotiation and operation, as shown in Figure 3. These messages might appear when the Quality Protocol option is enabled on an interface that is already running PPP.

Refer to
Online Course
for Illustration

2.4.1.3   Troubleshooting a PPP Configuration with Authentication

Authentication is a feature that needs to be implemented correctly or the security of your serial connection may be compromised. Always verify your configuration with the **show interfaces serial** command, in the same way as you did without authentication.

Note   Never assume your authentication configuration works without testing it using the previously covered show commands. If there are issues, debugging allows you to verify the issue is with authentication and correct any deficiencies. For debugging PPP authentication, use the **debug ppp authentication** command.

The figure shows an example output of the **debug ppp authentication** command. The following is an interpretation of the output:

Line 1 says that the router is unable to authenticate on interface Serial0 because the peer did not send a name.

Line 2 says the router was unable to validate the CHAP response because USERNAME pioneer was not found.

Line 3 says no password was found for pioneer. Other possible responses at this line might have been no name received to authenticate, unknown name, no secret for given name, short MD5 response received, or MD5 compare failed.

In the last line, the code 4 means that a failure has occurred. Other code values are as follows:

- 1 - Challenge
- 2 - Response
- 3 - Success
- 4 - Failure
- id - 3 is the ID number per LCP packet format
- len - 48 is the packet length without the header

Refer to Packet Tracer Activity for this chapter

2.4.1.4   Packet Tracer - Troubleshooting PPP with Authentication
Background/ Scenario

The routers at your company were configured by an inexperienced network engineer. Several errors in the configuration have resulted in connectivity issues. Your boss has asked you to troubleshoot and correct the configuration errors and document your work. Using your knowledge of PPP and standard testing methods, find and correct the errors. Make sure that all of the serial links use PPP CHAP authentication, and that all of the networks are reachable. The passwords are "cisco" and "class".

Refer to Lab Activity for this chapter

2.4.1.5   Lab - Troubleshooting Basic PPP with Authentication
In this lab, you will complete the following objectives:

- Part 1: Build the Network and Load Device Configurations
- Part 2: Troubleshoot the Data Link Layer
- Part 3: Troubleshoot the Network Layer

2.5   Summary

Refer to Online Course for Illustration

2.5.1.1   Class Activity - PPP Validation
PPP Validation

Three friends who are enrolled in the Cisco Networking Academy want to check their knowledge of PPP network configuration.

They set up a contest where each person will be tested on configuring PPP with defined PPP scenario requirements and varying options. Each person devises a different configuration scenario.

The next day they get together and test each other's configuration using their PPP scenario requirements.

Refer to **Packet Tracer Activity** for this chapter

2.5.1.2 Packet Tracer - Skills Integration Challenge

Background/Scenario

This activity allows you to practice a variety of skills including configuring VLANs, PPP with CHAP, static and default routing, using IPv4 and IPv6. Due to the sheer number of graded elements, feel free to click Check Results and Assessment Items to see if you correctly entered a graded command. Use the passwords "cisco" and "class" to access EXEC modes of the CLI for routers and switches.

Refer to **Online Course** for Illustration

2.5.1.3 Chapter 2: Point-to-Point Connections

Serial transmissions sequentially send one bit at a time over a single channel. A serial port is bidirectional. Synchronous serial communications require a clocking signal.

Point-to-Point links are usually more expensive than shared services; however, the benefits may outweigh the costs. Constant availability is important for some protocols, such as VoIP.

SONET is an optical network standard that uses STDM for efficient use of bandwidth. In the United States, OC transmission rates are standardized specifications for SONET.

The bandwidth hierarchy used by carriers is different in North America (T-carrier) and Europe (E-carrier). In North America, the fundamental line speed is 64 kbps, or DS0. Multiple DS0s are bundled together to provide higher line speeds.

The demarcation point is the point in the network where the responsibility of the service provider ends and the responsibility of the customer begins. The CPE, usually a router, is the DTE device. The DCE is usually a modem or CSU/DSU.

Cisco HDLC is a bit-oriented synchronous data link layer protocol extension of HDLC and is used by many vendors to provide multiprotocol support. This is the default encapsulation method used on Cisco synchronous serial lines.

Synchronous PPP is used to connect to non-Cisco devices, to monitor link quality, provide authentication, or bundle links for shared use. PPP uses HDLC for encapsulating datagrams. LCP is the PPP protocol used to establish, configure, test, and terminate the data link connection. LCP can optionally authenticate a peer using PAP or CHAP. A family of NCPs are used by the PPP protocol to simultaneously support multiple network layer protocols. Multilink PPP spreads traffic across bundled links by fragmenting packets and simultaneously sending these fragments over multiple links to same remote address, where they are reassembled.

PPP optionally supports authentication using PAP, CHAP, or both PAP and CHAP protocols. PAP sends authentication data in plaintext. CHAP uses a 3-way handshake, periodic challenge messaging, and a one-way hash that helps protect against playback attacks.

Go to the online course to take the quiz and exam.

Chapter 2 Quiz

This quiz is designed to provide an additional opportunity to practice the skills and knowledge presented in the chapter and to prepare for the chapter exam. You will be allowed multiple attempts and the grade does not appear in the gradebook.

Chapter 2 Exam

The chapter exam assesses your knowledge of the chapter content.

Your Chapter Notes

Branch Connections

3.0 Introduction

Refer to
Online Course
for Illustration

3.0.1.1 Chapter 3: Branch Connections

Broadband solutions provide teleworkers with high-speed connection options to business locations and to the Internet. Small branch offices can also connect using these same technologies. This chapter covers commonly used broadband solutions, such as cable, DSL, and wireless.

Note Teleworking is a broad term referring to conducting work by connecting to a workplace from a remote location, with the assistance of telecommunications.

ISPs value the Point-to-Point Protocol (PPP) because of the authentication, accounting, and link management features. Customers appreciate the ease and availability of the Ethernet connection. Ethernet links do not natively support PPP. A solution to this problem was created, PPP over Ethernet (PPPoE). This chapter covers the implementation of PPPoE.

Security is a concern when using the public Internet to conduct business. Virtual Private Networks (VPNs) are used to improve the security of data across the Internet. A VPN is used to create a private communication channel (also called tunnel) over a public network. Data can be secured by using encryption in this tunnel through the Internet and by using authentication to protect data from unauthorized access. VPN technology provides security options for data running over these connections. This chapter describes some basic VPN implementations.

Note VPNs rely on Internet Protocol Security (IPsec) to provide security across the Internet. IPsec is beyond the scope of this course.

Generic Routing Encapsulation (GRE) is a tunneling protocol developed by Cisco that can encapsulate a wide variety of protocol packet types inside IP tunnels. GRE creates a virtual point-to-point link to Cisco routers at remote points, over an IP internetwork. The chapter covers the basic GRE implementation.

The Border Gateway Protocol (BGP) is routing protocol used between autonomous systems. This chapter concludes with a discussion of BGP routing and an implementation of BGP in a single-homed network.

Refer to
Online Course
for Illustration

3.0.1.2 Class Activity - Broadband Varieties

Telework employment opportunities are expanding in your local area every day. You have been offered employment as a teleworker for a major corporation. The new employer requires teleworkers to have access the Internet to fulfill their job responsibilities.

Research the following broadband Internet connection types that are available in your geo-graphic area:

■ DSL

■ Cable

■ Satellite

Consider the advantages and disadvantages of each broadband variation as you notate your research, which may include cost, speed, security, and ease of implementation or installation.

3.1   Remote Access Connections

3.1.1   Broadband Connections

Refer to **Interactive Graphic** in online course

3.1.1.1   What is a Cable System?

Accessing the Internet through a cable network is a popular option used by teleworkers to access their enterprise network. The cable system uses a coaxial cable that carries radio frequency (RF) signals across the network. Coaxial cable is the primary medium used to build cable TV systems. Click here to learn more about the history of cable.

Modern cable systems offer customers advanced telecommunications services, including high-speed Internet access, digital cable television, and residential telephone service. Cable operators typically deploy hybrid fiber-coaxial (HFC) networks to enable high-speed transmission of data to cable modems located in a SOHO.

Click the highlighted areas in the figure to see more information about the components of a typical modern cable system.

The Data over Cable Service Interface Specification (DOCSIS) is the international standard for adding high-bandwidth data to an existing cable system.

Refer to **Interactive Graphic** in online course

3.1.1.2   Cable Components

Two types of equipment are required to send signals upstream and downstream on a cable system:

■ Cable Modem Termination System (CMTS) at the headend of the cable operator

■ Cable Modem (CM) on the subscriber end

Click the highlighted components in the figure for more information about how each device contributes to communication.

A headend CMTS communicates with CMs located in subscriber homes. The headend is actually a router with databases for providing Internet services to cable subscribers. The architecture is relatively simple, using an HFC network. The HFC network is a mixed optical-coaxial network in which optical fiber replaces the lower bandwidth coaxial cable. The fiber carries the same broadband content for Internet connections, telephone service, and streaming video as the coaxial cable carries.

In a modern HFC network, typically 500 to 2,000 active data subscribers are connected to a cable network segment, all sharing the upstream and downstream bandwidth. Under the new DOCSIS 3.1 standard, this bandwidth can be up to 10 Gb/s downstream and up to 1 Gb/s upstream.

Refer to Online Course for Illustration

3.1.1.3   What is DSL?

A Digital Subscriber Line (DSL) is a means of providing high-speed connections over installed copper wires. DSL is one of the key teleworker solutions available.

The figure shows a representation of bandwidth space allocation on a copper wire for Asymmetrical DSL (ADSL). The area labeled POTS (Plain Old Telephone System) identifies the frequency range used by the voice-grade telephone service. The area labeled ADSL represents the frequency space used by the upstream and downstream DSL signals. The area that encompasses both the POTS area and the ADSL area represents the entire frequency range supported by the copper wire pair.

Another form of DSL technology is symmetric DSL (SDSL). All forms of DSL service are categorized as ADSL or SDSL, and there are several varieties of each type. ADSL provides higher downstream bandwidth to the user than upload bandwidth. SDSL provides the same capacity in both directions.

The different varieties of DSL provide different bandwidths, some with capabilities exceeding 40 Mb/s. The transfer rates are dependent on the actual length of the local loop, and the type and condition of the cabling. For satisfactory ADSL service, the loop must be less than 3.39 miles (5.46 km).

Refer to Interactive Graphic in online course

3.1.1.4   DSL Connections

Service providers deploy DSL connections in the local loop. The connection is set up between a pair of modems on either end of a copper wire that extends between the customer premises equipment (CPE) and the DSL access multiplexer (DSLAM). A DSLAM is the device located at the Central Office (CO) of the provider and concentrates connections from multiple DSL subscribers. A DSLAM is often built into an aggregation router.

Figure 1 shows the equipment needed to provide a DSL connection to a SOHO. The two important components are the DSL transceiver and the DSLAM:

- **Transceiver** - Connects the computer of the teleworker to the DSL. Usually the transceiver is a DSL modem connected to the computer using a USB or Ethernet cable. Typically, DSL transceivers are built into small routers with multiple switch ports suitable for home office use.

- **DSLAM** - Located at the CO of the carrier, the DSLAM combines individual DSL connections from users into one high-capacity link to an ISP, and therefore, to the Internet.

A micro filter (also known as a DSL filter) allows analog devices such as phones or fax machines to be connected and are required to be installed when DSL is being used. Figure 2 depicts modern DSL routers and broadband aggregation routers. The advantage that DSL has over cable technology is that DSL is not a shared medium. Each user has a separate direct connection to the DSLAM. Adding users does not impede performance, unless the DSLAM Internet connection to the ISP, or the Internet, becomes saturated.

Refer to
Interactive Graphic
in online course

3.1.1.5   Wireless Connection

Developments in broadband wireless technology are increasing wireless availability through three main technologies:

- Municipal Wi-Fi
- Cellular/mobile
- Satellite Internet

Municipal Wi-Fi

Many municipal governments, often working with service providers, are deploying wireless networks. Some of these networks provide high-speed Internet access at no cost or for substantially less than the price of other broadband services. Other cities reserve their Wi-Fi networks for official use, providing police, fire fighters, and city workers remote access to the Internet and municipal networks.

Most municipal wireless networks use a mesh of interconnected access points, as shown in Figure 1. Each access point is in range and can communicate with at least two other access points. The mesh blankets a particular area with radio signals.

Cellular/Mobile

Mobile phones use radio waves to communicate through nearby cell towers. The mobile phone has a small radio antenna. The provider has a much larger antenna that sits at the top of a tower, as shown in Figure 2.

Three common terms that are used when discussing cellular/mobile networks include:

- **Wireless Internet** - A general term for Internet services from a mobile phone or from any device that uses the same technology.

- **2G/3G/4G Wireless** - Major changes to the mobile phone companies' wireless networks through the evolution of the second, third, and fourth generations of wireless mobile technologies.

- **Long-Term Evolution (LTE)** - A newer and faster technology considered to be part of 4G technology.

Cellular/mobile broadband access consists of various standards. Variations include 2G using GSM, CDMA, or TDMA; 3G using UMTS, CDMA2000, EDGE, or HSPA+; and 4G, using LTE. A mobile phone subscription does not necessarily include a mobile broadband subscription. Cellular speeds continue to increase. For example, LTE Category 10 supports up to 450 Mb/s download and 100 Mb/s upload.

Satellite Internet

Satellite Internet services are used in locations where land-based Internet access is not available, or for temporary installations that are mobile. Internet access using satellites is available worldwide, including for providing Internet access to vessels at sea, airplanes in flight, and vehicles moving on land.

Figure 3 illustrates a two-way satellite system that provides Internet access to a home subscriber. Upload speeds are about one-tenth of the download speed. Download speeds range from 5 Mb/s to 25 Mb/s.

The primary installation requirement is for the antenna to have a clear view toward the equator, where most orbiting satellites are stationed. Trees and heavy rains can affect reception of the signals.

Note WiMAX (Worldwide Interoperability for Microwave Access) is a wireless technology for both fixed and mobile implementations. WiMAX may still be relevant for some areas of the world. Click here to read about Intel Capital's recent investments in WiMAX. However, in most of the world, WiMAX has largely been replaced by LTE for mobile access and cable or DSL for fixed access. Sprint shut down its WiMAX networks in early 2016. Click here for more information on the rise and fall of WiMAX.

> Refer to
> **Interactive Graphic**
> in online course

3.1.1.6 Activity - Identify Broadband Connection Terminology

3.1.2 Select a Broadband Connection

> Refer to
> **Online Course**
> for Illustration

3.1.2.1 Comparing Broadband Solutions

Each broadband solution has advantages and disadvantages. The ideal is to have a fiber-optic cable directly connected to the SOHO network. Some locations have only one option, such as cable or DSL. Some locations only have broadband wireless options for Internet connectivity.

If there are multiple broadband solutions available, a cost-versus-benefit analysis should be performed to determine the best solution.

Some factors to consider in making a decision include:

- **Cable** - Bandwidth is shared by many users, upstream data rates are often slow during high-usage hours in areas with over-subscription.

- **DSL** - Limited bandwidth that is distance sensitive (in relation to the ISP's central office), upstream rate is proportionally quite small compared to downstream rate.

- **Fiber-to-the-Home** - Requires fiber installation directly to the home (shown in the figure).

- **Cellular/Mobile** - Coverage is often an issue, even within a SOHO where bandwidth is relatively limited.

- **Wi-Fi Mesh** - Most municipalities do not have a mesh network deployed; if it is available and the SOHO is in range, then it is a viable option.

- **Satellite** - Expensive, limited capacity per subscriber; often provides access where no other access is possible.

> Refer to
> **Lab Activity**
> for this chapter

3.1.2.2 Lab - Researching Broadband Internet Access Technologies

In this lab, you will complete the following objectives:

- Part 1: Investigate Broadband Distribution
- Part 2: Research Broadband Access Options for Specific Scenarios

3.2   PPPoE

3.2.1   PPPoE Overview

Refer to
Interactive Graphic
in online course

3.2.1.1   PPPoE Motivation

In addition to understanding the various technologies available for broadband Internet access, it is also important to understand the underlying data link layer protocol used by the ISP to form a connection.

A commonly used data link layer protocol by ISPs is PPP. PPP can be used on all serial links including those links created with dial-up analog and ISDN modems. To this day, the link from a dialup user to an ISP, using analog modems, likely uses PPP. Figure 1 shows a basic representation of that analog dial connection with PPP.

Additionally, ISPs often use PPP as the data link protocol over broadband connections. There are several reasons for this. First, PPP supports the ability to assign IP addresses to remote ends of a PPP link. With PPP enabled, ISPs can use PPP to assign each customer one public IPv4 address. More importantly, PPP supports CHAP authentication. ISPs often want to use CHAP to authenticate customers because during authentication, ISPs can check accounting records to determine whether the customer's bill is paid, prior to letting the customer connect to the Internet.

These technologies came to market in the following order, with varying support for PPP:

1. Analog modems for dialup that could use PPP and CHAP

2. ISDN for dialup that could use PPP and CHAP

3. DSL, which did not create a point-to-point link and could not support PPP and CHAP

ISPs value PPP because of the authentication, accounting, and link management features. Customers appreciate the ease and availability of the Ethernet connection. However, Ethernet links do not natively support PPP. PPP over Ethernet (PPPoE) provides a solution to this problem. As shown in Figure 2, PPPoE allows the sending of PPP frames encapsulated inside Ethernet frames.

Refer to
Online Course
for Illustration

3.2.1.2   PPPoE Concepts

As shown in the figure, the customer's router is usually connected to a DSL modem using an Ethernet cable. PPPoE creates a PPP tunnel over an Ethernet connection. This allows PPP frames to be sent across the Ethernet cable to the ISP from the customer's router. The modem converts the Ethernet frames to PPP frames by stripping the Ethernet headers. The modem then transmits these PPP frames on the ISP's DSL network.

3.2.2   Implement PPPoE

Refer to
Interactive Graphic
in online course

3.2.2.1   PPPoE Configuration

With the ability to send and receive PPP frames between the routers, the ISP could continue to use the same authentication model as with analog and ISDN. To make it all work, the client and ISP routers need additional configuration, including PPP configuration, as shown in Figure 1. To understand the configuration, consider the following:

1. To create a PPP tunnel, the configuration uses a dialer interface. A dialer interface is a virtual interface. The PPP configuration is placed on the dialer interface, not the physical interface. The dialer interface is created using the **interface dialer** *number* command. The client can configure a static IP address, but will more likely be automatically assigned a public IP address by the ISP.

2. The PPP CHAP configuration usually defines one-way authentication; therefore, the ISP authenticates the customer. The hostname and password configured on the customer router must match the hostname and password configured on the ISP router. Notice in the figure that the CHAP username and password match the settings on the ISP router.

3. The physical Ethernet interface that connects to the DSL modem is then enabled with the command **pppoe enable** that enables PPPoE and links the physical interface to the dialer interface. The dialer interface is linked to the Ethernet interface with the **dialer pool** and **pppoe-client** commands, using the same number. The dialer interface number does not have to match the dialer pool number.

4. The maximum transmission unit (MTU) should be set down to 1492, versus the default of 1500, to accommodate the PPPoE headers.

Use the Syntax Checker in Figure 2 to practice configuring PPPoE.

> Refer to **Interactive Graphic** in online course

3.2.2.2 PPPoE Verification

As shown in Figure 1, the customer's router is connected to the ISP router using DSL. Both routers have been configured for PPPoE. The **show ip interface brief** command is issued on R1 to verify the IPv4 address automatically assigned to the dialer interface by the ISP router.

As shown in Figure 2, the **show interface dialer** command on R1, verifies the MTU and PPP encapsulation configured on the dialer interface.

Figure 3 displays the routing table on R1.

Notice that two /32 host routes for 10.0.0.0 have been installed in R1's routing table. The first host route is for the address assigned to the dialer interface. The second host route is the IPv4 address of the ISP. The installation of these two host routes is the default behavior for PPPoE.

As shown in Figure 4, the **show pppoe session** command is used to display information about currently active PPPoE sessions. The output displays the local and remote Ethernet MAC addresses of both routers. The Ethernet MAC addresses can be verified by using the **show interfaces** command on each router.

> Refer to **Online Course** for Illustration

3.2.2.3 PPPoE Troubleshooting

After ensuring that the client router and DSL modem are connected with the proper cables, one or more of the following reasons is usually the cause of a PPPoE connection not functioning properly:

■ Failure in the PPP negotiation process

■ Failure in the PPP authentication process

■ Failure to adjust the TCP maximum segment size

Refer to
Online Course
for Illustration

3.2.2.4   PPPoE Negotiation

Verify PPP negotiation using the **debug ppp negotiation** command. Figure 1 displays part of the debug output after R1's G0/1 interface has been enabled.

There are four main points of failure in a PPP negotiation:

- No response from the remote device (the ISP)
- Link Control Protocol (LCP) not open
- Authentication failure
- IP Control Protocol (IPCP) failure

Refer to
Interactive Graphic
in online course

3.2.2.5   PPPoE Authentication

After confirming with the ISP that they use CHAP, verify that the CHAP username and password are correct. Figure 1 shows the CHAP configuration on the dialer2 interface.

Re-examining the output of the **debug ppp negotiation** command in Figure 2, verifies that the CHAP username is correct.

If the CHAP username or password were incorrect, the output from the **debug ppp negotiation** command would show an authentication failure message such as shown in Figure 3.

Refer to
Interactive Graphic
in online course

3.2.2.6   PPPoE MTU Size

Accessing some web pages might be a problem with PPPoE. When the client requests a web page, a TCP 3-way handshake occurs between the client and the web server. During the negotiation, the client specifies the value of its TCP maximum segment size (MSS). The TCP MSS is the maximum size of the data portion in the TCP segment.

A host determines the value of its MSS field by subtracting the IP and TCP headers from the Ethernet maximum transmission unit (MTU). On an Ethernet interface, the default MTU is 1500 bytes. Subtracting the IPv4 header of 20 bytes and the TCP header of 20 bytes, the default MSS size will be 1460 bytes, as shown in Figure 1.

The default MSS size is 1460 bytes, when the default MTU is 1500 bytes. However, PPPoE supports an MTU of only 1492 bytes in order to accommodate the additional 8-byte PPPoE header shown in Figure 2.

You can verify the PPPoE MTU size in running configuration, as shown in Figure 3. This disparity between the host and PPPoE MTU size can cause the router to drop 1500-byte packets and terminate TCP sessions over the PPPoE network.

The **ip tcp adjust-mss** *max-segment-size* interface command helps prevent TCP sessions from being dropped by adjusting the MSS value during the TCP 3-way handshake. In most cases, the optimum value for the *max-segment-size* argument is 1452 bytes. Figure 4 shows this configuration on R1's LAN interface.

The TCP MSS value of 1452, plus the 20-byte IPv4 header, the 20-byte TCP header, and the 8-byte PPPoE header adds up to a 1500-byte MTU as shown in Figure 2.

Refer to
Lab Activity
for this chapter

3.2.2.7 Lab - Configuring a Router as a PPPoE Client for DSL Connectivity

In this lab, you will complete the following objectives:

- Part 1: Build the Network
- Part 2: Configure the ISP Router
- Part 3: Configure the Cust1 Router

Refer to
Lab Activity
for this chapter

3.2.2.8 Lab - Troubleshoot PPPoE

In this lab, you will compete the following objectives:

- Part 1: Build the Network
- Part 2: Troubleshoot PPPoE on Cust1

3.3 VPNs

3.3.1 Fundamentals of VPNs

Refer to
Online Course
for Illustration

3.3.1.1 Introducing VPNs

Organizations need secure, reliable, and cost-effective ways to interconnect multiple networks, such as allowing branch offices and suppliers to connect to a corporation's headquarter network. Additionally, with the growing number of teleworkers, enterprises have an increasing need for secure, reliable, and cost-effective ways to connect employees working in small office/home office (SOHO) and other remote locations, with resources on corporate sites.

As shown in the figure, organizations use VPNs to create an end-to-end private network connection over third-party networks, such as the Internet. The tunnel eliminates the distance barrier and enables remote users to access central site network resources. A VPN is a private network created via tunneling over a public network, usually the Internet. A VPN is a communications environment in which access is strictly controlled to permit peer connections within a defined community of interest.

The first VPNs were strictly IP tunnels that did not include authentication or encryption of the data. For example, Generic Routing Encapsulation (GRE) is a tunneling protocol developed by Cisco that can encapsulate a wide variety of network layer protocol packet types inside IP tunnels but it doesn't support encryption. This creates a virtual point-to-point link to Cisco routers at remote points over an IP internetwork.

Today, a secure implementation of VPN with encryption, such as IPsec VPNs, is what is usually meant by virtual private networking.

To implement VPNs, a VPN gateway is necessary. The VPN gateway could be a router, a firewall, or a Cisco Adaptive Security Appliance (ASA). An ASA is a standalone firewall device that combines firewall, VPN concentrator, and intrusion prevention functionality into one software image.

Refer to
Online Course
for Illustration

3.3.1.2 Benefits of VPNs

As shown in the figure, a VPN uses virtual connections that are routed through the Internet from the private network of an organization to the remote site or employee host. The information from a private network is securely transported over the public network, to form a virtual network.

The benefits of a VPN include the following:

- **Cost savings** - VPNs enable organizations to use cost-effective, third-party Internet transport to connect remote offices and remote users to the main site; therefore, eliminating expensive, dedicated WAN links and modem banks. Furthermore, with the advent of cost-effective, high-bandwidth technologies, such as DSL, organizations can use VPNs to reduce their connectivity costs while simultaneously increasing remote connection bandwidth.

- **Scalability** - VPNs enable organizations to use the Internet infrastructure within ISPs and devices, which makes it easy to add new users. Therefore, organizations are able to add large amounts of capacity without adding significant infrastructure.

- **Compatibility with broadband technology** - VPNs allow mobile workers and telecommuters to take advantage of high-speed, broadband connectivity, such as DSL and cable, to access to their organizations' networks. Broadband connectivity provides flexibility and efficiency. High-speed, broadband connections also provide a cost-effective solution for connecting remote offices.

- **Security** - VPNs can include security mechanisms that provide the highest level of security by using advanced encryption and authentication protocols that protect data from unauthorized access.

Refer to
Interactive Graphic
in online course

3.3.1.3 Activity - Identify the Benefits of VPNs

3.3.2 Types of VPNs

Refer to
Online Course
for Illustration

3.3.2.1 Site-to-Site VPNs

A site-to-site VPN is created when devices on both sides of the VPN connection are aware of the VPN configuration in advance, as shown in the figure. The VPN remains static, and internal hosts have no knowledge that a VPN exists. In a site-to-site VPN, end hosts send and receive normal TCP/IP traffic through a VPN "gateway". The VPN gateway is responsible for encapsulating and encrypting outbound traffic for all traffic from a particular site. The VPN gateway then sends it through a VPN tunnel over the Internet to a peer VPN gateway at the target site. Upon receipt, the peer VPN gateway strips the headers, decrypts the content, and relays the packet toward the target host inside its private network.

A site-to-site VPN is an extension of a classic WAN network. Site-to-site VPNs connect entire networks to each other, for example, they can connect a branch office network to a company headquarters network. In the past, a leased line or Frame Relay connection was required to connect sites, but because most corporations now have Internet access, these connections can be replaced with site-to-site VPNs.

Refer to **Online Course** for Illustration

3.3.2.2 Remote Access VPNs

Where a site-to-site VPN is used to connect entire networks, a remote-access VPN supports the needs of telecommuters, mobile users, and extranet, consumer-to-business traffic. A remote-access VPN is created when VPN information is not statically set up, but instead allows for dynamically changing information, and can be enabled and disabled. Remote-access VPNs support a client/server architecture, where the VPN client (remote host) gains secure access to the enterprise network via a VPN server device at the network edge, as shown in the figure.

Remote-access VPNs are used to connect individual hosts that must access their company network securely over the Internet. Internet connectivity used by telecommuters is typically a broadband connection.

VPN client software may need to be installed on the mobile user's end device; for example, each host may have Cisco AnyConnect Secure Mobility Client software installed. When the host tries to send any traffic, the Cisco AnyConnect VPN Client software encapsulates and encrypts this traffic. The encrypted data is then sent over the Internet to the VPN gateway at the edge of the target network. Upon receipt, the VPN gateway behaves as it does for site-to-site VPNs.

Note The Cisco AnyConnect Secure Mobility Client software builds on prior Cisco Any-Connect VPN Client and Cisco VPN Client offerings to improve the always-on VPN experience across more laptop and smart phone-based mobile devices. This client supports IPv6.

Refer to **Interactive Graphic** in online course

3.3.2.3 DMVPN

Dynamic Multipoint VPN (DMVPN) is a Cisco software solution for building multiple VPNs in an easy, dynamic, and scalable manner. The goal is to simplify the configuration while easily and flexibly connecting central office sites with branch sites. This is called hub-to-spoke, as shown in Figure 1.

With DMVPNs, branch sites can also communicate directly with other branch sites, as shown in Figure 2.

DMVPN is built using the following technologies:

- Next Hop Resolution Protocol (NHRP)
- Multipoint Generic Routing Encapsulation (mGRE) tunnels
- IP Security (IPsec) encryption

NHRP is a Layer 2 resolution and caching protocol similar to Address Resolution Protocol (ARP). NHRP creates a distributed mapping database of public IP addresses for all tunnel spokes. NHRP is a client server protocol consisting of the NHRP hub known as the Next Hop Server (NHS), and the NHRP spokes known as the Next Hop Clients (NHCs).

Generic Routing Encapsulation (GRE) is a tunneling protocol developed by Cisco that can encapsulate a wide variety of protocol packet types inside IP tunnels. An mGRE tunnel interface allows a single GRE interface to support multiple IPsec tunnels. With mGRE, dynamically allocated tunnels are created through a permanent tunnel source at the hub and dynamically allocated tunnel destinations, created as necessary, at the spokes. This reduces the size and simplifies the complexity of the configuration.

Like other VPN types, DMVPN relies on IPsec to provide secure transport of private information over public networks, such as the Internet.

Refer to
Interactive Graphic
in online course

3.3.2.4   Activity - Compare Types of VPNs

3.4   GRE

3.4.1   GRE Overview

Refer to
Online Course
for Illustration

3.4.1.1   GRE Introduction

Generic Routing Encapsulation (GRE) is one example of a basic, non-secure, site-to-site VPN tunneling protocol. GRE is a tunneling protocol developed by Cisco that can encapsulate a wide variety of protocol packet types inside IP tunnels. GRE creates a virtual point-to-point link to Cisco routers at remote points, over an IP internetwork.

GRE is designed to manage the transportation of multiprotocol and IP multicast traffic between two or more sites, that may only have IP connectivity. It can encapsulate multiple protocol packet types inside an IP tunnel.

As shown in the figure, a tunnel interface supports a header for each of the following:

- An encapsulated protocol (or passenger protocol), such as IPv4, IPv6, AppleTalk, DECnet, or IPX

- An encapsulation protocol (or carrier), such as GRE

- A transport delivery protocol, such as IP, which is the protocol that carries the encapsulated protocol

Refer to
Online Course
for Illustration

3.4.1.2   GRE Characteristics

GRE is a tunneling protocol developed by Cisco that can encapsulate a wide variety of protocol packet types inside IP tunnels, creating a virtual point-to-point link to Cisco routers at remote points over an IP internetwork. IP tunneling using GRE enables network expansion across a single-protocol backbone environment. It does this by connecting multiprotocol subnetworks in a single-protocol backbone environment.

GRE has these characteristics:

- GRE is defined as an IETF standard (RFC 2784).

- In the outer IP header, 47 is used in the protocol field to indicate that a GRE header will follow.

- GRE encapsulation uses a protocol type field in the GRE header to support the encapsulation of any OSI Layer 3 protocol. Protocol Types are defined in RFC 1700 as "EtherTypes".

- GRE itself is stateless; by default, it does not include any flow-control mechanisms.

- GRE does not include any strong security mechanisms to protect its payload.

- The GRE header, together with the tunneling IP header indicated in the figure, creates at least 24 bytes of additional overhead for tunneled packets.

Refer to
Interactive Graphic
in online course

3.4.1.3 Activity - Identify GRE Characteristics

3.4.2 Implement GRE

Refer to
Interactive Graphic
in online course

3.4.2.1 Configure GRE

GRE is used to create a VPN tunnel between two sites, as shown in Figure 1. To implement a GRE tunnel, the network administrator must first learn the IP addresses of the endpoints. After that, there are five steps to configuring a GRE tunnel:

Step 1. Create a tunnel interface using the **interface tunnel number** command.

Step 2. Configure an IP address for the tunnel interface. This is normally a private IP address.

Step 3. Specify the tunnel source IP address.

Step 4. Specify the tunnel destination IP address.

Step 5. (Optional) Specify GRE tunnel mode as the tunnel interface mode. GRE tunnel mode is the default tunnel interface mode for Cisco IOS software.

The sample configuration in Figure 2 illustrates a basic GRE tunnel configuration for router R1.

The configuration of R2 in Figure 3 mirrors the configuration of R1.

The minimum configuration requires specification of the tunnel source and destination addresses. The IP subnet must also be configured to provide IP connectivity across the tunnel link. Both tunnel interfaces have the tunnel source set as the local serial S0/0/0 interface and the tunnel destination set as the peer router serial S0/0/0 interface. A private IP address is commonly assigned to the tunnel interface on both routers. OSPF has also been configured to exchange routes over the GRE tunnel.

The individual GRE tunnel command descriptions are displayed in Figure 4.

Note   When configuring GRE tunnels, it can be difficult to remember which IP networks are associated with the physical interfaces and which IP networks are associated with the tunnel interfaces. Remember that before a GRE tunnel is created, the physical interfaces have already been configured. The **tunnel source** and **tunnel destination** commands reference the IP addresses of the preconfigured physical interfaces. The **ip address** command on the tunnel interfaces refers to an IP network (usually a private IP network) specifically selected for the purposes of the GRE tunnel.

Refer to
Interactive Graphic
in online course

3.4.2.2 Verify GRE

There are several commands that can be used to monitor and troubleshoot GRE tunnels. To determine whether the tunnel interface is up or down, use the **show ip interface brief** command, as shown in Figure 1.

To verify the state of a GRE tunnel, use the **show interface tunnel** command. The line protocol on a GRE tunnel interface is up as long as there is a route to the tunnel destination. Before implementing a GRE tunnel, IP connectivity must already be in effect between the

IP addresses of the physical interfaces on opposite ends of the potential GRE tunnel. The tunnel transport protocol is displayed in the output, also shown in Figure 1.

If OSPF has also been configured to exchange routes over the GRE tunnel, verify that an OSPF adjacency has been established over the tunnel interface using the **show ip ospf neighbor** command. In Figure 2, note that the peering address for the OSPF neighbor is on the IP network created for the GRE tunnel.

In Figure 3, use the Syntax Checker to configure and verify a GRE tunnel on R2 followed by R1.

GRE is considered a VPN because it is a private network that is created by tunneling over a public network. Using encapsulation, a GRE tunnel creates a virtual point-to-point link to Cisco routers at remote points over an IP internetwork. The advantages of GRE are that it can be used to tunnel non-IP traffic over an IP network, allowing for network expansion by connecting multiprotocol subnetworks across a single-protocol backbone environment. GRE also supports IP multicast tunneling. This means that routing protocols can be used across the tunnel, enabling dynamic exchange of routing information in the virtual network. Finally, it is common practice to create IPv6 over IPv4 GRE tunnels, where IPv6 is the encapsulated protocol and IPv4 is the transport protocol. In the future, these roles will likely be reversed as IPv6 takes over as the standard IP protocol.

However, GRE does not provide encryption or any other security mechanisms. Therefore, data sent across a GRE tunnel is not secure. If secure data communication is needed, IPsec or SSL VPNs should be configured.

Refer to **Interactive Graphic** in online course

3.4.2.3   Troubleshoot GRE

Issues with GRE are usually due to one or more of the following misconfigurations:

- The tunnel interface IP addresses are not on the same network or the subnet masks do not match.

- The interfaces for the tunnel source and/or tunnel destination are not configured with the correct IP address or are in the down state.

- Static or dynamic routing is not properly configured.

Use the **show ip interface brief** command on both routers to verify that the tunnel interface is up and configured with the correct IP addresses for the physical interface and the tunnel interface. Also, verify that the source interface on each router is up and configured with the correct IP addresses, as shown in Figure 1.

Routing can cause an issue. Both routers need a default route pointing to the Internet. Also, both routers will need the correct dynamic or static routing configured. You can use the **show ip ospf neighbor** command to verify neighbor adjacency, as shown on the previous page. Regardless of the routing used, you can also use **show ip route** to verify that networks are being passed between the two routers, as shown in Figure 2.

Refer to **Packet Tracer Activity** for this chapter

3.4.2.4   Packet Tracer - Configuring GRE

You are the network administrator for a company which wants to set up a GRE tunnel to a remote office. Both networks are locally configured, and need only the tunnel configured.

Refer to **Packet Tracer Activity** for this chapter

3.4.2.5   Packet Tracer - Troubleshooting GRE

A junior network administrator was hired to set up a GRE tunnel between two sites and was unable to complete the task. You have been asked to correct configuration errors in the company network.

Refer to **Lab Activity** for this chapter

3.4.2.6   Lab - Configuring a Point-to-Point GRE VPN Tunnel

In this lab, you will complete the following objectives:

■ Part 1: Configure Basic Device Settings

■ Part 2: Configure a GRE Tunnel

■ Part 3: Enable Routing over the GRE Tunnel

3.5   eBGP

3.5.1   BGP Overview

Refer to **Online Course** for Illustration

3.5.1.1   IGP and EGP Routing Protocols

RIP, EIGRP and OSPF are Interior Gateway Protocols (IGPs). ISPs and their customers, such as corporations and other enterprises, usually use an IGP to route traffic within their networks. IGPs are used to exchange routing information within a company network or an autonomous system (AS).

Border Gateway Protocol (BGP) is an Exterior Gateway Protocol (EGP) used for the exchange of routing information between autonomous systems, such as ISPs, companies, and content providers (e.g., YouTube, Netflix, etc.).

In BGP, every AS is assigned a unique 16-bit or 32-bit AS number which uniquely identifies it on the Internet. An example of how IGPs are used is shown in the figure.

Note   There are also private AS numbers. However, private AS numbers are beyond the scope of this course.

Internal routing protocols use a specific metric, such as OSPF's cost, for determining the best paths to destination networks. BGP does not use a single metric like IGPs. BGP routers exchange several path attributes including a list of AS numbers (hop by hop) necessary to reach a destination network. For example, in Figure 1 AS 65002 may use the AS-path of 65003 and 65005 to reach a network within the content provider AS 65005. BGP is known as a path vector routing protocol.

Note   AS-path is one of several attributes that may be used by BGP to determine best path. However, path attributes and BGP best path determination are beyond the scope of this course.

BGP updates are encapsulated over TCP on port 179. Therefore, BGP inherits the connection-oriented properties of TCP, which ensures that BGP updates are transmitted reliably.

IGP routing protocols are used to route traffic within the same organization and administered by a single organization. In contrast, BGP is used to route between networks administered by two different organizations. BGP is used by an AS to advertise its networks and in some cases, networks that it learned about from other autonomous systems, to the rest of the Internet.

Refer to
Online Course
for Illustration

3.5.1.2   eBGP and iBGP

Two routers exchanging BGP routing information are known as BGP peers. As shown in the figure, there are two types of BGP:

- **External BGP (eBGP)** - External BGP is the routing protocol used between routers in different autonomous systems.

- **Internal BGP (iBGP)** - Internal BGP is the routing protocol used between routers in the same AS.

This course focuses on eBGP only.

Note   There are some differences in how BGP operates depending on whether the two routers are eBGP peers or iBGP peers. However, these differences are beyond the scope of this course.

3.5.2   BGP Design Considerations

Refer to
Online Course
for Illustration

3.5.2.1   When to use BGP

The use of BGP is most appropriate when an AS has connections to multiple autonomous systems. This is known as multi-homed. Each AS in the figure is multi-homed because each AS has connections to at least two other autonomous systems or BGP peers.

Before running BGP, it is important that the network administrator has a good understanding of BGP. A misconfiguration of a BGP router could have negative effects throughout the entire Internet.

Refer to
Online Course
for Illustration

3.5.2.2   When not to use BGP

BGP should not be used when at least one of the following conditions exist:

- There is a single connection to the Internet or another AS. This is known as single-homed. In this case, Company-A may run an IGP with the ISP or, Company-A and the ISP will each use static routes, as shown in the figure. Although it is recommended only in unusual situations, for the purposes of this course, you will configure single-homed BGP.

- When there is a limited understanding of BGP. A misconfiguration of a BGP router can have far reaching affects beyond the local AS, negatively impacting routers throughout the Internet.

Note   There are some single-homed situations where BGP may be appropriate, such as the need for a specific routing policy. However, routing policies are beyond the scope of this course.

Refer to
Interactive Graphic
in online course

3.5.2.3 BGP Options

BGP is used by autonomous systems to advertise networks that originated within their AS or in the case of ISPs, the networks that originated from other autonomous systems.

For example, a company connecting to their ISP using BGP would advertise their network addresses to their ISP. The ISP would then advertise these networks to other ISPs (BGP peers). Eventually, all other autonomous systems on the Internet would learn about the networks initially originated by the company.

There are three common ways an organization can choose to implement BGP in a multi-homed environment:

Default Route Only

ISPs advertise a default route to Company-A, as shown in Figure 1. The arrows indicate that the default is configured on the ISPs, not on the Company-A. This is the simplest method to implement BGP. However, because the company only receives a default route from both ISPs, sub-optimal routing may occur. For example, Company-A may choose to use ISP-1's default route when sending packets to a destination network in ISP-2's AS.

Default Route and ISP Routes

ISPs advertise their default route and their network to Company-A, as shown in Figure 2. This option allows Company-A to forward traffic to the appropriate ISP for networks advertised by that ISP. For example, Company-A would choose ISP-1 for networks advertised by ISP-1. For all other networks, one of the two default routes can be used, which means sub-optimal routing may still occur for all other Internet routes.

All Internet Routes

ISPs advertise all Internet routes to Company-A, as shown in Figure 3. Because Company-A receives all Internet routes from both ISPs, Company-A can determine which ISP to use as the best path to forward traffic for any network. Although this solves the issue of sub-optimal routing, the Company-A's BGP router must contain all Internet routes, which would currently include routes to over 550,000 networks.

Refer to
Interactive Graphic
in online course

3.5.2.4 Activity - Identify BPG Terminology and Designs

3.5.3 eBGP Branch Configuration

Refer to
Online Course
for Illustration

3.5.3.1 Steps to Configure eBGP

To implement eBGP for this course, you will need to complete the following tasks:

Step 1. Enable BGP routing.

Step 2. Configure BGP neighbor(s) (peering).

Step 3. Advertise network(s) originating from this AS.

The figure lists the command syntax and a description for basic eBGP configuration.

Refer to
Interactive Graphic
in online course

3.5.3.2   BGP Sample Configuration

In this a single-homed BGP topology, Company-A in AS 65000 uses eBGP to advertise its 198.133.219.0/24 network to ISP-1 at AS 65001. ISP-1 advertises a default route in its eBGP updates to Company-A.

Note   BGP is usually not necessary in single-homed AS. It is used here to provide a simple configuration example.

Figure 1 shows the BGP configuration for Company-A. Customers typically use private IPv4 address space for internal devices within their own network. Using NAT, the Company-A router translates these private IPv4 addresses to one of its public IPv4 addresses, advertised by BGP to the ISP.

The **router bgp** command enables BGP and identifies the AS number for Company-A. A router can belong to only a single AS, so only a single BGP process can run on a router.

The **neighbor** command identifies the BGP peer and its AS number. Notice that the ISP AS number is different than the Company-A AS number. This informs the BGP process that the neighbor is in a different AS and is therefore, an external BGP neighbor.

The **mask** option must be used when the network advertised is different than its classful equivalent. In this example, the 198.133.219.0/24 is equivalent to a class C network. Class C networks have a /24 subnet mask, so in this case the **mask** option is not required. If Customer-A was advertising the 198.133.0.0/16 network, then the **mask** option would be required. Otherwise BGP would advertise the network with a /24 classful mask.

The **network** command enters the *network-address* into the local BGP table. The BGP table contains all routes learned via BGP or advertised using BGP. eBGP will then advertise the *network-address* to its eBGP neighbors.

Note   In contrast to an IGP protocol, the *network-address* used in the **network** command does not have to be a directly connected network. The router only needs to have a route to this network in its routing table.

Figure 2 shows the BGP configuration for ISP-1.

The eBGP commands on the ISP-1 router are similar to the configuration on Company-A. Notice how the **network 0.0.0.0** command is used to advertise a default network to Company-A.

Note   Although the **network 0.0.0.0** command is a valid BGP configuration option, there are better ways to advertise a default route in eBGP. However, these methods are beyond the scope of this course.

Refer to
Interactive Graphic
in online course

3.5.3.3   Verify eBGP

Three commands can be used to verify eBGP, as shown in Figure 1.

Figure 2 shows the output for Company-A's IPv4 routing table. Notice how the origin code **B** identifies that the route was learned using BGP. Specifically, in this example, Company-A has received a BGP advertised default route from ISP-1.

Figure 3 shows the output of Company-A's BGP table. The first entry 0.0.0.0 with a next hop of 209.165.201.1 is the default route advertised by ISP-1. The AS path displays the single AS of 65001 because the 0.0.0.0/0 network advertised by ISP-1, originated from the same AS. Most BGP table entries show multiple autonomous system numbers in the path, listing the sequence of AS numbers required to reach the destination network.

The second entry 198.133.219.0/24 is the network advertised by the Company-A router to ISP-1. The next hop address of 0.0.0.0 indicates that the 198.133.219.0/24 network originated from this router.

Figure 4 displays the status of BGP connection on Company-A. The first line displays the local IPv4 address used to peer with another BGP neighbor and this router's local AS number. The address and AS number of the remote BGP neighbor is shown at the bottom of the output.

Use the Syntax Checker in Figure 5 to practice configuring and verifying BGP.

Refer to **Packet Tracer Activity** for this chapter

3.5.3.4   Packet Tracer - Configure and Verify eBGP

In this activity, you will configure and verify the operation of eBGP between autonomous systems 65001 and 65002.

Refer to **Lab Activity** for this chapter

3.5.3.5   Lab - Configure and Verify eBGP

In this lab, you will complete the following objectives:

- Build the Network and Configure Basic Device Settings

- Configure eBGP on R1

- Verify eBGP Configuration

3.6   Summary

Refer to **Online Course** for Illustration

3.6.1.1   Class Activity - VPN Planning Design

Your small- to medium-sized business has received quite a few new contracts lately. This has increased the need for teleworkers and workload outsourcing. The new contract vendors and clients will also need access to your network as the projects progress.

As network administrator for the business, you recognize that VPNs must be incorporated as a part of your network strategy to support secure access by the teleworkers, employees, and vendors or clients.

To prepare for implementation of VPNs on the network, you devise a planning checklist to bring to the next department meeting for discussion.

Refer to **Packet Tracer Activity** for this chapter

3.6.1.2   Packet Tracer - Skills Integration Challenge

In this skills integration challenge, the XYZ Corporation uses a combination of eBGP, PPP, and GRE WAN connections. Other technologies include DHCP, default routing, OSPF for IPv4, and SSH configurations.

Refer to
Lab Activity
for this chapter

3.6.1.3   Lab - Configure a Branch Connection

In this lab, you will configure two separate WAN connections, a BGP route over a PPPoE connection, and a BGP route over a GRE tunnel. This lab is a test case scenario and does not represent a realistic BGP implementation.

- Part 1: Build the Network and Load Device Configurations

- Part 2: Configure a PPPoE Client Connection

- Part 3: Configure a GRE Tunnel

- Part 4: Configure BGP over PPPoE and BGP over a GRE Tunnel

Refer to
Online Course
for Illustration

3.6.1.4   Chapter 3: Summary

Broadband transmission is provided by a wide range of technologies, including DSL, fiber-to-the-home, coaxial cable systems, wireless, and satellite. This transmission requires additional components at the home end and at the corporate end. Broadband wireless solutions include municipal Wi-Fi, cellular/mobile, and satellite Internet. Municipal Wi-Fi mesh networks are not widely deployed. Cellular/mobile coverage can be limited and bandwidth can be an issue. Satellite Internet is relatively expensive and limited, but it may be the only method to provide access.

If multiple broadband connections are available to a particular location, a cost-benefit analysis should be performed to determine the best solution. The best solution may be to connect to multiple service providers to provide redundancy and reliability.

PPPoE is a popular data link protocol for connecting remote networks to their ISPs. PPPoE provides the flexibility of PPP and the convenience of Ethernet.

VPNs are used to create a secure end-to-end private network connection over a third party network, such as the Internet. GRE is a basic, non-secure site-to-site VPN tunneling protocol that can encapsulate a wide variety of protocol packet types inside IP tunnels, thus allowing an organization to deliver other protocols through an IP-based WAN. Today it is primarily used to deliver IP multicast traffic or IPv6 traffic over an IPv4 unicast-only connection.

BGP is the routing protocol implemented between autonomous systems. Three basic design options for eBGP are as follows:

- The ISP advertises a default route only to the customer

- The ISP advertises a default route and all of its routes to the customer

- The ISP advertises all Internet routes to the customer

Implementing eBGP in a single-homed network only requires a few commands.

Go to the online course to take the quiz and exam.

Chapter 3 Quiz

This quiz is designed to provide an additional opportunity to practice the skills and knowledge presented in the chapter and to prepare for the chapter exam. You will be allowed multiple attempts and the grade does not appear in the gradebook.

Chapter 3 Exam

The chapter exam assesses your knowledge of the chapter content.

Your Chapter Notes

Access Control Lists

4.0 Introduction

Refer to
Online Course
for Illustration

4.0.1.1 Chapter 4: Access Control Lists

One of the most important skills a network administrator needs is mastery of access control lists (ACLs). ACLs provide packet filtering capabilities to control traffic flow.

Network designers use firewalls to protect networks from unauthorized use. Firewalls are hardware or software solutions that enforce network security policies. Consider a lock on a door to a room inside a building. The lock allows only authorized users with a key or access card to pass through the door. Similarly, a firewall filters unauthorized or potentially dangerous packets from entering the network.

On a Cisco router, you can configure a simple firewall that provides basic traffic filtering capabilities using ACLs. Administrators use ACLs to filter traffic, allowing or blocking specified packets on their networks.

This chapter begins with a review of ACLs and standard IPv4 ACL configuration. The chapter then explains how to configure and troubleshoot extended IPv4 ACLs and IPv6 ACLs on a Cisco router as part of a security solution. Included are tips, considerations, recommendations, and general guidelines on how to use ACLs. In addition, this chapter includes an opportunity to develop your mastery of ACLs with a series of lessons, activities, and lab exercises.

4.1 Standard ACL Operation and Configuration Review

4.1.1 ACL Operation Overview

Refer to
Interactive Graphic
in online course

4.1.1.1 ACLs and the Wildcard Mask

Note This section includes a brief review of standard IPv4 ACL operation and configuration. If you require additional review, refer to Chapter 7, Access Control Lists in the *Routing and Switching Essentials v6* course.

An ACL is a sequential list of permit or deny statements, known as access control entries (ACEs). ACEs are also commonly called ACL statements. When network traffic passes through an interface configured with an ACL, the router compares the information within the packet against each ACE, in sequential order, to determine if the packet matches one of the ACEs.

IPv4 ACEs include the use of wildcard masks. A wildcard mask is a string of 32 binary digits used by the router to determine which bits of the address to examine for a match.

Figure 1 shows how different wildcard masks filter IPv4 addresses. In the example, remember that binary 0 signifies a bit that must match, and binary 1 signifies a bit that can be ignored.

Figure 2 provides three examples of wildcard masks that match subnets.

In the first example the wildcard mask stipulates that every bit in the IPv4 192.168.1.1 must match exactly.

In the second example, the wildcard mask stipulates that anything will match.

In the third example, the wildcard mask stipulates that any host within the 192.168.1.0/24 network will match.

Refer to **Interactive Graphic** in online course

4.1.1.2   Applying ACLs to an Interface

ACLs can be configured to apply to inbound traffic and outbound traffic as shown in Figure 1. The last statement of an ACL is always an implicit deny. This statement is automatically inserted at the end of each ACL even though it is not visible in show command output.

As shown in Figure 2, you can configure one ACL per protocol, per direction, per interface:

- **One ACL per protocol** - To control traffic flow on an interface, an ACL must be defined for each protocol enabled on the interface.

- **One ACL per direction** - ACLs control traffic in one direction at a time on an interface. Two separate ACLs must be created to control inbound and outbound traffic.

- **One ACL per interface** - ACLs control traffic for an interface, for example, GigabitEthernet 0/0.

Refer to **Interactive Graphic** in online course

4.1.1.3   A TCP Conversation

Administrators can control network traffic based on a number of characteristics, including the TCP port being requested. It is easier to understand how an ACL filters traffic by examining the dialogue that occurs during a TCP conversation, such as when requesting a webpage.

When a client requests data from a web server, IP manages the communication between the PC (source) and the server (destination). TCP manages the communication between the web browser (application) and the network server software.

The animation shown in Figure 1 illustrates how a TCP/IP conversation takes place. TCP segments are marked with flags that denote their purpose: a SYN starts (synchronizes) the session; an ACK is an acknowledgment that an expected segment was received, and a FIN finishes the session. A SYN/ACK acknowledges that the transfer is synchronized. TCP data segments include the higher level protocol needed to direct the application data to the correct application.

The TCP data segment also identifies the port which matches the requested service. Figure 2 shows ranges of UDP and TCP ports. Figure 3 shows a listing of well-known port numbers.

Refer to
Online Course
for Illustration

4.1.1.4   ACL Packet Filtering

Packet filtering controls access to a network by analyzing the incoming and outgoing packets and forwarding them or discarding them based on given criteria. Packet filtering can occur at Layer 3 or Layer 4. Standard ACLs only filter at Layer 3. Extended ACLs filter at Layer 3 and Layer 4.

For example, an ACL could be configured to logically, "Permit web access to users from network A but deny all other services to network A users. Deny HTTP access to users from network B, but permit network B users to have all other access." Refer to the figure to examine the decision path the packet filter uses to accomplish this task.

For this scenario, the packet filter looks at each packet as follows:

- If the packet is a TCP SYN from Network A using Port 80, it is allowed to pass. All other access is denied to those users.

- If the packet is a TCP SYN from Network B using Port 80, it is blocked. However, all other access is permitted.

This is just a simple example. Multiple rules can be configured to further permit or deny services to specific users.

Refer to
Interactive Graphic
in online course

4.1.1.5   Activity - Determine the Correct Wildcard Mask

4.1.1.6   Activity - ACL Operation

Refer to
Interactive Graphic
in online course

4.1.2   Types of IPv4 ACLs

Refer to
Interactive Graphic
in online course

4.1.2.1   Standard and Extended IPv4 ACLs

The two types of Cisco IPv4 ACLs are standard and extended.

Standard ACLs can be used to permit or deny traffic only from source IPv4 addresses. The destination of the packet and the ports involved are not evaluated. The example in Figure 1 allows all traffic from the 192.168.30.0/24 network. Because of the implied "deny any" at the end, all traffic except for traffic coming from the 192.168.30.0/24 network is blocked with this ACL. Standard ACLs are created in global configuration mode.

Extended ACLs filter IPv4 packets based on several attributes:

- Protocol type

- Source IPv4 address

- Destination IPv4 address

- Source TCP or UDP ports

- Destination TCP or UDP ports

- Optional protocol type information for finer control

In Figure 2, ACL 103 permits traffic originating from any address on the 192.168.30.0/24 network to any IPv4 network if the destination host port is 80 (HTTP). Extended ACLs are created in global configuration mode.

Note   ACL command syntax is discussed in more detail later in this chapter.

4.1.2.2   Numbered and Named ACLs

Standard and extended ACLs can be created using either a number or a name to identify the ACL and its list of statements.

Using numbered ACLs is an effective method for determining the ACL type on smaller networks with more homogeneously defined traffic. However, a number does not provide information about the purpose of the ACL. For this reason, a name can be used to identify a Cisco ACL.

The figure summarizes the rules to follow to designate numbered ACLs and named ACLs.

4.1.2.3   Where to Place ACLs

Every ACL should be placed where it has the greatest impact on efficiency. As shown in the figure, the basic rules are:

- **Extended ACLs** - Locate extended ACLs as close as possible to the source of the traffic to be filtered. This way, undesirable traffic is denied close to the source network without crossing the network infrastructure.

- **Standard ACLs** - Because standard ACLs do not specify destination addresses, place them as close to the destination as possible. If a standard ACL was placed at the source of the traffic, the "permit" or "deny" will occur based on the given source address no matter where the traffic is destined.

Placement of the ACL and therefore, the type of ACL used, may also depend a variety of factors:

- **The extent of the network administrator's control** - Placement of the ACL can depend on whether or not the network administrator has control of both the source and destination networks.

- **Bandwidth of the networks involved** - Filtering unwanted traffic at the source prevents transmission of the traffic before it consumes bandwidth on the path to a destination. This is especially important in low bandwidth networks.

- **Ease of configuration** - If a network administrator wants to deny traffic coming from several networks, one option is to use a single standard ACL on the router closest to the destination. The disadvantage is that traffic from these networks will use bandwidth unnecessarily. An extended ACL could be used on each router where the traffic originated. This will save bandwidth by filtering the traffic at the source, but requires creating extended ACLs on multiple routers.

Note   For CCNA certification, the general rule is that extended ACLs are placed as close as possible to the source and standard ACLs are placed as close as possible to the destination.

Refer to
Online Course
for Illustration

4.1.2.4   Standard ACL Placement Example

In the figure, the administrator wants to prevent traffic originating in the 192.168.10.0/24 network from reaching the 192.168.30.0/24 network.

If the standard ACL is placed on the outbound interface of R1 (not shown in figure), this would prevent traffic on the 192.168.10.0/24 network from reaching any networks that are reachable through the Serial 0/0/0 interface of R1.

Following the basic placement guidelines of placing the standard ACL close to the destination, the figure shows two possible interfaces on R3 to apply the standard ACL:

- **R3 S0/0/1 interface** - Applying a standard ACL to prevent traffic from 192.168.10.0/24 from entering the S0/0/1 interface will prevent this traffic from reaching 192.168.30.0/24 and all other networks that are reachable by R3. This includes the 192.168.31.0/24 network. Because the intent of the ACL is to filter traffic destined only for 192.168.30.0/24, a standard ACL should not be applied to this interface.

- **R3 G0/0 interface** - Applying the standard ACL to traffic exiting the G0/0 interface will filter packets from 192.168.10.0/24 to 192.168.30.0/24. This will not affect other networks that are reachable by R3. Packets from 192.168.10.0/24 will still be able to reach 192.168.31.0/24.

Refer to
Online Course
for Illustration

4.1.2.5   Extended ACL Placement Example

The basic rule for placing an extended ACL is to place it as close to the source as possible. This prevents unwanted traffic from being sent across multiple networks only to be denied when it reaches its destination. However, network administrators can only place ACLs on devices that they control. Therefore, placement must be determined in the context of where the control of the network administrator extends.

In the figure, the administrator of Company A, which includes the 192.168.10.0/24 and 192.168.11.0/24 networks (referred to as .10 and .11 in this example) wants to control traffic to Company B. Specifically, the administrator wants to deny Telnet and FTP traffic from the .11 network to Company B's 192.168.30.0/24 (.30, in this example) network. At the same time, all other traffic from the .11 network must be permitted to leave Company A without restriction.

There are several ways to accomplish these goals. An extended ACL on R3 that blocks Telnet and FTP from the .11 network would accomplish the task, but the administrator does not control R3. In addition, this solution also allows unwanted traffic to cross the entire network, only to be blocked at the destination. This affects overall network efficiency.

A better solution is to place an extended ACL on R1 that specifies both source and destination addresses (.11 network and .30 network, respectively), and enforces the rule, "Telnet and FTP traffic from the .11 network is not allowed to go to the .30 network." The figure shows two possible interfaces on R1 to apply the extended ACL:

- **R1 S0/0/0 interface (outbound)** - One possibility is to apply an extended ACL outbound on the S0/0/0 interface. Because the extended ACL can examine both source and destination addresses, only FTP and Telnet packets from 192.168.11.0/24 will be denied. Other traffic from 192.168.11.0/24 and other networks will be forwarded by R1. The disadvantage of placing the extended ACL on this interface is that all traffic exiting S0/0/0 must be processed by the ACL including packets from 192.168.10.0/24.

■ **R1 G0/1 interface (inbound)** - Applying an extended ACL to traffic entering the G0/1 interface means that only packets from the 192.168.11.0/24 network are subject to ACL processing on R1. Because the filter is to be limited to only those packets leaving the 192.168.11.0/24 network, applying the extended ACL to G0/1 is the best solution.

Refer to **Interactive Graphic** in online course

4.1.2.6 Activity - Placing Standard and Extended ACLs

4.1.3 Standard IPv4 ACL Implementation

Refer to **Interactive Graphic** in online course

4.1.3.1 Configure a Standard IPv4 ACL

The full syntax of the standard ACL command is as follows:

```
Router(config)# access-list access-list-number { deny | permit |
   remark } source [ source-wildcard ] [ log ]
```

Figure 1 provides a detailed explanation of the syntax for a standard ACL.

ACEs can permit or deny an individual host or a range of host addresses. To create numbered ACL 10 that permits a specific host with the IPv4 address 192.168.10.10, you would enter:

```
R1(config)# access-list 10 permit 192.168.10.0 0.0.0.255
```

As shown in Figure 2, to create a statement that will permit a range of IPv4 addresses in a numbered ACL 10 that permits all IPv4 addresses in the network 192.168.10.0/24, you would enter:

```
R1(config)# access-list 10 permit 192.168.10.0 0.0.0.255
```

To remove the ACL, the global configuration **no access-list 10** command is used. Issuing the **show access-list** command confirms that access list 10 has been removed.

As shown in Figure 3, the **remark** keyword is used for documentation and makes access lists a great deal easier to understand. When reviewing the ACL in the configuration using the **show running-config** command, the remark is also displayed.

Refer to **Online Course** for Illustration

4.1.3.2 Apply a Standard IPv4 ACL

After a standard IPv4 ACL is configured, it is linked to an interface using the **ip access-group** command in interface configuration mode:

```
Router(config-if)# ip access-group { access-list-number | access-list-
   name } { in | out }
```

To remove an ACL from an interface, first enter the **no ip access-group** command on the interface, and then enter the global **no access-list** command to remove the entire ACL.

The figure shows an example of an ACL designed to permit a single network. Only traffic from the 192.168.10.0/24 network will be permitted out the Serial 0/0/0 interface.

Refer to **Interactive Graphic** in online course

4.1.3.3 Named Standard IPv4 ACLs

Figure 1 shows the steps required to create a standard named ACL.

Step 1. Starting from the global configuration mode, use the **ip access-list** command to create a named ACL. ACL names are alphanumeric, case sensitive, and must be unique. The **ip access-list standard** *name* command is used to create a standard named ACL. After entering the command, the router is in standard (std) named ACL (nacl) configuration mode as indicated by the second prompt in the Figure 1.

Step 2. From the named ACL configuration mode, use **permit** or **deny** statements to specify one or more conditions for determining whether a packet is forwarded or dropped. You can use **remark** to add a comment to the ACL.

Step 3. Apply the ACL to an interface using the **ip access-group** *name* command. Specify whether the ACL should be applied to packets as they enter the interface (**in**) or applied to packets as they exit the interface (**out**).

Figure 2 shows the commands used to configure a standard named ACL on router R1, interface G0/0, which denies host 192.168.11.10 access to the 192.168.10.0 network. The ACL is named NO_ACCESS.

Refer to
Interactive Graphic
in online course

4.1.3.4   Verify ACLs

As shown in Figure 1, the **show ip interface** command is used to verify the ACL on the interface. The output from this command includes the number or name of the access list and the direction in which the ACL was applied. The output shows router R1 has the access list 1 applied to its S0/0/0 outbound interface and the access list NO_ACCESS applied to its g0/0 interface also in the outbound direction.

The example in Figure 2 shows the result of issuing the **show access-lists** command on router R1. To view an individual access list use the **show access-lists** command followed by the access list number or name. The NO_ACCESS statements may look strange. Notice that sequence number 15 is displayed prior to sequence number 10. This is a result of the router internal process and will be discussed later in this section.

Refer to **Packet Tracer Activity** for this chapter

4.1.3.5   Packet Tracer - Configure Standard IPv4 ACLs

In this activity, you will practice configuring standard IPv4 ACLs to restrict traffic on the network. The next two pages include video demonstrations of this activity.

Refer to **Video**
in online course

4.1.3.6   Video Demonstration - Standard ACL Configuration Part 1

Click Play in the figure to view a demonstration of Part 1 in the Packet Tracer activity "Configure Standard IPv4 ACLs".

Click here to read the transcript of this video.

Refer to **Video**
in online course

4.1.3.7   Video Demonstration - Standard ACL Configuration Part 2

Click Play in the figure to view a demonstration of Part 2 in the Packet Tracer activity "Configure Standard IPv4 ACLs".

Click here to read the transcript of this video.

4.2   Extended IPv4 ACLs

4.2.1   Structure of an Extended IPv4 ACLs

Refer to
Online Course
for Illustration

4.2.1.1   Extended ACLs

Testing Packets with Extended ACLs

For more precise traffic-filtering control, extended IPv4 ACLs can be created. Extended ACLs are numbered 100 to 199 and 2000 to 2699, providing a total of 799 possible extended numbered ACLs. Extended ACLs can also be named.

Extended ACLs are used more often than standard ACLs because they provide a greater degree of control. As shown in the figure, like standard ACLs, extended ACLs have the ability to check source addresses of packets, but they also have the ability to check the destination address, protocols, and port numbers (or services). This provides a greater range of criteria on which to base the ACL. For example, one extended ACL can allow email traffic from a network to a specific destination while denying file transfers and web browsing.

Refer to
Interactive Graphic
in online course

4.2.1.2   Filtering Ports and Services

The ability to filter on protocol and port number allows network administrators to build very specific extended ACLs. An application can be specified by configuring either the port number or the name of a well-known port.

Figure 1 shows some examples of how an administrator specifies a TCP or UDP port number by placing it at the end of the extended ACL statement. Logical operations can be used, such as equal (eq), not equal (neq), greater than (gt), and less than (lt).

Figure 2 shows how to display a list of port numbers and keywords that can be used when building an ACL using the command:

```
R1(config)# access-list 101 permit tcp any any eq ?
```

4.2.2   Configure Extended IPv4 ACLs

Refer to
Interactive Graphic
in online course

4.2.2.1   Configuring Extended ACLs

The procedural steps for configuring extended ACLs are the same as for standard ACLs. The extended ACL is first configured, and then it is activated on an interface. However, the command syntax and parameters are more complex to support the additional features provided by extended ACLs.

Note   The internal logic applied to the ordering of standard ACL statements does not apply to extended ACLs. The order in which the statements are entered during configuration is the order they are displayed and processed.

Figure 1 shows the common command syntax for extended IPv4 ACLs. Note that there are many keywords and parameters for extended ACLs. It is not necessary to use all of the keywords and parameters when configuring an extended ACL. Recall that the **?** can be used to get help when entering complex commands.

Figure 2 shows an example of an extended ACL. In this example, the network administrator has configured ACLs to restrict network access to allow website browsing only from the LAN attached to interface G0/0 to any external network. ACL 103 allows traffic coming from any address on the 192.168.10.0 network to go to any destination, subject to the limitation that the traffic is using ports 80 (HTTP) and 443 (HTTPS) only.

The nature of HTTP requires that traffic flow back into the network from websites accessed from internal clients. The network administrator wants to restrict that return traffic to HTTP exchanges from requested websites, while denying all other traffic. ACL 104 does that by blocking all incoming traffic, except for previously established connections. The permit statement in ACL 104 allows inbound traffic using the **established** parameter.

The **established** parameter allows only responses to traffic that originates from the 192.168.10.0/24 network to return to that network. A match occurs if the returning TCP segment has the ACK or reset (RST) bits set, which indicates that the packet belongs to an existing connection. Without the **established** parameter in the ACL statement, clients could send traffic to a web server, but not receive traffic returning from the web server.

4.2.2.2 Applying Extended ACLs to Interfaces

> Refer to
> **Online Course**
> for Illustration

In the previous example, the network administrator configured an ACL to allow users from the 192.168.10.0/24 network to browse both insecure and secure websites. Even though it has been configured, the ACL will not filter traffic until it is applied to an interface. To apply an ACL to an interface, first consider whether the traffic to be filtered is going in or out. When a user on the internal LAN accesses a website on the Internet, traffic is traffic going out to the Internet. When an internal user receives an email from the Internet, traffic is coming into the local router. However, when applying an ACL to an interface, in and out take on different meanings. From an ACL consideration, in and out are in reference to the router interface.

In the topology in the figure, R1 has three interfaces. It has a serial interface, S0/0/0, and two Gigabit Ethernet interfaces, G0/0 and G0/1. Recall that an extended ACL should typically be applied close to the source. In this topology the interface closest to the source of the target traffic is the G0/0 interface.

Web request traffic from users on the 192.168.10.0/24 LAN is inbound to the G0/0 interface. Return traffic from established connections to users on the LAN is outbound from the G0/0 interface. The example applies the ACL to the G0/0 interface in both directions. The inbound ACL, 103, checks for the type of traffic. The outbound ACL, 104, checks for return traffic from established connections. This will restrict 192.168.10.0 Internet access to allow only website browsing.

Note The access lists could have been applied to the S0/0/0 interface but in that case, the router's ACL process would have to examine all packets entering the router, not only traffic to and from 192.168.11.0. This would cause unnecessary processing by the router.

4.2.2.3 Filtering Traffic with Extended ACLs

> Refer to
> **Interactive Graphic**
> in online course

The example shown in Figure 1 denies FTP traffic from subnet 192.168.11.0 that is going to subnet 192.168.10.0, but permits all other traffic. Remember that FTP uses TCP ports 20 and 21; therefore, the ACL requires both port name keywords **ftp** and **ftp-data** or **eq 20** and **eq 21** to deny FTP.

If using port numbers instead of port names, the commands would be written as:

access-list 101 deny tcp 192.168.11.0 0.0.0.255 192.168.10.0 0.0.0.255 eq 20

access-list 101 deny tcp 192.168.11.0 0.0.0.255 192.168.10.0 0.0.0.255 eq 21

To prevent the implied **deny any** statement at the end of the ACL from blocking all traffic, the **permit ip any any** statement is added. Without at least one **permit** statement in an ACL, all traffic on the interface where that ACL was applied would be dropped. The ACL should be applied inbound on the G0/1 interface so that traffic from the 192.168.11.0/24 LAN is filtered as it enters the router interface.

The example shown in Figure 2, denies Telnet traffic from any source to the 192.168.11.0/24 LAN, but allows all other IP traffic. Because traffic destined for the 192.168.11.0/24 LAN is outbound on interface G0/1, the ACL would be applied to G0/1 using the **out** keyword. Note the use of the **any** keywords in the permit statement. This permit statement is added to ensure that no other traffic is blocked.

Note   The examples in Figures 1 and 2 both use the **permit ip any any** statement at the end of the ACL. For greater security the **permit 192.168.11.0 0.0.0.255 any** command may be used.

4.2.2.4   Creating Named Extended ACLs

Refer to Online Course for Illustration

Named extended ACLs are created in essentially the same way that named standard ACLs are created. Follow these steps to create an extended ACL, using names:

Step 1.   From global configuration mode, use the **ip access-list extended** *name* command to define a name for the extended ACL.

Step 2.   In named ACL configuration mode, specify the conditions to **permit** or **deny**.

Step 3.   From interface configuration mode, apply the named ACL using the **ip access-group** [**in** | **out**] *name* command.

Step 4.   Return to privileged EXEC mode and verify the ACL with the **show access-lists** *name* command.

Step 5.   Save the entries in the configuration file with the **copy running-config startup-config** command.

To remove a named extended ACL, use the **no ip access-list extended** *name* global configuration command.

The figure shows the named versions of the ACLs created in the previous examples. The named ACL, SURFING, permits the users on the 192.168.10.0/24 LAN to access web sites. The named ACL, BROWSING, allows the return traffic from established connections. Using the ACL names, the rules are applied inbound and outbound on the G0/0 interface.

4.2.2.5   Verifying Extended ACLs

Refer to Online Course for Illustration

After an ACL has been configured and applied to an interface, use Cisco IOS **show** commands to verify the configuration. In the figure, the top example shows the Cisco IOS command used to display the contents of all ACLs. The bottom example shows the result of issuing the **show ip interface g0/0** command on router R1.

Unlike standard ACLs, extended ACLs do not implement the same internal logic and hashing function. The output and sequence numbers displayed in the **show access-lists** command output is the order in which the statements were entered. Host entries are not automatically listed prior to range entries.

The **show ip interface** command is used to verify the ACL on the interface and the direction in which it was applied. The output from this command includes the number or name of the access list and the direction in which the ACL was applied. The capitalized ACL names BROWSING and SURFING stand out in the screen output.

After an ACL configuration has been verified, the next step is to confirm that the ACLs work as planned; blocking and permitting traffic as expected.

The guidelines discussed earlier in this section, suggest that ACLs should be configured on a test network and then implemented on the production network.

Refer to
Online Course
for Illustration

4.2.2.6   Editing Extended ACLs

An extended ACL can be editing in one of two ways:

- **Method 1 Text editor** - Using this method, the ACL is copied and pasted into the text editor where the changes are made. The current access list is removed using the **no access-list** command. The modified ACL is then pasted back into the configuration.

- **Method 2 Sequence numbers** - Sequence numbers can be used to delete or insert an ACL statement. The **ip access-list extended** *name* command is used to enter named-ACL configuration mode. If the ACL is numbered instead of named, the ACL number is used in the *name* parameter. ACEs can be inserted or removed.

In the figure the administrator needs to edit the ACL named SURFING to correct a typo in the source network statement. To view the current sequence numbers, the **show access-lists** command is used. The statement to be edited is identified as statement 10. The original statement is removed with the **no** *sequence_#* command. The corrected statement is added replacing the original statement.

Refer to
Interactive Graphic
in online course

4.2.2.7   Activity - Creating an Extended ACL Statement

4.2.2.8   Activity - Evaluating Extended ACEs

Refer to
Interactive Graphic
in online course

4.2.2.9   Activity - ACL Testlet

Refer to
Interactive Graphic
in online course

4.2.2.10   Packet Tracer - Configuring Extended ACLs - Scenario 1
Scenario

Refer to **Packet Tracer Activity** for this chapter

Two employees need access to services provided by the server. PC1 only needs FTP access while PC2 only needs web access. Both computers will be able to ping the server, but not each other.

Refer to **Packet Tracer Activity** for this chapter

4.2.2.11   Packet Tracer - Configuring Extended ACLs - Scenario 2
Scenario

In this scenario, devices on one LAN are allowed to remotely access devices in another LAN using the Telnet protocol. Besides ICMP, all traffic from other networks is denied.

Refer to **Packet Tracer Activity** for this chapter

4.2.2.12   Packet Tracer - Configuring Extended ACLs - Scenario 3
Background / Scenario

In this scenario, specific devices on the LAN are allowed to access various services on servers that are located on the Internet.

Refer to **Lab Activity** for this chapter

4.2.2.13   Lab - Configuring and Verifying Extended ACLs
In this lab, you will complete the following objectives:

- Part 1: Set Up the Topology and Initialize Devices
- Part 2: Configure Devices and Verify Connectivity
- Part 3: Configure and Verify Extended Numbered and Named ACLs
- Part 4: Modify and Verify Extended ACLs

4.3   IPv6 ACLs

4.3.1   IPv6 ACL Creation

Refer to **Online Course** for Illustration

4.3.1.1   Types of IPv6 ACLs

IPv6 ACLs are similar to IPv4 ACLs in both operation and configuration. Being familiar with IPv4 access lists makes IPv6 ACLs easy to understand and configure.

In IPv4 there are two types of ACLs, standard and extended. Both types of ACLs can be either numbered or named ACLs.

With IPv6, there is only one type of ACL, which is equivalent to an IPv4 extended named ACL. There are no numbered ACLs in IPv6.

An IPv4 ACL and an IPv6 ACL cannot share the same name.

Refer to **Online Course** for Illustration

4.3.1.2   Comparing IPv4 and IPv6 ACLs

Although IPv4 and IPv6 ACLs are similar, there are three significant differences between them:

- The first difference is the command used to apply an IPv6 ACL to an interface. IPv4 uses the command **ip access-group** to apply an IPv4 ACL to an IPv4 interface. IPv6 uses the **ipv6 traffic-filter** command to perform the same function for IPv6 interfaces.

- Unlike IPv4 ACLs, IPv6 ACLs do not use wildcard masks. Instead, the prefix-length is used to indicate how much of an IPv6 source or destination address should be matched.

■ The last major difference has to with the addition of two implicit permit statements at the end of each IPv6 access list. At the end of every IPv4 standard or extended ACL is an implicit **deny any** or **deny ip any any**. IPv6 includes a similar **deny ipv6 any any** statement at the end of each IPv6 ACL. The difference is IPv6 also includes two other implicit statements by default: **permit icmp any any nd-na** and **permit icmp any any nd-ns**.

These two statements allow the router to participate in the IPv6 equivalent of ARP for IPv4. Recall that ARP is used in IPv4 to resolve Layer 3 addresses to Layer 2 MAC addresses. As shown in the figure, IPv6 uses ICMP Neighbor Discovery (ND) messages to accomplish the same thing. ND uses Neighbor Solicitation (NS) and Neighbor Advertisement (NA) messages.

ND messages are encapsulated in IPv6 packets and require the services of the IPv6 network layer while ARP for IPv4 does not use Layer 3. Because IPv6 uses the Layer 3 service for neighbor discovery, IPv6 ACLs need to implicitly permit ND packets to be sent and received on an interface. Specifically, both Neighbor Discovery - Neighbor Advertisement (nd-na) and Neighbor Discovery - Neighbor Solicitation (nd-ns) messages are permitted.

4.3.2   Configuring IPv6 ACLs

Refer to
Online Course
for Illustration

4.3.2.1   Configuring IPv6 Topology

Figure 1 shows the topology that will be used for configuring IPv6 ACLs. The topology is similar to the previous IPv4 topology except for the IPv6 addressing scheme. There are three 2001:DB8:CAFE::/64 subnets:

■ 2001:DB8:CAFE:10::/64

■ 2001:DB8:CAFE:11::/64

■ 2001:DB8:CAFE:30::/64

Two serial networks connect the three routers:

■ 2001:DB8:FEED:1::/64

■ 2001:DB8:FEED:2::/64

Figures 2, 3, and 4 show the IPv6 address configuration for each router. The **show ipv6 interface brief** command is used to verify the address and the state of the interface.

Note   The **no shutdown** command and the **clock rate** command are not shown.

Refer to
Interactive Graphic
in online course

4.3.2.2   Configuring IPv6 ACLs

In IPv6 there are only named ACLs. The configuration is similar to that of an IPv4 extended named ACL.

Figure 1 shows the command syntax for IPv6 ACLs. The syntax is similar to the syntax used for an IPv4 extended ACL. One significant difference is the use of the IPv6 prefix-length instead of an IPv4 wildcard mask.

There are three basic steps to configure an IPv6 ACL:

Step 1.   From global configuration mode, use the **ipv6 access-list** *name* command to create an IPv6 ACL. Like IPv4 named ACLs, IPv6 names are alphanumeric, case sensitive, and must be unique. Unlike IPv4, there is no need for a standard or extended option.

Step 2.   From the named ACL configuration mode, use the **permit** or **deny** statements to specify one or more conditions to determine if a packet is forwarded or dropped.

Step 3.   Return to privileged EXEC mode with the **end** command.

Figure 2 demonstrates the steps to create an IPv6 ACL with a simple example based on the previous topology. The first statement names the IPv6 access list NO-R3-LAN-ACCESS. Similar to IPv4 named ACLs, capitalizing IPv6 ACL names is not required, but makes them stand out when viewing the running-config output.

The second statement denies all IPv6 packets from the 2001:DB8:CAFE:30::/64 destined for any IPv6 network. The third statement allows all other IPv6 packets.

Figure 3 shows the ACL in context with the topology.

Refer to
Online Course
for Illustration

4.3.2.3   Applying an IPv6 ACL to an Interface

After an IPv6 ACL is configured, it is linked to an interface using the **ipv6 traffic-filter** command:

```
Router(config-if)# ipv6 traffic-filter access-list-name { in | out }
```

The figure shows the NO-R3-LAN-ACCESS ACL configured previously and the commands used to apply the IPv6 ACL inbound to the S0/0/0 interface. Applying the ACL to the inbound S0/0/0 interface will deny packets from 2001:DB8:CAFE:30::/64 to both of the LANs on R1.

To remove an ACL from an interface, first enter the **no ipv6 traffic-filter** command on the interface, and then enter the global **no ipv6 access-list** command to remove the access list.

Note   IPv4 and IPv6 both use the **access-class** command to apply an access list to VTY ports.

Refer to
Interactive Graphic
in online course

4.3.2.4   IPv6 ACL Examples

Deny FTP

The topology for the examples is shown in Figure 1.

In the first example (Figure 2), router R1 is configured with an IPv6 access list to deny FTP traffic to 2001:DB8:CAFE:11::/64. Ports for both FTP data (port 20) and FTP control (port 21) need to be blocked. Because the filter is applied inbound on the G0/0 interface on R1, only traffic from the 2001:DB8:CAFE:10::/64 network will be denied.

Restricted Access

In the second example (Figure 3), an IPv6 ACL is configured to give the LAN on R3 limited access to the LANs on R1. Comments are added in the configuration to document the ACL. The following features have been labelled in the ACL:

1. The first two permit statements allow access from any device to the web server at 2001:DB8:CAFE:10::10.

2. All other devices are denied access to the 2001:DB8:CAFE:10::/64 network.

3. PC3 at 2001:DB8:CAFE:30::12 is permitted Telnet access to PC2 which has the IPv6 address 2001:DB8:CAFE:11::11.

4. All other devices are denied Telnet access to PC2.

5. All other IPv6 traffic is permitted to all other destinations.

6. The IPv6 access list is applied to interface G0/0 in the inbound direction, so only the 2001:DB8:CAFE:30::/64 network is affected.

Refer to **Interactive Graphic** in online course

4.3.2.5 Verifying IPv6 ACLs

The commands used to verify an IPv6 access list are similar to those used for IPv4 ACLs. Using these commands, the IPv6 access list RESTRICTED-ACCESS that was configured previously can be verified. Figure 1 shows the output of the **show ipv6 interface** command. The output confirms that RESTRICTED-ACCESS ACL is configured inbound on the G0/0 interface.

As shown in Figure 2, the **show access-lists** command displays all access lists on the router including both IPv4 and IPv6 ACLs. Notice that with IPv6 ACLs the sequence numbers occur at the end of the statement and not the beginning as with IPv4 access lists. Although the statements appear in the order they were entered, they are not always incremented by 10. This is because the remark statements that were entered use a sequence number but are not displayed in the output of the **show access-lists** command.

Similar to extended ACLs for IPv4, IPv6 access lists are displayed and processed in the order the statements are entered. Remember, IPv4 standard ACLs use an internal logic which changes their order and processing sequence.

As shown in Figure 3, the output from the **show running-config** command includes all of the ACEs and remark statements. Remark statements can come before or after **permit** or **deny** statements but should be consistent in their placement.

Refer to **Packet Tracer Activity** for this chapter

4.3.2.6 Packet Tracer - Configuring IPv6 ACLs

Objectives

- Part 1: Configure, Apply, and Verify an IPv6 ACL
- Part 2: Configure, Apply, and Verify a Second IPv6 ACL

Refer to **Lab Activity** for this chapter

4.3.2.7 Lab - Configuring and Verifying IPv6 ACLs

In this lab, you will complete the following objectives:

- Part 1: Set Up the Topology and Initialize Devices
- Part 2: Configure Devices and Verify Connectivity

- Part 3: Configure and Verify IPv6 ACLs
- Part 4: Edit IPv6 ACLs

4.4   Troubleshoot ACLs

4.4.1   Processing Packets with ACLs

Refer to
Interactive Graphic
in online course

4.4.1.1   Inbound and Outbound ACL Logic

Inbound ACL Logic

Figure 1 shows the logic for an inbound ACL. If the information in a packet header and an ACL statement match, the rest of the statements in the list are skipped, and the packet is permitted or denied as specified by the matched statement. If a packet header does not match an ACL statement, the packet is tested against the next statement in the list. This matching process continues until the end of the list is reached.

At the end of every ACL is a statement is an implicit **deny any** statement. This statement is not shown in output. This final implied statement applied to all packets for which conditions did not test true. This final test condition matches all other packets and results in a "deny" action. Instead of proceeding into or out of an interface, the router drops all of these remaining packets. This final statement is often referred to as the "implicit deny any statement" or the "deny all traffic" statement. Because of this statement, an ACL should have at least one permit statement in it; otherwise, the ACL blocks all traffic.

Outbound ACL Logic

Figure 2 shows the logic for an outbound ACL. Before a packet is forwarded to an outbound interface, the router checks the routing table to see if the packet is routable. If the packet is not routable, it is dropped and is not tested against the ACEs. Next, the router checks to see whether the outbound interface is grouped to an ACL. If the outbound interface is not grouped to an ACL, the packet can be sent to the output buffer. Examples of outbound ACL operation are as follows:

- **No ACL applied to the interface** - If the outbound interface is not grouped to an outbound ACL, the packet is sent directly to the outbound interface.

- **ACL applied to the interface** - If the outbound interface is grouped to an outbound ACL, the packet is not sent out on the outbound interface until it is tested by the combination of ACEs that are associated with that interface. Based on the ACL tests, the packet is permitted or denied.

For outbound lists, "permit" means to send the packet to the output buffer, and "deny" means to discard the packet.

Refer to
Interactive Graphic
in online course

4.4.1.2   ACL Logic Operations

ACL and Routing and ACL Processes on a Router

The figure shows the logic of routing and ACL processes. When a packet arrives at a router interface, the router process is the same, whether ACLs are used or not. As a frame enters an interface, the router checks to see whether the destination Layer 2 address matches its interface Layer 2 address, or whether the frame is a broadcast frame.

If the frame address is accepted, the frame information is stripped off and the router checks for an ACL on the inbound interface. If an ACL exists, the packet is tested against the statements in the list.

If the packet matches a statement, the packet is either permitted or denied. If the packet is accepted, it is then checked against routing table entries to determine the destination interface. If a routing table entry exists for the destination, the packet is then switched to the outgoing interface, otherwise the packet is dropped.

Next, the router checks whether the outgoing interface has an ACL. If an ACL exists, the packet is tested against the statements in the list.

If the packet matches a statement, it is either permitted or denied.

If there is no ACL or the packet is permitted, the packet is encapsulated in the new Layer 2 protocol and forwarded out the interface to the next device.

Refer to
Interactive Graphic
in online course

4.4.1.3   Standard ACL Decision Process

Standard ACLs only examine the source IPv4 address. The destination of the packet and the ports involved are not considered.

The decision process for a standard ACL is mapped in the figure. Cisco IOS software tests addresses against the conditions in the ACL one by one. The first match determines whether the software accepts or rejects the address. Because the software stops testing conditions after the first match, the order of the conditions is critical. If no conditions match, the address is rejected.

Refer to
Interactive Graphic
in online course

4.4.1.4   Extended ACL Decision Process

The figure shows the logical decision path used by an extended ACL built to filter on source and destination addresses, and protocol and port numbers. In this example, the ACL first filters on the source address, then on the port and protocol of the source. It then filters on the destination address, then on the port and protocol of the destination, and makes a final permit or deny decision.

Recall that entries in ACLs are processed one after the other, so a 'No' decision does not necessarily equal a 'Deny'. As you go through the logical decision path, note that a 'No' means go to the next entry until a condition is matched.

Refer to
Interactive Graphic
in online course

4.4.1.5   Activity - Place in Order the Steps of the ACL Decision Making Process

4.4.2   Common ACLs Errors

Refer to
Online Course
for Illustration

4.4.2.1   Troubleshooting IPv4 ACLs - Example 1

Using the **show** commands described earlier reveals most of the common ACL errors. The most common errors are entering ACEs in the wrong order and not applying adequate criteria to the ACL rules.

In the figure, host 192.168.10.10 has no Telnet connectivity with 192.168.30.12. When viewing the output of the **show access-lists** command, matches are shown for the first deny statement. This is an indicator that this statement has been matched by traffic.

Solution - Look at the order of the ACEs. Host 192.168.10.10 has no connectivity with 192.168.30.12 because of the order of rule 10 in the access list. Because the router processes ACLs from the top down, statement 10 denies host 192.168.10.10, so statement 20 can never be matched. Statements 10 and 20 should be reversed. The last line allows all other non-TCP traffic that falls under IP (ICMP, UDP, etc.).

Refer to **Online Course** for Illustration

4.4.2.2   Troubleshooting IPv4 ACLs - Example 2

In the figure, the 192.168.10.0/24 network cannot use TFTP to connect to the 192.168.30.0/24 network.

Solution - The 192.168.10.0/24 network cannot use TFTP to connect to the 192.168.30.0/24 network because TFTP uses the transport protocol UDP. Statement 30 in access list 120 allows all other TCP traffic. However, because TFTP uses UDP instead of TCP, it is implicitly denied. Recall that the implied deny any statement does not appear in **show access-lists** output and therefore matches are not shown.

Statement 30 should be **ip any any**.

This ACL works whether it is applied to G0/0 of R1, or S0/0/1 of R3, or S0/0/0 of R2 in the incoming direction. However, based on the rule about placing extended ACLs closest to the source, the best option is to place it inbound on G0/0 of R1 because it allows undesirable traffic to be filtered without crossing the network infrastructure.

Refer to **Online Course** for Illustration

4.4.2.3   Troubleshooting IPv4 ACLs - Example 3

In the figure, the 192.168.11.0/24 network can use Telnet to connect to 192.168.30.0/24, but according to company policy, this connection should not be allowed. The results of the **show access-lists 130** command indicate that the permit statement has been matched.

Solution - The 192.168.11.0/24 network can use Telnet to connect to the 192.168.30.0/24 network because the Telnet port number in statement 10 of access list 130 is listed in the wrong position in the ACL statement. Statement 10 currently denies any source packet with a port number that is equal to Telnet. To deny Telnet traffic inbound on G0/1, deny the destination port number that is equal to Telnet, for example, **10 deny tcp 192.168.11.0 0.0.0.255 192.168.30.0 0.0.0.255 eq telnet**.

Refer to **Online Course** for Illustration

4.4.2.4   Troubleshooting IPv4 ACLs - Example 4

In the figure, host 192.168.30.12 is able to Telnet to connect to 192.168.31.12, but company policy states that this connection should not be allowed. Output from the **show access-lists 140** command indicate that the permit statement has been matched.

Solution - Host 192.168.30.12 can use Telnet to connect to 192.168.31.12 because there are no rules that deny host 192.168.30.12 or its network as the source. Statement 10 of access list 140 denies the router interface on which traffic enters the router. The host IPv4 address in statement 10 should be 192.168.30.12.

Refer to
Online Course
for Illustration

4.4.2.5   Troubleshooting IPv4 ACLs - Example 5

In the figure, host 192.168.30.12 can use Telnet to connect to 192.168.31.12, but according to the security policy, this connection should not be allowed. Output from the **show access-lists 150** command indicate that no matches have occurred for the deny statement as expected.

Solution - Host 192.168.30.12 can use Telnet to connect to 192.168.31.12 because of the direction in which access list 150 is applied to the G0/1 interface. Statement 10 denies any source address to connect to host 192.168.31.12 using Telnet. However, this filter should be applied outbound on G0/1 to filter correctly.

Refer to
Interactive Graphic
in online course

4.4.2.6   Troubleshooting IPv6 ACLs - Example 1

Similar to IPv4 ACLs, use the **show ipv6 access-list** and **show running-config** commands to reveal typical IPv6 ACL errors.

In Figure 1, R1 is configured with an IPv6 ACL to deny FTP access from the :10 network to the :11 network. However, after configuring the ACL, PC1 is still able to connect to the FTP server running on PC2. Referring to the output for the **show ipv6 access-list** command in Figure 2, matches are shown for the permit statement but not the deny statements.

Solution: The ACEs in the ACL reveal no problems in their order, or in the criteria of their rules. The next step is to consider how the ACL is applied at the interface using the **ipv6 traffic-filter** command. Did the ACL get applied using the correct name, the correct interface, and in the correct direction? To check for interface configuration errors, display the running configuration, as shown in Figure 2.

The ACL was applied using the correct name, but not the correct direction. The direction, in or out, is from the perspective of the router, meaning the ACL is currently applied to traffic before it is forwarded out the G0/0 interface and enters the :10 network. To correct the issue, remove the ipv6 traffic-filter NO-FTP-TO-11 out and replace it with ipv6 traffic-filter NO-FTP-TO-11 in, as shown in Figure 3. Now PC1's attempts to access the FTP server are denied, as verified with the **show ipv6 access-list** command.

Refer to
Interactive Graphic
in online course

4.4.2.7   Troubleshooting IPv6 ACLs - Example 2

In the figure, R3 is configured with an IPv6 ACL named RESTRICTED-ACCESS that should enforce the following policy for the R3 LAN:

- Permit access to the :10 network

- Deny access to the :11 network

- Permit SSH access to the PC at 2001:DB8:CAFE:11::11

However, after configuring the ACL, PC3 cannot reach the 10 network or the 11 network, and it cannot SSH into the host at 2001:DB8:CAFE:11::11.

Solution: In this situation the problem is not with how the ACL was applied. At the interface, the ACL is not misspelled and the direction and location are correct, as shown in Figure 2. A close look at the IPv6 ACL reveals that the problem is with the order and criteria of the ACE rules. The first permit statement should allow access to the :10 network. However, the administrator configured a host statement and did not specify a prefix. In this case, only access to the 2001:DB8:CAFE:10:: host is allowed.

To correct this issue, remove the host argument and change the prefix to /64. You can do this without removing the ACL by replacing the ACE using the sequence number 10, as shown in Figure 3.

The second error in the ACL is the order of the next two statements. The policy specifies that hosts on the R3 LAN should be able to SSH into host 2001:DB8:CAFE:11::11. However, the deny statement for :11 network is listed before the permit statement. Therefore, all attempts to access the :11 network are denied before the statement permitting SSH access can be evaluated. After a match is made, no further statements are analyzed. To correct this issue, you will need to remove the statements first, and then enter them in the correct order, as shown in Figure 4.

Refer to
Interactive Graphic
in online course

4.4.2.8   Troubleshooting IPv6 ACLs - Example 3

In Figure 1, R1 is configured with an IPv6 ACL named DENY-ACCESS that should enforce the following policy for the R3 LAN:

- Permit access to the :11 network from the :30 network

- Deny access to the :10 network

Figure 2 shows the configuration and application of the IPv6 ACL.

The DENY-ACCESS ACL is supposed to permit access to the :11 network from the :30 network while denying access to the :10 network. However, after applying the ACL to the interface the :10 network is still reachable from the :30 network.

Solution: In this situation, the problem is not with how the ACL statements were written but with the location of the ACL. Because IPv6 ACLs must be configured with both a source and a destination, they should be applied closest to the source of the traffic. The DENY-ACCESS ACL was applied in the outbound direction on the R1 G0/1 interface which is closest to the destination. As a result, traffic to the :10 network is completely unaffected because it reaches the :10 network through the other LAN interface, G0/0. You could apply the ACL inbound on the R1 S0/0/0 interface. However, because we have control over R3, the best location would be to configure and apply the ACL closest to the source of the traffic. Figure 3 shows the removal of the ACL on R1 and the correct configuration and application of the ACL on R3.

Refer to **Packet
Tracer Activity**
for this chapter

4.4.2.9   Packet Tracer - Troubleshooting IPv4 ACLs

Scenario

Create a network that has the following three policies implemented:

- Hosts from the 192.168.0.0/24 network are unable to access any TCP service of Server3.

- Hosts from the 10.0.0.0/8 network are unable to access the HTTP service of Server1.

- Hosts from the 172.16.0.0/16 network are unable to access the FTP service of Server2.

Refer to **Packet Tracer Activity** for this chapter

4.4.2.10   Packet Tracer - Troubleshooting IPv6 ACLs

The following three policies have been implemented on the network:

- Hosts from the 2001:DB8:CAFE::/64 network do not have HTTP access to the other networks.

- Hosts from the 2001:DB8:CAFE:1::/64 network are prevented from access to the FTP service on Server2.

- Hosts from the 2001:DB8:CAFE:1::/64 and 2001:DB8:CAFE:2::/64 networks are prevented from accessing R1 via SSH.

No other restrictions should be in place. Unfortunately, the rules that have been implemented are not working correctly. Your task is to find and fix the errors related to the access lists on R1.

Refer to **Lab Activity** for this chapter

4.4.2.11   Lab - Troubleshooting ACL Configuration and Placement

In this lab, you will complete the following objectives:

- Part 1: Build the Network and Configure Basic Device Settings

- Part 2: Troubleshoot Internal Access

- Part 3: Troubleshoot Remote Access

4.5   Summary

Refer to **Packet Tracer Activity** for this chapter

4.5.1.1   Packet Tracer - Skills Integration Challenge

In this challenge activity, you will finish the addressing scheme, configure routing, and implement named access control lists.

Refer to **Online Course** for Illustration

4.5.1.2   Chapter 4: Access Control Lists

By default a router does not filter traffic. Traffic that enters the router is routed solely based on information within the routing table.

Packet filtering controls access to a network by analyzing the incoming and outgoing packets and passing or dropping them based on criteria such as the source IP address, destination IP addresses, and the protocol carried within the packet. A packet-filtering router uses rules to determine whether to permit or deny traffic. A router can also perform packet filtering at Layer 4, the transport layer.

An ACL is a sequential list of permit or deny statements. The last statement of an ACL is always an implicit deny any statement which blocks all traffic. To prevent the implied deny any statement at the end of the ACL from blocking all traffic, the **permit ip any any** statement can be added.

When network traffic passes through an interface configured with an ACL, the router compares the information within the packet against each entry, in sequential order, to determine if the packet matches one of the statements. If a match is found, the packet is processed accordingly.

ACLs are configured to apply to inbound traffic or to apply to outbound traffic.

Standard ACLs can be used to permit or deny traffic only from a source IPv4 addresses. The destination of the packet and the ports involved are not evaluated. The basic rule for placing a standard ACL is to place it close to the destination.

Extended ACLs filter packets based on several attributes: protocol type, source or destination IPv4 address, and source or destination ports. The basic rule for placing an extended ACL is to place it as close to the source as possible.

The **access-list** global configuration command defines a standard ACL with a number in the range of 1 through 99 or an extended ACL with numbers in the range of 100 to 199 and 2000 to 2699. Both standard and extended ACLs can be named instead of numbered. The **ip access-list standard** *name* is used to create a standard named ACL, whereas the command **ip access-list extended** *name* is for an extended access list. IPv4 ACEs include the use of wildcard masks.

After an ACL is configured, it is linked to an interface using the **ip access-group** command in interface configuration mode. A device an only have one ACL per protocol, per direction, per interface.

To remove an ACL from an interface, first enter the **no ip access-group** command on the interface, and then enter the global **no access-list** command to remove the entire ACL.

The **show running-config** and **show access-lists** commands are used to verify ACL configuration. The **show ip interface** command is used to verify the ACL on the interface and the direction in which it was applied.

The **access-class** command configured in line configuration mode restricts incoming and outgoing connections between a particular VTY and the addresses in an access list.

Like IPv4 named ACLs, IPv6 names are alphanumeric, case sensitive, and must be unique. Unlike IPv4, there is no need for a standard or extended option.

From global configuration mode, use the **ipv6 access-list** *name* command to create an IPv6 ACL. Unlike IPv4 ACLs, IPv6 ACLs do not use wildcard masks. Instead, the prefix-length is used to indicate how much of an IPv6 source or destination address should be matched.

After an IPv6 ACL is configured, it is linked to an interface using the **ipv6 traffic-filter** command.

Go to the online course to take the quiz and exam.

Chapter 4 Quiz

This quiz is designed to provide an additional opportunity to practice the skills and knowledge presented in the chapter and to prepare for the chapter exam. You will be allowed multiple attempts and the grade does not appear in the gradebook.

Chapter 4 Exam

The chapter exam assesses your knowledge of the chapter content.

Your Chapter Notes

Network Security and Monitoring

5.0 Introduction

Refer to
Online Course
for Illustration

5.0.1.1 Chapter 5: Network Security and Monitoring

A secure network is only as strong as its weakest link and Layer 2 is potentially the weakest link. Common Layer 2 attacks include CDP reconnaissance, Telnet exploitation, MAC address table flooding, VLAN attacks, and DHCP related attacks. Network administrators must know how to mitigate these attacks, and well as securing administrative access using AAA and securing port access using 802.1X.

Monitoring an operational network can provide a network administrator with information to proactively manage the network and to report network usage statistics to others. Link activity, error rates, and link status are a few of the factors that help a network administrator determine the health and usage of a network. Collecting and reviewing this information over time enables a network administrator to see and project growth, and may enable the administrator to detect and replace a failing part before it completely fails. SNMP is commonly used to collect device information.

Network traffic must be monitored for malicious traffic. Network administrators use port analyzers and IPS devices to help with this task. However, the switched infrastructure does not enable port mirroring by default. Cisco SPAN must be implemented to enable port mirroring. This enables the switch to send duplicate traffic to port analyzers or IPS devices for monitoring of malicious, or questionable traffic.

This chapter covers common LAN security threats and how to mitigate them. It then covers SNMP and how to enable it to monitor a network, and how to implement local SPAN to capture and monitor traffic with port analyzers or IPS devices.

Refer to
Online Course
for Illustration

5.0.1.2 Class Activity – Network Maintenance Development

Network Maintenance Development

Currently, there are no formal policies or procedures for recording problems experienced on your company's network. Furthermore, when network problems occur, you must try many methods to find the causes and this approach takes time.

You know there must be a better way to resolve these issues. You decide to create a network maintenance plan to keep repair records and pinpoint the causes of errors on the network.

5.1   LAN Security

5.1.1   LAN Security Attacks

Refer to
Online Course
for Illustration

5.1.1.1   Common LAN Attacks

Organizations commonly implement security solutions using routers, firewalls, Intrusion Prevention System (IPSs), and VPN devices. These protect the elements in Layer 3 up through Layer 7.

Layer 2 LANs are often considered to be a safe and secure environment. However, as shown in the figure, if Layer 2 is compromised then all layers above it are also affected. Today, with BYOD and more sophisticated attacks, LANs have become more vulnerable.

For example, a disgruntled employee with internal network access could capture Layer 2 frames. This could render all of the security implemented in layers 3 and above useless. The attacker could also wreak havoc on the Layer 2 LAN networking infrastructure and create DoS situations. Therefore, in addition to protecting Layer 3 to Layer 7, network security professionals must also mitigate threats against the Layer 2 LAN infrastructure.

The first step in mitigating attacks on the Layer 2 infrastructure is to understand the underlying operation of Layer 2 and the threats posed by the Layer 2 infrastructure.

Common attacks against the Layer 2 LAN infrastructure include:

- CDP Reconnaissance Attack
- Telnet Attacks
- MAC Address Table Flooding Attack
- VLAN Attacks
- DHCP Attacks

The first two attacks are focused on gaining administrative access to the network device. The remaining attacks are focused on disrupting the network operation. Other more sophisticated attacks exist. However, the focus of this section is on common Layer 2 attacks.

Note   For more information on Layer 2 attacks, refer to the CCNA Security course.

Refer to
Online Course
for Illustration

5.1.1.2   CDP Reconnaissance Attack

The Cisco Discovery Protocol (CDP) is a proprietary Layer 2 link discovery protocol. It is enabled on all Cisco devices by default. CDP can automatically discover other CDN-enabled devices and help auto-configure their connection. Network administrators also use CDP to help configure and troubleshoot network devices.

CDP information is sent out CDP-enabled ports in periodic, unencrypted broadcasts. CDP information includes the IP address of the device, IOS software version, platform, capabilities, and the native VLAN. The device receiving the CDP message updates its CDP database.

CDP information is extremely useful in network troubleshooting. For example, CDP can be used to verify Layer 1 and 2 connectivity. If an administrator cannot ping a directly connected interface, but still receives CDP information, then the problem is most likely related to the Layer 3 configuration.

However, the information provided by CDP can also be used by an attacker to discover network infrastructure vulnerabilities.

In the figure, a sample Wireshark capture displays the contents of a CDP packet. The attacker is able to identify the Cisco IOS software version used by the device. This allows the attacker to determine whether there were any security vulnerabilities specific to that particular version of IOS.

CDP broadcasts are sent unencrypted and unauthenticated. Therefore, an attacker could interfere with the network infrastructure by sending crafted CDP frames containing bogus device information to directly-connected Cisco devices.

To mitigate the exploitation of CDP, limit the use of CDP on devices or ports. For example, disable CDP on edge ports that connect to untrusted devices.

To disable CDP globally on a device, use the **no cdp run** global configuration mode command. To enable CDP globally, use the **cdp run** global configuration command.

To disable CDP on a port, use the **no cdp enable** interface configuration command. To enable CDP on a port, use the **cdp enable** interface configuration command.

Note   Link Layer Discovery Protocol (LLDP) in also vulnerable to reconnaissance attacks. Configure **no lldp run** to disable LLDP globally. To disable LLDP on the interface, configure **no lldp transmit** and **no lldp receive**.

Refer to
Online Course
for Illustration

5.1.1.3   Telnet Attacks

The ability to remotely manage a switched LAN infrastructure is an operational requirement; therefore, it must be supported.

However, the Telnet protocol is inherently insecure and can be leveraged by an attacker to gain remote access to a Cisco network device. There are tools available that allow an attacker to launch attacks against the vty lines on the switch.

There are two types of Telnet attacks:

- **Brute Force Password Attack** – The attacker may use a list of common passwords, dictionary words, and variations of words to discover the administrative password. If the password is not discovered by the first phase, a second phase begins. The attacker uses specialized password auditing tools such as those shown in the figure. The software creates sequential character combinations in an attempt to guess the password. Given enough time and the right conditions, a brute force password attack can crack almost all passwords.

- **Telnet DoS Attack** – The attacker continuously requests Telnet connections in an attempt to render the Telnet service unavailable and preventing an administrator from remotely accessing a switch. This can be combined with other direct attacks on the network as part of a coordinated attempt to prevent the network administrator from accessing core devices during the breach.

There are several way to mitigate against Telnet attacks:

- Use SSH, rather than Telnet for remote management connections.

- Use strong passwords that are changed frequently. A strong password should have a mix of upper and lowercase letters and should include numerals and symbols (special characters).

- Limit access to the vty lines using an access control list (ACL) permitting only administrator devices and denying all other devices.

- Authenticate and authorize administrative access to the device using AAA with either TACACS+ or RADIUS protocols.

Refer to
Interactive Graphic
in online course

5.1.1.4   MAC Address Table Flooding Attack

One of the most basic and common LAN switch attacks is the MAC address flooding attack. This attack is also known as a MAC address table overflow attack, or a CAM table overflow attack.

Consider what happens when a switch receives incoming frames. The MAC address table in a switch contains the MAC addresses associated with each physical port, and the associated VLAN for each port. When a Layer 2 switch receives a frame, the switch looks in the MAC address table for the destination MAC address. All Catalyst switch models use a MAC address table for Layer 2 switching. As frames arrive on switch ports, the source MAC addresses are recorded in the MAC address table. If an entry exists for the MAC address, the switch forwards the frame to the correct port. If the MAC address does not exist in the MAC address table, the switch floods the frame out of every port on the switch, except the port where the frame was received.

Figures 1 through 3 illustrate this default switch behaviour.

In Figure 1, host A sends traffic to host B. The switch receives the frames and adds the source MAC address of host A to its MAC address table. The switch then looks up the destination MAC address in its MAC address table. If the switch does not find the destination MAC in the MAC address table, it copies the frame and floods (broadcasts) it out of every switch port, except the port where it was received.

In Figure 2, host B receives and processes the frame. It then sends a reply to host A. The switch receives the incoming frame from host B. The switch then adds the source MAC address and port assignment for host B to its MAC address table. The switch then looks for the destination MAC address in its MAC address table and forwards the frames out of Port 1 towards host A.

The MAC address table of the switch eventually learns all MAC addresses connected to it and forwards frames between communicating ports only. In Figure 3 for example, any frame sent by host A (or any other host) to host B is forwarded out port 2 of the switch. It is not broadcasted out every port because the switch knows the location of the destination MAC address.

An attacker can exploit this default switch behaviour to create a MAC address flooding attack. MAC address tables are limited in size. MAC flooding attacks exploit this limitation with fake source MAC addresses until the switch MAC address table is full and the switch is overwhelmed.

Figures 4 and 5 illustrate how a MAC address table flooding attack is generated.

In Figure 4, an attacker uses a network attack tool and continuously sends frames with fake, randomly-generated source and destination MAC addresses to the switch. The switch keeps updating its MAC address table with the information in the fake frames.

Eventually, the MAC address table becomes full of fake MAC addresses and enters into what is known as fail-open mode. In this mode, the switch broadcasts all frames to all machines on the network. As a result, the attacker can capture all of the frames, even frames that are not addressed to its MAC address table.

In Figure 5, the switch is in fail-open mode and broadcasts all received frames out of every port. Therefore, frames sent from host A to host B are also broadcast out of port 3 on the switch and seen by the attacker.

Configure port security on the switch to mitigate MAC address table overflow attacks.

Refer to **Online Course** for Illustration

5.1.1.5 VLAN Attacks

The VLAN architecture simplifies network maintenance and improves performance, but it also opens the door to abuse. There are a variety of VLAN related attacks that exist.

The figure illustrates one type of VLAN threat which is the switch spoofing attack. The attacker attempts to gain VLAN access by configuring a host to spoof a switch and use the 802.1Q trunking protocol and the Cisco-proprietary Dynamic Trunking Protocol (DTP) feature to trunk with the connecting switch. If successful and the switch establishes a trunk link with the host and the attacker can then access all the VLANS on the switch and hop (i.e., send and receive) traffic on all the VLANs.

There are several ways to mitigate VLAN attacks:

- Explicitly configure access links
- Explicitly disable auto trunking
- Manually enable trunk links
- Disable unused ports, make them access ports, and assign them to a black hole VLAN
- Change the default native VLAN
- Implement port security

Refer to **Online Course** for Illustration

5.1.1.6 DHCP Attacks

DHCP is the protocol that automatically assigns a host a valid IP address out of a DHCP pool.

There are two types of DHCP attacks which can be performed against a switched network:

- **DHCP spoofing attack** - An attacker configures a fake DHCP server on the network to issue IP addresses to clients. This type of attack forces the clients to use both a false Domain Name System (DNS) server and a computer which is under the control of the attacker as their default gateway.

- **DHCP starvation attack** - An attacker floods the DHCP server with bogus DHCP requests and eventually leases all of the available IP addresses in the DHCP server pool. After these IP addresses are issued, the server cannot issue any more addresses, and this situation produces a denial-of-service (DoS) attack as new clients cannot obtain network access.

Note   A DoS attack is any attack that is used to overload specific devices and network services with illegitimate traffic, thereby preventing legitimate traffic from reaching those resources.

DHCP starvation is often used before a DHCP spoofing attack to deny service to the legitimate DHCP server. This makes it easier to introduce a fake DHCP server into the network.

Configure DHCP snooping and port security on the switch to mitigate DHCP attacks.

Refer to **Interactive Graphic** in online course

5.1.1.7   Activity – Identify Common Security Attacks

5.1.2   LAN Security Best Practices

Refer to **Interactive Graphic** in online course

5.1.2.1   Secure the LAN

As noted at the beginning of this chapter, security is only as strong as the weakest link in the system, and Layer 2 is considered to be that weakest link. Therefore, Layer 2 security solutions must be implemented to help secure a network.

Many network management protocols including Telnet, Syslog, SNMP, TFTP, and FTP are insecure. There are several strategies to help secure Layer 2 of a network:

- Always use secure variants of these protocols such as SSH, SCP, SSL, SNMPv3, and SFTP.
- Always use strong passwords and change them often.
- Enable CDP on select ports only.
- Secure Telnet access.
- Use a dedicated management VLAN where nothing but management traffic resides.
- Use ACLs to filter unwanted access.

The figure highlights four Cisco switch security solutions to help mitigate Layer 2 attacks.

This topic covers several Layer 2 security solutions:

- Mitigating MAC address table flooding attacks using port security
- Mitigating VLAN attacks
- Mitigating DHCP attacks using DHCP snooping
- Securing administrative access using AAA
- Securing device access using 802.1X port authentication

Note   IP Source Guard (IPSG) and Dynamic ARP Inspection (DAI) are advanced switch security solutions discussed in the CCNA Security course.

Refer to **Online Course** for Illustration

5.1.2.2   Mitigate MAC Address Flooding Table Attacks

The simplest and most effective method to prevent MAC table flooding attacks is to enable port security.

Port security allows an administrator to statically specify MAC addresses for a port, or to permit the switch to dynamically learn a limited number of MAC addresses. By limiting the number of permitted MAC addresses on a port to one, port security can be used to control unauthorized expansion of the network, as shown in the figure.

When MAC addresses are assigned to a secure port, the port does not forward frames with source MAC addresses outside the group of defined addresses. When a port configured with port security receives a frame, the source MAC address of the frame is compared to the list of secure source addresses that were manually configured, or auto configured (learned), on the port.

If a port is configured as a secure port and the maximum number of MAC addresses is reached, any additional attempts to connect by unknown MAC addresses will generate a security violation. The figure summarizes these points.

Refer to **Online Course** for Illustration

5.1.2.3   Mitigate VLAN Attacks

The figure shows the best way to prevent basic VLAN attacks:

- Disable DTP (auto trunking) negotiations on non-trunking ports by using the **switchport mode access** interface configuration command.

- Manually enable the trunk link on a trunking port using the **switchport mode trunk** interface configuration command.

- Disable DTP (auto trunking) negotiations on trunking ports using the **switchport non-negotiate** interface configuration command.

- Set the native VLAN to be something other than VLAN 1. Set it on an unused VLAN using the **switchport trunk native vlan** *vlan_number* interface configuration mode command.

- Disable unused ports and assign them to an unused VLAN.

Refer to **Online Course** for Illustration

5.1.2.4   Mitigate DHCP Attacks

A DHCP spoofing attack occurs when a rogue DHCP server is connected to the network and provides false IP configuration parameters to legitimate clients. DHCP spoofing is dangerous because clients can be leased IP information for malicious DNS server addresses, malicious default gateways, and malicious IP assignments.

Security best practices recommend using DHCP snooping to mitigate DHCP spoofing attacks.

When DHCP snooping is enabled on an interface or VLAN and a switch receives a DHCP packet on an untrusted port, the switch compares the source packet information with that held in the DHCP Snooping Binding Database. The switch will deny packets containing any of the following information:

- Unauthorized DHCP server messages coming from an untrusted port

- Unauthorized DHCP client messages not adhering to the DHCP Snooping Binding Database or rate limits

In a large network, the DHCP Snooping Binding Database may take time to build after it is enabled. For example, it could take two days for DHCP snooping to complete the database if DHCP lease time is four days.

DHCP snooping recognizes two types of ports:

- **Trusted DHCP ports** - Only ports connecting to upstream DHCP servers should be trusted. These ports should lead to legitimate DHCP servers replying with DHCP Offer and DHCP Ack messages. Trusted ports must be explicitly identified in the configuration.

- **Untrusted ports** - These ports connect to hosts that should not be providing DHCP server messages. By default, all switch ports are untrusted.

The figure provides a visual example of how DHCP snooping ports should be assigned on a network. Notice how the trusted ports always lead to the legitimate DHCP server while all other ports (i.e., access ports connecting to endpoints) are untrusted by default.

Note For more information on DHCP snooping, refer to the CCNA Security course.

Refer to
Interactive Graphic
in online course

5.1.2.5 Secure Administrative Access using AAA

To keep malicious users from gaining access to sensitive network equipment and services, administrators must enable access control. Access control limits who or what can use specific resources. It also limits the services or options that are available after access is granted.

There are different methods of implementing authentication on a Cisco device, and each method offers varying levels of security. The Authentication, Authorization, and Accounting (AAA) framework is used to help secure device access. AAA Authentication can be used to authenticate users for administrative access or it can be used to authenticate users for remote network access.

Cisco provides two common methods of implementing AAA services:

- **Local AAA Authentication** - Local AAA uses a local database for authentication. This method is sometimes known as self-contained authentication. This method stores usernames and passwords locally in the Cisco router, and users authenticate against the local database. Local AAA is ideal for small networks.

- **Server-Based AAA Authentication** - Server-based AAA authentication is much a more scalable solution. With server-based method, the router accesses a central AAA server. The AAA server contains the usernames and password for all users and serves as a central authentication system for all infrastructure devices.

Figure 1 illustrates how local AAA authentication works:

- The client establishes a connection with the router.

- The AAA router prompts the user for a username and password.

- The router authenticates the username and password using the local database, and the user is provided access to the network based on the information in the local database.

Figure 2 illustrates how server-based AAA authentication works:

- The client establishes a connection with the router.

- The AAA router prompts the user for a username and password.

- The router authenticates the username and password using a remote AAA server.

As shown in Figure 3, the AAA-enabled router uses either the Terminal Access Controller Access Control System (TACACS+) protocol or the Remote Authentication Dial-In User Service (RADIUS) protocol to communicate with the AAA server. While both protocols can be used to communicate between a router and AAA servers, TACACS+ is considered the more secure protocol. This is because all TACACS+ protocol exchanges are encrypted, while RADIUS only encrypts the user's password. RADIUS does not encrypt user names, accounting information, or any other information carried in the RADIUS message.

Note   For more information on AAA, refer to the CCNA Security course.

Refer to
Online Course
for Illustration

5.1.2.6   Secure Device Access using 802.1X

Network user authentication can be provided with AAA server-based authentication. The 802.1X protocol/standard can be used to authenticate network devices on the corporate network. There is another protocol used to secure computers connecting to a LAN.

The IEEE 802.1X standard defines a port-based access control and authentication protocol. IEEE 802.1X restricts unauthorized workstations from connecting to a LAN through publicly accessible switch ports. The authentication server authenticates each workstation that is connected to a switch port before making available any services offered by the switch or the LAN.

With 802.1X port-based authentication, the devices in the network have specific roles, as shown in the figure:

- **Client (Supplicant)** – This is usually the 802.1X-enabled port on the device. The device requests access to LAN and switch services and then responds to requests from the switch. In the figure, the device is a PC running 802.1X-compliant client software. Another client supplicant is the 802.1X-compliant wireless device such as a laptop or tablet.

- **Switch (Authenticator)** – This controls physical access to the network based on the authentication status of the client. The switch acts as an intermediary (proxy) between the client and the authentication server. It requests identifying information from the client, verifies that information with the authentication server, and relays a response to the client. The switch uses a RADIUS software agent, which is responsible for encapsulating and de-encapsulating the EAP (Extensible Authentication Protocol) frames and interacting with the authentication server. Another device that could act as authenticator is a wireless access point acting as the intermediary between the wireless client and the authentication server.

- **Authentication server** – This performs the actual authentication of the client. The authentication server validates the identity of the client and notifies the switch or other authenticator such as a wireless access point whether the client is authorized to access the LAN and switch services. Because the switch acts as the proxy, the authentication service is transparent to the client. The RADIUS security system with EAP extensions is the only supported authentication server.

Note   For more information on 802.1X, refer to the CCNA Security course.

Refer to
Interactive Graphic
in online course

5.1.2.7   Activity: Identify the Security Best Practice

5.2   SNMP

5.2.1   SNMP Operation

Refer to
Online Course
for Illustration

5.2.1.1   Introduction to SNMP

Simple Network Management Protocol (SNMP) was developed to allow administrators to manage nodes such as servers, workstations, routers, switches, and security appliances, on an IP network. It enables network administrators to monitor and manage network performance, find and solve network problems, and plan for network growth.

SNMP is an application layer protocol that provides a message format for communication between managers and agents. The SNMP system consists of three elements:

- SNMP manager

- SNMP agents (managed node)

- Management Information Base (MIB)

To configure SNMP on a networking device, it is first necessary to define the relationship between the manager and the agent.

The SNMP manager is part of a network management system (NMS). The SNMP manager runs SNMP management software. As shown in the figure, the SNMP manager can collect information from an SNMP agent using the "get" action and can change configurations on an agent using the "set" action. In addition, SNMP agents can forward information directly to a network manager using "traps".

The SNMP agent and MIB reside on SNMP client devices. Network devices that must be managed, such as switches, routers, servers, firewalls, and workstations, are equipped with an SMNP agent software module. MIBs store data about the device and operational statistics and are meant to be available to authenticated remote users. The SNMP agent is responsible for providing access to the local MIB.

SNMP defines how management information is exchanged between network management applications and management agents. The SNMP manager polls the agents and queries the MIB for SNMP agents on UDP port 161. SNMP agents send any SNMP traps to the SNMP manager on UDP port 162.

Refer to
Interactive Graphic
in online course

5.2.1.2   SNMP Operation

SNMP agents that reside on managed devices collect and store information about the device and its operation. This information is stored by the agent locally in the MIB. The SNMP manager then uses the SNMP agent to access information within the MIB.

There are two primary SNMP manager requests, get and set. A get request is used by the NMS to query the device for data. A set request is used by the NMS to change configuration variables in the agent device. A set request can also initiate actions within a device. For example, a set can cause a router to reboot, send a configuration file, or receive a configuration file. The SNMP manager uses the get and set actions to perform the operations described in the table in Figure 1.

The SNMP agent responds to SNMP manager requests as follows:

- **Get an MIB variable** - The SNMP agent performs this function in response to a GetRequest-PDU from the network manager. The agent retrieves the value of the requested MIB variable and responds to the network manager with that value.

- **Set an MIB variable** - The SNMP agent performs this function in response to a SetRequest-PDU from the network manager. The SNMP agent changes the value of the MIB variable to the value specified by the network manager. An SNMP agent reply to a set request includes the new settings in the device.

Figure 2 illustrates the use of an SNMP GetRequest to determine if interface G0/0 is up/up.

Refer to
Interactive Graphic
in online course

5.2.1.3   SNMP Agent Traps

An NMS periodically polls the SNMP agents residing on managed devices, by querying the device for data using the get request. Using this process, a network management application can collect information to monitor traffic loads and to verify device configurations of managed devices. The information can be displayed via a GUI on the NMS. Averages, minimums, or maximums can be calculated, the data can be graphed, or thresholds can be set to trigger a notification process when the thresholds are exceeded. For example, an NMS can monitor CPU utilization of a Cisco router. The SNMP manager samples the value periodically and presents this information in a graph for the network administrator to use in creating a baseline, creating a report, or viewing real time information.

Periodic SNMP polling does have disadvantages. First, there is a delay between the time that an event occurs and the time that it is noticed (via polling) by the NMS. Second, there is a trade-off between polling frequency and bandwidth usage.

To mitigate these disadvantages, it is possible for SNMP agents to generate and send traps to inform the NMS immediately of certain events. Traps are unsolicited messages alerting the SNMP manager to a condition or event on the network. Examples of trap conditions include, but are not limited to, improper user authentication, restarts, link status (up or down), MAC address tracking, closing of a TCP connection, loss of connection to a neighbor, or other significant events. Trap-directed notifications reduce network and agent resources, by eliminating the need for some of SNMP polling requests.

Figure 1 illustrates the use of an SNMP trap to alert the network administrator that interface G0/0 has failed. The NMS software can send the network administrator a text message, pop up a window on the NMS software, or turn the router icon red in the NMS GUI.

The exchange of all SNMP messages is illustrated in Figure 2.

Refer to
Online Course
for Illustration

5.2.1.4   SNMP Versions

There are several versions of SNMP:

- **SNMPv1** - The Simple Network Management Protocol, a Full Internet Standard, defined in RFC 1157.

- **SNMPv2c** - Defined in RFCs 1901 to 1908; utilizes community-string-based Administrative Framework.

- **SNMPv3** - Interoperable standards-based protocol originally defined in RFCs 2273 to 2275; provides secure access to devices by authenticating and encrypting packets over the network. It includes these security features: message integrity to ensure that a packet was not tampered with in transit; authentication to determine that the message is from a valid source, and encryption to prevent the contents of a message from being read by an unauthorized source.

All versions use SNMP managers, agents, and MIBs. Cisco IOS software supports the above three versions. Version 1 is a legacy solution and not often encountered in networks today; therefore, this course focuses on versions 2c and 3.

Both SNMPv1 and SNMPv2c use a community-based form of security. The community of managers able to access the agent's MIB is defined by an ACL and password.

Unlike SNMPv1, SNMPv2c includes a bulk retrieval mechanism and more detailed error message reporting to management stations. The bulk retrieval mechanism retrieves tables and large quantities of information, minimizing the number of round-trips required. The SNMPv2c improved error-handling includes expanded error codes that distinguish different kinds of error conditions. These conditions are reported through a single error code in SNMPv1. Error return codes in SNMPv2c include the error type.

Note   SNMPv1 and SNMPv2c offer minimal security features. Specifically, SNMPv1 and SNMPv2c can neither authenticate the source of a management message nor provide encryption. SNMPv3 is most currently described in RFCs 3410 to 3415. It adds methods to ensure the secure transmission of critical data between managed devices.

SNMPv3 provides for both security models and security levels. A security model is an authentication strategy set up for a user and the group within which the user resides. A security level is the permitted level of security within a security model. A combination of the security level and the security model determine which security mechanism is used when handling an SNMP packet. Available security models are SNMPv1, SNMPv2c, and SNMPv3.

The table in the figure identifies the characteristics of the different combinations of security models and levels.

A network administrator must configure the SNMP agent to use the SNMP version supported by the management station. Because an agent can communicate with multiple SNMP managers, it is possible to configure the software to support communications using SNMPv1, SNMPv2c, or SNMPv3.

Refer to **Video** in online course

5.2.1.5   Community Strings

For SNMP to operate, the NMS must have access to the MIB. To ensure that access requests are valid, some form of authentication must be in place.

SNMPv1 and SNMPv2c use community strings that control access to the MIB. Community strings are plaintext passwords. SNMP community strings authenticate access to MIB objects.

There are two types of community strings:

- **Read-only (ro)** - Provides access to the MIB variables, but does not allow these variables to be changed, only read. Because security is minimal in version 2c, many organizations use SNMPv2c in read-only mode.

- **Read-write (rw)** - Provides read and write access to all objects in the MIB.

To view or set MIB variables, the user must specify the appropriate community string for read or write access.

Click Play in the figure to see an animation about how SNMP operates with the community string.

Note   Plaintext passwords are not considered a security mechanism. This is because plaintext passwords are highly vulnerable to man-in-the-middle attacks, in which they are compromised through the capture of packets.

Refer to
Interactive Graphic
in online course

5.2.1.6   Management Information Base Object ID

The MIB organizes variables hierarchically. MIB variables enable the management software to monitor and control the network device. Formally, the MIB defines each variable as an object ID (OID). OIDs uniquely identify managed objects in the MIB hierarchy. The MIB organizes the OIDs based on RFC standards into a hierarchy of OIDs, usually shown as a tree.

The MIB tree for any given device includes some branches with variables common to many networking devices and some branches with variables specific to that device or vendor.

RFCs define some common public variables. Most devices implement these MIB variables. In addition, networking equipment vendors, like Cisco, can define their own private branches of the tree to accommodate new variables specific to their devices. Figure 1 shows portions of the MIB structure defined by Cisco Systems, Inc. Note how the OID can be described in words or numbers to help locate a particular variable in the tree. OIDs belonging to Cisco, are numbered as follows: .iso (1).org (3).dod (6).internet (1).private (4). enterprises (1).cisco (9). Therefore the OID is 1.3.6.1.4.1.9.

Because the CPU is one of the key resources, it should be measured continuously. CPU statistics should be compiled on the NMS and graphed. Observing CPU utilization over an extended time period allows the administrator to establish a baseline estimate for CPU utilization. Threshold values can then be set relative to this baseline. When CPU utilization exceeds this threshold, notifications are sent. An SNMP graphing tool can periodically poll SNMP agents, such as a router, and graph the gathered values. Figure 2 illustrates 5-minute samples of router CPU utilization over the period of a few weeks.

The data is retrieved via the snmpget utility, issued on the NMS. Using the snmpget utility, one can manually retrieve real-time data or have the NMS run a report which would give you a period of time that you could use the data to get the average. The snmpget utility requires that the SNMP version, the correct community, the IP address of the network device to query, and the OID number are set. Figure 3 demonstrates the use of the freeware snmpget utility, which allows quick retrieval of information from the MIB.

Figure 3 shows a sample snmpget utility command with several parameters, including:

- `-v2c` - version of SNMP

- `-c community` - SNMP password, called a community string

- `10.250.250.14` - IP address of monitored device

- `1.3.6.1.4.1.9.2.1.58.0` - OID of MIB variable

The last line shows the response. The output shows a shortened version of the MIB variable. It then lists the actual value in the MIB location. In this case, the 5-minute exponential moving average of the CPU busy percentage is 11 percent. The utility gives some insight into the basic mechanics of how SNMP works. However, working with long MIB variable names like 1.3.6.1.4.1.9.2.1.58.0 can be problematic for the average user. More commonly, the network operations staff uses a network management product with an easy-to-use GUI, with the entire MIB data variable naming transparent to the user.

The Cisco SNMP Navigator on the http://cisco.com website allows a network administrator to research details about a particular OID. Figure 4 displays an example associated with a configuration change on a Cisco 2960 switch.

Refer to
Online Course
for Illustration

5.2.1.7 SNMPv3

Simple Network Management Protocol version 3 (SNMPv3) authenticates and encrypts packets over the network to provide secure access to devices. Adding authentication and encryption to SNMPv3 addresses the vulnerabilities of earlier versions of SNMP.

SNMPv3 authenticates and encrypts packets over the network to provide secure access to devices, as shown in the figure. This addressed the vulnerabilities of earlier versions of SNMP.

SNMPv3 provides three security features:

- **Message integrity and authentication** - Transmissions from the SNMP manager (NMS) to agents (managed nodes) can be authenticated to guarantee the identity of the sender and the integrity and timeliness of a message. This ensures that a packet has not been tampered with in transit, and is from a valid source.

- **Encryption** - SNMPv3 messages may be encrypted to ensure privacy. Encryption scrambles the contents of a packet to prevent it from being seen by an unauthorized source.

- **Access control** - Restricts SNMP managers to certain actions on specific portions of data. For example, you may not want the NMS to have full access to your firewall device.

Refer to
Interactive Graphic
in online course

5.2.1.8 Activity – Identify Characteristics of SNMP Versions

Refer to
Lab Activity
for this chapter

5.2.1.9 Lab – Researching Network Monitoring Software

In this lab, you will complete the following objectives:

- Part 1: Survey Your Understanding of Network Monitoring

- Part 2: Research Network Monitoring Tools

- Part 3: Select a Network Monitoring Tool

5.2.2   Configuring SNMP

Refer to
Online Course
for Illustration

5.2.2.1   Steps for Configuring SNMP

A network administrator can configure SNMPv2 to obtain network information from network devices. As shown in the figure, the basic steps to configuring SNMP are all in global configuration mode.

Step 1.   (Required) Configure the community string and access level (read-only or read-write) with the **snmp-server community** *string* **ro** | **rw** command.

Step 2.   (Optional) Document the location of the device using the **snmp-server location** *text* command.

Step 3.   (Optional) Document the system contact using the **snmp-server contact** *text* command.

Step 4.   (Optional) Restrict SNMP access to NMS hosts (SNMP managers) that are permitted by an ACL: define the ACL and then reference the ACL with the **snmp-server community** *string access-list-number-or-name* command. This command can be used both to specify a community string and to restrict SNMP access via ACLs. Step 1 and Step 4 can be combined into one step, if desired; the Cisco networking device combines the two commands into one if they are entered separately.

Step 5.   (Optional) Specify the recipient of the SNMP trap operations with the **snmp-server host** *host-id* [**version** {**1**| **2c** | **3** [**auth** | **noauth** | **priv**]}] *community-string* command. By default, no trap manager is defined.

Step 6.   (Optional) Enable traps on an SNMP agent with the **snmp-server enable traps** *notification-types* command. If no trap notification types are specified in this command, then all trap types are sent. Repeated use of this command is required if a particular subset of trap types is desired.

Note   By default, SNMP does not have any traps set. Without this command, SNMP managers must poll for all relevant information.

Refer to
Interactive Graphic
in online course

5.2.2.2   Verifying SNMP Configuration

There are several software solutions for viewing SNMP output. For our purposes, the Kiwi Syslog Server displays SNMP messages associated with SNMP traps.

PC1 and R1 are configured to demonstrate output on an SNMP Manager as related to SNMP traps.

As shown in Figure 1, PC1 is assigned the IP address 192.168.1.3/24. The Kiwi Syslog Server is installed on PC1.

After R1 is configured, whenever an event occurs which qualifies as a trap, the SNMP traps are sent to the SNMP manager. For instance, if an interface comes up, a trap is sent to the server. Configuration changes on the router also trigger SNMP traps to be sent to the SNMP manager. A list of over 60 trap notification types can be seen with the **snmp-server enable traps ?** command. In the configuration of R1, no trap notification types are specified in the **snmp-server enable traps** *notification-types* command, so all traps are sent.

In Figure 2, a check box is checked in the **Setup** menu to indicate that the network administrator wants SNMP manager software to listen for SNMP traps on UDP port 162.

In Figure 3, the top row of the displayed SNMP trap output indicates that interface GigabitEthernet0/0 changed state to up. Also, each time the global configuration mode is entered from privileged EXEC mode, a trap is received by the SNMP manager, as shown in the highlighted row.

To verify the SNMP configuration, use any of the variations of the **show snmp** privileged EXEC mode command. The most useful command is simply the **show snmp** command, as it displays the information that is commonly of interest when examining the SNMP configuration. Unless there is an involved SNMPv3 configuration, for the most part the other command options only display selected portions of the output of the **show snmp** command. Figure 4 provides an example of **show snmp** output.

The **show snmp** command output does not display information relating to the SNMP community string or, if applicable, the associated ACL. Figure 5 displays the SNMP community string and ACL information, using the **show snmp community** command.

Use the Syntax Checker in Figure 6 to configure and verify SNMP on R1.

Refer to
Online Course
for Illustration

5.2.2.3   SNMP Best Practices

While SNMP is very useful for monitoring and troubleshooting, as shown in the figure, it can also create security vulnerabilities. For this reason, prior to implementing SNMP, be mindful of security best practices.

Both SNMPv1 and SNMPv2c rely on SNMP community strings in plaintext to authenticate access to MIB objects. These community strings, as with all passwords, should be carefully chosen to ensure that they are not too easy to crack. Additionally, community strings should be changed at regular intervals and in accordance with network security policies. For example, the strings should be changed when a network administrator changes roles or leaves the company. If SNMP is used only to monitor devices, use read-only communities.

Ensure that SNMP messages do not spread beyond the management consoles. ACLs should be used to prevent SNMP messages from going beyond the required devices. ACLs should also be used on the monitored devices to limit access for management systems only.

SNMPv3 is recommended because it provides security authentication and encryption. There are a number of other global configuration mode commands that a network administrator can implement to take advantage of the authentication and encryption support in SNMPv3:

■ The **snmp-server group** *groupname* {v1 | v2c | v3 {auth | noauth | priv}} command creates a new SNMP group on the device.

■ The **snmp-server user** *username groupname* **v3** [encrypted] [auth {md5 | sha} auth-password] [priv {des | 3des | aes {128 | 192 | 256}} priv-password] command is used to add a new user to the SNMP group specified in the **snmp-server group** *groupname* command.

Refer to
Online Course
for Illustration

5.2.2.4   Steps for Configuring SNMPv3

SNMPv3 can be secured with the four steps. The figure shows the syntax. The following describes each step:

Step 1.   Configure a standard ACL that will permit access for authorized SNMP managers.

Step 2.   Configure an SNMP view with the **snmp-server view** global configuration command to identify which MIB Object Identifiers (OIDs) the SNMP manager will be able to read. Configuring a view is required to limit SNMP messages to read-only access.

Step 3.   Configure SNMP group features with the **snmp-server group** global configuration command. This command has following parameters (refer to the figure for the syntax):

■ Configures a name for the group.

■ Sets the SNMP version.

■ Specifies the required authentication and encryption.

■ Associates the view from Step 2 to the group.

■ Specifies read or read write access.

■ Filters the group with the ACL configured in Step 1.

Step 4.   Configure SNMP group user features with the **snmp-server user** global configuration command. The command has the following parameters:

■ Configures a username.

■ Associates the user with the group name that was configured in Step 3.

■ Sets the SNMP version.

■ Sets the authentication type. SHA is preferred and should be supported by the SNMP management software.

■ Sets the encryption type.

■ Configures an encryption password.

Refer to
Interactive Graphic
in online course

5.2.2.5   Verifying SNMPv3 Configuration

The example in Figure 1 configures a standard ACL named PERMIT-ADMIN. It is configured to permit only the 192.168.1.0/24 network. All hosts attached to this network will be allowed to access the SNMP agent running on R1.

An SNMP view is named SNMP-RO and is configured to include the entire ISO tree from the MIB. On a production network, the network administrator would probably configure this view to include only the MIB OIDs that were necessary for monitoring and managing the network.

An SNMP group is configured with the name ADMIN. SNMP is set to version 3 with authentication and encryption required. The group is allowed read-only access to the view (SNMP-RO). Access for the group is limited by the PERMIT-ADMIN ACL.

An SNMP user, BOB, is configured as a member of the group ADMIN. SNMP is set to version 3. Authentication is set to use SHA, and an authentication password is configured. Although R1 supports up to AES 256 encryption, the SNMP management software only supports AES 128. Therefore, the encryption is set to AES 128 and an encryption password is configured.

Use the Syntax Checker in Figure 2 to configure R1 with SNMPv3 authentication using an ACL.

Refer to
Lab Activity
for this chapter

5.2.2.6   Lab – Configuring SNMP

In this lab, you will complete the following objectives:

■ Part 1: Build the Network and Configure Basic Device Settings

■ Part 2: Configure an SNMP Manager and Agents

■ Part 3: Convert OID Codes with the Cisco SNMP Object Navigator

5.3   Cisco Switch Port Analyzer

5.3.1   SPAN Overview

Refer to
Online Course
for Illustration

5.3.1.1   Port Mirroring

A packet analyzer (also known as a sniffer, packet sniffer, or traffic sniffer) is a valuable tool to help monitor and troubleshoot a network. A packet analyzer is typically software that captures packets entering and exiting a network interface card (NIC). For example, Wireshark is a packet analyzer that is commonly used to capture and analyze packets on a local computer.

What if a network administrator wanted to capture packets from many other key devices and not just the local NIC? A solution is to configure networking devices to copy and send traffic going to ports of interest to a port connected to a packet analyzer. The administrator could then analyze network traffic from various sources in the network.

However, the basic operation of a modern switched network disables the packet analyzer ability to capture traffic from other sources. For instance, a user running Wireshark can only capture traffic going to their NIC. They cannot capture traffic between another host and a server. The reason is because a Layer 2 switch populates its MAC address table based on the source MAC address and the ingress port of the Ethernet frame. After the table is built, the switch only forwards traffic destined for a MAC address directly to the corresponding port. This prevents a packet analyzer connected to another port on the switch from "hearing" other switch traffic.

The solution to this dilemma is to enable port mirroring. The port mirroring feature allows a switch to copy and send Ethernet frames from specific ports to the destination port connected to a packet analyzer. The original frame is still forwarded in the usual manner.

An example of port mirroring is shown in the figure. Notice how traffic between PC1 and PC2 is also being sent to the laptop that has a packet analyzer installed.

Refer to
Online Course
for Illustration

5.3.1.2   Analyzing Suspicious Traffic

The Switched Port Analyzer (SPAN) feature on Cisco switches is a type of port mirroring that sends copies of the frame entering a port, out another port on the same switch. SPAN allows administrators or devices to collect and analyze traffic.

As shown in Figure 1, SPAN is commonly implemented to deliver traffic to specialized devices including:

- **Packet analyzers** - Using software such as Wireshark to capture and analyze traffic for troubleshooting purposes. For example, an administrator can capture traffic destined to a server to troubleshoot the sub-optimal operation of a network application.

- **Intrusion Protection Systems (IPSs)** - IPSs are focused on the security aspect of traffic and are implemented to detect network attacks as they happen, issuing alerts or even blocking the malicious packets as the attack takes place. IPSs are typically deployed as a service on an ISR G2 router or using a dedicated device.

While packet analyzers are commonly used for troubleshooting purposes, an IPS looks for specific patterns in traffic. As the traffic flows through the IPS, it analyzes traffic in real-time and takes action upon the discovery of malicious traffic patterns.

Modern networks are switched environments. Therefore, SPAN is crucial for effective IPS operation. SPAN can be implemented as either Local SPAN or Remote SPAN (RSPAN).

Refer to
Interactive Graphic
in online course

5.3.1.3   Local SPAN

Local SPAN is when traffic on a switch is mirrored to another port on that switch. Various terms are used to identify incoming and outgoing ports. The table in Figure 1 describes commonly used SPAN terms. Figure 2 identifies the SPAN ports.

A SPAN session is the association between source ports (or VLANs) and a destination port.

Traffic entering or leaving the source port (or VLAN) is replicated by the switch on the destination port. Although SPAN can support multiple source ports under the same session or an entire VLAN as the traffic source, a SPAN session does not support both. Both Layer 2 and Layer 3 ports can be configured as source ports.

There are three important things to consider when configuring SPAN:

- The destination port cannot be a source port, and the source port cannot be a destination port.

- The number of destination ports is platform-dependent. Some platforms allow for more than one destination port.

- The destination port is no longer a normal switch port. Only monitored traffic passes through that port.

The SPAN feature is said to be local when the monitored ports are all located on the same switch as the destination port. This feature is in contrast to Remote SPAN (RSPAN).

Refer to
Interactive Graphic
in online course

5.3.1.4   Remote SPAN

Remote SPAN (RSPAN) allows source and destination ports to be in different switches. RSPAN is useful when the packet analyzer or IPS is on a different switch than the traffic being monitored.

The table in Figure 1 describes RSPAN terms.

Figure 2 illustrates how RSPAN is forwarded between two switches. Notice how RSPAN extends SPAN by enabling remote monitoring of multiple switches across the network.

RSPAN uses two sessions. One session is used as the source and one session is used to copy or receive the traffic from a VLAN. The traffic for each RSPAN session is carried over trunk links in a user-specified RSPAN VLAN that is dedicated (for that RSPAN session) in all participating switches.

Note   Configuring RSPAN is covered in the CCNA Security course.

Refer to
Interactive Graphic
in online course

5.3.1.5   Activity – Identify SPAN Terminology

5.3.2   SPAN Configuration

Refer to
Interactive Graphic
in online course

5.3.2.1   Configuring Local SPAN

The SPAN feature on Cisco switches sends a copy of each frame entering the source port, out the destination port and toward the packet analyzer or IPS. A session number is used to identify a local SPAN session.

Figure 1 shows the syntax of the **monitor session** global configuration command. This command is used to associate a source port and a destination port with a SPAN session. A separate **monitor session** command is used for each session. A VLAN can be specified instead of a physical port.

For example, in Figure 2, PCA is connected to F0/1 and a computer with a packet analyzer application is connected to F0/2. The objective is to capture all the traffic that is sent or received by PCA on port F0/1 and send a copy of those frames to the packet analyzer (or IPS) on port F0/2. The SPAN session on the switch will copy all the traffic that it sends and receives on source port F0/1 to the destination port F0/2.

Refer to
Interactive Graphic
in online course

5.3.2.2   Verifying Local SPAN

The **show monitor** command is used to verify the SPAN session. The command displays the type of the session, the source ports for each traffic direction, and the destination port.

In the example shown in Figure 1, the session number is 1, the source port for both traffic directions is F0/1, and the destination port is F0/2. The ingress SPAN is disabled on the destination port, so only traffic that leaves the destination port is copied to that port.

Use the Syntax Checker in Figure 2 to configure and verify local SPAN.

Refer to
Lab Activity
for this chapter

5.3.2.3   Lab – Implement a Local SPAN

In this lab, you will complete the following objectives:

- Part 1: Build the Network and Verify Connectivity

- Part 2: Configure Local SPAN and Capture Copied Traffic with Wireshark

5.3.3   SPAN as a Troubleshooting Tool

Refer to
Online Course
for Illustration

5.3.3.1   Troubleshooting with SPAN Overview

SPAN allows administrators to troubleshoot network issues. For example, a network application may be taking too long to execute tasks. To investigate, a network administrator may use SPAN to duplicate and redirect traffic to a packet analyzer such as Wireshark. The administrator can then analyze the traffic from all devices to troubleshoot sub-optimal operation of the network application.

Older systems with faulty NICs can also cause issues. If SPAN is enabled on a switch to send traffic to a packet analyzer, a network technician can detect and isolate the end device causing the excess traffic, as shown in the figure.

Refer to
Lab Activity
for this chapter

5.3.3.2   Lab – Troubleshoot LAN Traffic Using SPAN

In this lab, you will complete the following objectives:

- Part 1: Build the Network and Verify Connectivity
- Part 2: Configure Local SPAN and Capture Copied Traffic with Wireshark

5.4   Summary

Refer to
Online Course
for Illustration

5.4.1.1   Chapter 5: Network Security and Monitoring

At Layer 2, a number of vulnerabilities exist that require specialized mitigation techniques:

- MAC address table flooding attacks are addressed with port security.
- VLAN attacks are controlled by disabling DTP and following basic guidelines for configuring trunk ports.
- DHCP attacks are addressed with DHCP snooping.

The SNMP protocol has three elements: the Manager, the Agent, and the MIB. The SNMP manager resides on the NMS, while the Agent and the MIB are on the client devices. The SNMP Manager can poll the client devices for information, or it can use a TRAP message that tells a client to report immediately if the client reaches a particular threshold. SNMP can also be used to change the configuration of a device. SNMPv3 is the recommended version because it provides security. SNMP is a comprehensive and powerful remote management tool. Nearly every item available in a **show** command is available through SNMP.

Switched Port Analyzer (SPAN) is used to mirror the traffic going to and/or coming from the host. It is commonly implemented to support traffic analyzers or IPS devices.

Go to the online course to take the quiz and exam.

Chapter 5 Quiz

This quiz is designed to provide an additional opportunity to practice the skills and knowledge presented in the chapter and to prepare for the chapter exam. You will be allowed multiple attempts and the grade does not appear in the gradebook.

Chapter 5 Exam

The chapter exam assesses your knowledge of the chapter content.

Your Chapter Notes

Quality of Service

6.0 Introduction

Refer to **Online Course** for Illustration

6.0.1.1 Chapter 6: Quality of Service

In today's networks, users expect content to be immediately available. But if the traffic exceeds the bandwidth of the links between the source of the content and the user, how do network administrators ensure a quality experience? Quality of Service (QoS) tools can be designed into the network to guarantee that certain traffic types, such as voice and video, are prioritized over traffic that is not as time-sensitive, such as email and web browsing.

This chapter describes network transmission quality, traffic characteristics, queueing algorithms, QoS models, and QoS implementation techniques.

6.1 QoS Overview

6.1.1 Network Transmission Quality

Refer to **Video** in online course

6.1.1.1 Video Tutorial - The Purpose of QoS

Click Play for a brief explanation of the purpose of QoS.

Click here to read the transcript of this video.

Refer to **Online Course** for Illustration

6.1.1.2 Prioritizing Traffic

Quality of Service (QoS) is an ever increasing requirement of networks today. New applications available to users, such as voice and live video transmissions, create higher expectations for quality delivery.

Congestion occurs when multiple communication lines aggregate onto a single device such as a router, and then much of that data is placed on fewer outbound interfaces, or onto a slower interface. Congestion can also occur when large data packets prevent smaller packets from being transmitted in a timely manner.

When the volume of traffic is greater than what can be transported across the network, devices queue, or hold, the packets in memory until resources become available to transmit them. Queuing packets causes delay because new packets cannot be transmitted until previous packets have been processed. If the number of packets to be queued continues to increase, the memory within the device fills up and packets are dropped. One QoS technique that can help with this problem is to classify data into multiple queues, as shown in the figure.

Note A device implements QoS only when it is experiencing some type of congestion.

Refer to
Interactive Graphic
in online course

6.1.1.3 Bandwidth, Congestion, Delay, and Jitter

Network bandwidth is measured in the number of bits that can be transmitted in a single second, or bits per second (bps). For example, a network device may be described as having the capability to perform at 10 gigabits per second (Gbps).

Network congestion causes delay. An interface experiences congestion when it is presented with more traffic than it can handle. Network congestion points are strong candidates for QoS mechanisms. Figure 1 shows three examples of typical congestion points.

Delay or latency refers to the time it takes for a packet to travel from the source to the destination. Two types of delays are fixed and variable. A fixed delay is a specific amount of time a specific process takes, such as how long it takes to place a bit on the transmission media. A variable delay take an unspecified amount of time and is affected by factors such as how much traffic is being processed.

The sources of delay are summarized in table in Figure 2.

Jitter is the variation in the delay of received packets. At the sending side, packets are sent in a continuous stream with the packets spaced evenly apart. Due to network congestion, improper queuing, or configuration errors, the delay between each packet can vary instead of remaining constant. Both delay and jitter need to be controlled and minimized to support real-time and interactive traffic.

Refer to
Interactive Graphic
in online course

6.1.1.4 Packet Loss

Without any QoS mechanisms in place, packets are processed in the order in which they are received. When congestion occurs, network devices such as routers and switches can drop packets. This means that time-sensitive packets, such as real-time video and voice, will be dropped with the same frequency as data that is not time-sensitive, such as email and web browsing.

For example, when a router receives a Real-Time Protocol (RTP) digital audio stream for Voice over IP (VoIP), it must compensate for the jitter that is encountered. The mechanism that handles this function is the playout delay buffer. The playout delay buffer must buffer these packets and then play them out in a steady stream as shown in Figure 1. The digital packets are later converted back to an analog audio stream.

If the jitter is so large that it causes packets to be received out of the range of this buffer, the out-of-range packets are discarded and dropouts are heard in the audio, as shown in Figure 2.

For losses as small as one packet, the digital signal processor (DSP) interpolates what it thinks the audio should be and no problem is audible to the user. However, when jitter exceeds what the DSP can do to make up for the missing packets, audio problems are heard.

Packet loss is a very common cause of voice quality problems on an IP network. In a properly designed network, packet loss should be near zero. The voice codecs used by the DSP can tolerate some degree of packet loss without a dramatic effect on voice quality. Network engineers use QoS mechanisms to classify voice packets for zero packet loss. Bandwidth is guaranteed for the voice calls by giving priority to voice traffic over traffic that is not time-sensitive.

Refer to
Interactive Graphic
in online course

6.1.1.5   Activity - Identify Network Transmission Quality Terminology

6.1.2   Traffic Characteristics

Refer to **Video**
in online course

6.1.2.1   Video Tutorial - Traffic Characteristics

Click Play for an overview of how QoS can be used to treat packets differently based on the characteristics of the traffic.

Click here to read the transcript of this video.

Refer to
Online Course
for Illustration

6.1.2.2   Network Traffic Trends

In the early 2000s, the predominant types of IP traffic were voice and data. Voice traffic has a predictable bandwidth need and known packet arrival times. Data traffic is not real-time and has unpredictable bandwidth need. Data traffic can temporarily burst, as when a large file is being downloaded. This bursting can consume the entire bandwidth of a link.

More recently, video traffic has become the increasingly important to business communications and operations. According to the Cisco Virtual Networking Index (VNI), video traffic represented 67% of all traffic in 2014. By 2019, video will represent 80% of all traffic. In addition, mobile video traffic will increase over 600% from 113,672 TB to 768,334 TB.

The type of demands voice, video, and data traffic place on the network are very different.

Refer to
Online Course
for Illustration

6.1.2.3   Voice

Voice traffic is predictable and smooth, as shown in the figure. However, voice is very sensitive to delays and dropped packets; there is no reason to re-transmit voice if packets are lost. Therefore, voice packets must receive a higher priority than other types of traffic. Therefore, it must receive a higher priority. For example, Cisco products use the RTP port range 16384 to 32767 to prioritize voice traffic. Voice can tolerate a certain amount of latency, jitter, and loss without any noticeable effects. Latency should be no more than 150 milliseconds (ms). Jitter should be no more than 30 ms, and voice packet loss should be no more than 1%. Voice traffic requires at least 30 Kbps of bandwidth.

Refer to
Interactive Graphic
in online course

6.1.2.4   Video

Without QoS and a significant amount of extra bandwidth capacity, video quality typically degrades. The picture appears blurry, jagged, or in slow motion. The audio portion of the feed may become unsynchronized with the video.

Video traffic tends to be unpredictable, inconsistent, and bursty compared to voice traffic. Compared to voice, video is less resilient to loss and has a higher volume of data per packet, as shown in Figure 1. Notice how voice packets arrive every 20 ms and are a predictable 200 bytes each. In contrast, the number and size of video packets varies every 33 ms based on the content of the video. For example, if the video stream consists of content that is not changing much from frame to frame, then the video packets will be small and fewer are required to maintain acceptable user experience. However, if the video steam consists of content that is rapidly changing, such as in an action sequence in a movie, then the video packets will be larger and more are required per 33 ms time slot to maintain an acceptable user experience.

Figure 2 summarizes the characteristics of video traffic. UDP ports, such as 554 used for the Real-Time Streaming Protocol (RSTP), should be given priority over other, less time-sensitive, network traffic. Similar to voice, video can tolerate a certain amount of latency, jitter, and loss without any noticeable affects. Latency should be no more than 400 milliseconds (ms). Jitter should be no more than 50 ms, and video packet loss should be no more than 1%. Video traffic requires at least 384 Kbps of bandwidth.

Refer to
Interactive Graphic
in online course

6.1.2.5   Data

Most applications use either TCP or UDP. Unlike UDP, TCP performs error recovery. Data applications that have no tolerance for data loss, such as email and web pages, use TCP to ensure that, if packets are lost in transit, they will be resent. Data traffic can be smooth or bursty. Network control traffic is usually smooth and predictable. When there is a topology change, the network control traffic may burst for a few seconds. But the capacity of today's networks can easily handle the increase in network control traffic as the network converges.

However, some TCP applications can be very greedy, consuming a large portion of network capacity. FTP will consume as much bandwidth as it can get when you download a large file, such as a movie or game. Figure 1 summarizes data traffic characteristics.

Although data traffic is relatively insensitive to drops and delays compared to voice and video, a network administrator still needs to consider the quality of the user experience, sometimes referred to as Quality of Experience or QoE. The two main factors a network administrator needs to ask about the flow of data traffic are the following:

- Does the data come from an interactive application?

- Is the data mission critical?

Figure 2 compares these two factors.

Refer to
Interactive Graphic
in online course

6.1.2.6   Activity - Compare Traffic Characteristics

6.1.3   Queueing Algorithms

Refer to **Video**
in online course

6.1.3.1   Video Tutorial - QoS Algorithms

Click Play for an overview of the different types of QoS queueing algorithms.

Click here to read the transcript of this video.

Refer to
Online Course
for Illustration

6.1.3.2   Queuing Overview

The QoS policy implemented by the network administrator becomes active when congestion occurs on the link. Queuing is a congestion management tool that can buffer, prioritize, and, if required, reorder packets before being transmitted to the destination. A number of queuing algorithms are available. For the purposes of this course, we will focus on the following:

- First-In, First-Out (FIFO)

- Weighted Fair Queuing (WFQ)

- Class-Based Weighted Fair Queuing (CBWFQ)

- Low Latency Queuing (LLQ)

Refer to
Online Course
for Illustration

6.1.3.3   First In First Out (FIFO)

In its simplest form, FIFO queuing, also known as first-come, first-served (FCFS) queuing, involves buffering and forwarding of packets in the order of arrival.

FIFO has no concept of priority or classes of traffic and consequently, makes no decision about packet priority. There is only one queue, and all packets are treated equally. Packets are sent out an interface in the order in which they arrive, as shown in the figure. Although some traffic is more important or time-sensitive based on the priority classification, notice that the traffic is sent out in the order it is received.

When FIFO is used, important or time-sensitive traffic can be dropped when congestion occurs on the router or switch interface. When no other queuing strategies are configured, all interfaces except serial interfaces at E1 (2.048 Mbps) and below use FIFO by default. (Serial interfaces at E1 and below use WFQ by default.)

FIFO, which is the fastest method of queuing, is effective for large links that have little delay and minimal congestion. If your link has very little congestion, FIFO queuing may be the only queuing you need to use.

Refer to
Online Course
for Illustration

6.1.3.4   Weighted Fair Queuing (WFQ)

WFQ is an automated scheduling method that provides fair bandwidth allocation to all network traffic. WFQ applies priority, or weights, to identified traffic and classifies it into conversations or flows, as shown in the figure.

WFQ then determines how much bandwidth each flow is allowed relative to other flows. The flow-based algorithm used by WFQ simultaneously schedules interactive traffic to the front of a queue to reduce response time. It then fairly shares the remaining bandwidth among high-bandwidth flows. WFQ allows you to give low-volume, interactive traffic, such as Telnet sessions and voice, priority over high-volume traffic, such as FTP sessions. When multiple file transfers flows are occurring simultaneously, the transfers are given comparable bandwidth.

WFQ classifies traffic into different flows based on packet header addressing, including such characteristics as source and destination IP addresses, MAC addresses, port numbers, protocol, and Type of Service (ToS) value. The ToS value in the IP header can be used to classify traffic. ToS will be discussed later in the chapter.

Low-bandwidth traffic streams, which comprise the majority of traffic, receive preferential service, allowing their entire offered loads to be sent in a timely fashion. High-volume traffic streams share the remaining capacity proportionally among themselves.

Limitations

WFQ is not supported with tunneling and encryption because these features modify the packet content information required by WFQ for classification.

Although WFQ automatically adapts to changing network traffic conditions, it does not offer the degree of precision control over bandwidth allocation that CBWFQ offers.

Refer to
Online Course
for Illustration

6.1.3.5   Class-Based Weighted Fair Queuing (CBWFQ)

CBWFQ extends the standard WFQ functionality to provide support for user-defined traffic classes. For CBWFQ, you define traffic classes based on match criteria including protocols, access control lists (ACLs), and input interfaces. Packets satisfying the match criteria for a class constitute the traffic for that class. A FIFO queue is reserved for each class, and traffic belonging to a class is directed to the queue for that class, as shown in the figure.

When a class has been defined according to its match criteria, you can assign it characteristics. To characterize a class, you assign it bandwidth, weight, and maximum packet limit. The bandwidth assigned to a class is the guaranteed bandwidth delivered to the class during congestion.

To characterize a class, you also specify the queue limit for that class, which is the maximum number of packets allowed to accumulate in the queue for the class. Packets belonging to a class are subject to the bandwidth and queue limits that characterize the class.

After a queue has reached its configured queue limit, adding more packets to the class causes tail drop or packet drop to take effect, depending on how class policy is configured. Tail drop means a router simply discards any packet that arrives at the tail end of a queue that has completely used up its packet-holding resources. This is the default queuing response to congestion. Tail drop treats all traffic equally and does not differentiate between classes of service.

Refer to **Online Course** for Illustration

6.1.3.6 Low Latency Queuing (LLQ)

The LLQ feature brings strict priority queuing (PQ) to CBWFQ. Strict PQ allows delay-sensitive data such as voice to be sent before packets in other queues. LLQ provides strict priority queuing for CBWFQ, reducing jitter in voice conversations, as shown in the figure.

Without LLQ, CBWFQ provides WFQ based on defined classes with no strict priority queue available for real-time traffic. The weight for a packet belonging to a specific class is derived from the bandwidth you assigned to the class when you configured it. Therefore, the bandwidth assigned to the packets of a class determines the order in which packets are sent. All packets are serviced fairly based on weight; no class of packets may be granted strict priority. This scheme poses problems for voice traffic that is largely intolerant of delay, especially variation in delay. For voice traffic, variations in delay introduce irregularities of transmission manifesting as jitter in the heard conversation.

With LLQ, delay-sensitive data is sent first, before packets in other queues are treated. LLQ allows delay-sensitive data such as voice to be sent first (before packets in other queues), giving delay-sensitive data preferential treatment over other traffic. Although it is possible to enqueue various types of real-time traffic to the strict priority queue, Cisco recommends that only voice traffic be directed to the priority queue.

Refer to **Interactive Graphic** in online course

6.1.3.7 Activity - Compare Queuing Algorithms

6.2 QoS Mechanisms

6.2.1 QoS Models

Refer to **Video** in online course

6.2.1.1 Video Tutorial - QoS Models

Click Play for an overview of the QoS best-effort model, integrated services model, and differentiated services model.

Click here to read the transcript of this video.

Refer to
Online Course
for Illustration

6.2.1.2   Selecting an Appropriate QoS Policy Model

How can QoS be implemented in a network? The three models for implementing QoS are:

- Best-effort model

- Integrated services (IntServ)

- Differentiated services (DiffServ)

The table in the figure summarizes these three models. QoS is really implemented in a network using either IntServ or DiffServ. While IntServ provides the highest guarantee of QoS, it is very resource-intensive and therefore, limited in scalability. In contrast, DiffServ is less resource-intensive and more scalable. The two are sometimes co-deployed in network QoS implementations.

Refer to
Online Course
for Illustration

6.2.1.3   Best-Effort

The basic design of the Internet provides for best-effort packet delivery and provides no guarantees. This approach is still predominant on the Internet today and remains appropriate for most purposes. The best-effort model treats all network packets in the same way, so an emergency voice message is treated the same way a digital photograph attached to an email is treated. Without QoS, the network cannot tell the difference between packets and, as a result, cannot treat packets preferentially.

The best-effort model is similar in concept to sending a letter using standard postal mail. Your letter is treated exactly the same as every other letter. With the best-effort model, the letter may never arrive, and, unless you have a separate notification arrangement with the letter recipient, you may never know that the letter did not arrive.

The table in the figure lists the benefits and drawbacks of the best effort model.

Refer to
Interactive Graphic
in online course

6.2.1.4   Integrated Services

The needs of real-time applications, such as remote video, multimedia conferencing, visualization, and virtual reality, motivated the development of the IntServ architecture model in 1994 (RFC 1633, 2211, and 2212). IntServ is a multiple-service model that can accommodate multiple QoS requirements.

IntServ provides a way to deliver the end-to-end QoS that real-time applications require by explicitly managing network resources to provide QoS to specific user packet streams, sometimes called microflows. It uses resource reservation and admission-control mechanisms as building blocks to establish and maintain QoS. This practice is similar to a concept known as "hard QoS." Hard QoS guarantees traffic characteristics, such as bandwidth, delay, and packet-loss rates, from end to end. Hard QoS ensures both predictable and guaranteed service levels for mission-critical applications.

Figure 1 is a simple illustration of the IntServ model.

IntServ uses a connection-oriented approach inherited from telephony network design. Each individual communication must explicitly specify its traffic descriptor and requested resources to the network. The edge router performs admission control to ensure that available resources are sufficient in the network. The IntServ standard assumes that routers along a path set and maintain the state for each individual communication.

In the IntServ model, the application requests a specific kind of service from the network before sending data. The application informs the network of its traffic profile and requests a particular kind of service that can encompass its bandwidth and delay requirements. IntServ uses the Resource Reservation Protocol (RSVP) to signal the QoS needs of an application's traffic along devices in the end-to-end path through the network. If network devices along the path can reserve the necessary bandwidth, the originating application can begin transmitting. If the requested reservation fails along the path, the originating application does not send any data.

The edge router performs admission control based on information from the application and available network resources. The network commits to meeting the QoS requirements of the application as long as the traffic remains within the profile specifications. The network fulfills its commitment by maintaining the per-flow state and then performing packet classification, policing, and intelligent queuing based on that state.

The table in Figure 2 lists the benefits and drawbacks of the IntServ model.

Refer to
Interactive Graphic
in online course

6.2.1.5 Differentiated Services

The differentiated services (DiffServ) QoS model specifies a simple and scalable mechanism for classifying and managing network traffic and providing QoS guarantees on modern IP networks. For example, DiffServ can provide low-latency guaranteed service to critical network traffic such as voice or video while providing simple best-effort traffic guarantees to non-critical services such as web traffic or file transfers.

The DiffServ design overcomes the limitations of both the best-effort and IntServ models. The DiffServ model is described in RFCs 2474, 2597, 2598, 3246, 4594. DiffServ can provide an "almost guaranteed" QoS while still being cost-effective and scalable.

The DiffServ model is similar in concept to sending a package using a delivery service. You request (and pay for) a level of service when you send a package. Throughout the package network, the level of service you paid for is recognized and your package is given either preferential or normal service, depending on what you requested.

DiffServ is not an end-to-end QoS strategy because it cannot enforce end-to-end guarantees. However, DiffServ QoS is a more scalable approach to implementing QoS. Unlike IntServ and hard QoS in which the end-hosts signal their QoS needs to the network, DiffServ does not use signaling. Instead, DiffServ uses a "soft QoS" approach. It works on the provisioned-QoS model, where network elements are set up to service multiple classes of traffic each with varying QoS requirements.

Figure 1 is a simple illustration of the DiffServ model.

As a host forwards traffic to a router, the router classifies the flows into aggregates (classes) and provides the appropriate QoS policy for the classes. DiffServ enforces and applies QoS mechanisms on a hop-by-hop basis, uniformly applying global meaning to each traffic class to provide both flexibility and scalability. For example, DiffServ could be configured to group all TCP flows as a single class, and allocate bandwidth for that class, rather than for the individual flows as IntServ would do. In addition to classifying traffic, DiffServ minimizes signaling and state maintenance requirements on each network node.

Specifically, DiffServ divides network traffic into classes based on business requirements. Each of the classes can then be assigned a different level of service. As the packets traverse a network, each of the network devices identifies the packet class and services the packet according to that class. It is possible to choose many levels of service with DiffServ. For example, voice traffic from IP phones is usually given preferential treatment over all other application traffic, email is generally given best-effort service, and nonbusiness traffic can either be given very poor service or blocked entirely.

Figure 2 lists the benefits and drawbacks of the DiffServ model.

Note   Modern networks primarily use the DiffServ model. However, due to the increasing volumes of delay- and jitter-sensitive traffic, IntServ and RSVP are sometimes co-deployed.

Refer to
Interactive Graphic
in online course

6.2.1.6   Activity - Compare QoS Models

6.2.2   QoS Implementation Techniques

Refer to **Video**
in online course

6.2.2.1   Video Tutorial - QoS Implementation Techniques

Click Play for an overview of classification, marking, trust boundaries, congestion avoidance, shaping and policing.

Click here to read the transcript of this video

Refer to
Online Course
for Illustration

6.2.2.2   Avoiding Packet Loss

Packet loss is usually the result of congestion on an interface. Most applications that use TCP experience slowdown because TCP automatically adjusts to network congestion. Dropped TCP segments cause TCP sessions to reduce their window sizes. Some applications do not use TCP and cannot handle drops (fragile flows).

The following approaches can prevent drops in sensitive applications:

- Increase link capacity to ease or prevent congestion.

- Guarantee enough bandwidth and increase buffer space to accommodate bursts of traffic from fragile flows. There are several mechanisms available in Cisco IOS QoS software that can guarantee bandwidth and provide prioritized forwarding to drop-sensitive applications. Examples being WFQ, CBWFQ, and LLQ.

- Prevent congestion by dropping lower-priority packets before congestion occurs. Cisco IOS QoS provides queuing mechanisms that start dropping lower-priority packets before congestion occurs. An example being weighted random early detection (WRED).

Refer to
Interactive Graphic
in online course

6.2.2.3   QoS Tools

There are three categories of QoS tools, as described in the table in Figure 1:

- Classification and marking tools

- Congestion avoidance tools

- Congestion management tools

Refer to Figure 2 to help understand the sequence of how these tools are used when QoS is applied to packet flows.

As shown in the figure, ingress packets (gray squares) are classified and their respective IP header is marked (colored squares). To avoid congestion, packets are then allocated resources based on defined policies. Packets are then queued and forwarded out the egress interface based on their defined QoS shaping and policing policy.

Note   Classification and marking can be done on ingress or egress, whereas other QoS actions such queuing and shaping are usually done on egress.

Refer to
Online Course
for Illustration

6.2.2.4   Classification and Marking

Before a packet can have a QoS policy applied to it, the packet has to be classified. Classification and marking allows us to identify or "mark" types of packets. Classification determines the class of traffic to which packets or frames belong. Only after traffic is marked can policies be applied to it.

How a packet is classified depends on the QoS implementation. Methods of classifying traffic flows at Layer 2 and 3 include using interfaces, ACLs, and class maps. Traffic can also be classified at Layers 4 to 7 using Network Based Application Recognition (NBAR).

Note   NBAR is a classification and protocol discovery feature of Cisco IOS software that works with QoS features. NBAR is out of scope for this course.

Marking means that we are adding a value to the packet header. Devices receiving the packet look at this field to see if it matches a defined policy. Marking should be done as close to the source device as possible. This establishes the trust boundary.

How traffic is marked usually depends on the technology. The table in the figure describes some the marking fields used in various technologies. The decision of whether to mark traffic at Layers 2 or 3 (or both) is not trivial and should be made after consideration of the following points:

- Layer 2 marking of frames can be performed for non-IP traffic.

- Layer 2 marking of frames is the only QoS option available for switches that are not "IP aware".

- Layer 3 marking will carry the QoS information end-to-end.

Refer to
Interactive Graphic
in online course

6.2.2.5   Marking at Layer 2

802.1Q is the IEEE standard that supports VLAN tagging at layer 2 on Ethernet networks. When 802.1Q is implemented, two fields are added to the Ethernet Frame. As shown in Figure 1, these two fields are inserted into the Ethernet frame following the source MAC address field.

The 802.1Q standard also includes the QoS prioritization scheme known as IEEE 802.1p. The 802.1p standard uses the first three bits in the Tag Control Information (TCI) field. Known as the Priority (PRI) field, this 3-bit field identifies the Class of Service (CoS) markings. Three bits means that a Layer 2 Ethernet frame can be marked with one of eight levels of priority (values 0–7) as displayed in Figure 2.

Refer to
Interactive Graphic
in online course

6.2.2.6 Marking at Layer 3

IPv4 and IPv6 specify an 8-bit field in their packet headers to mark packets. As shown in Figure 1, both IPv4 and IPv6 support an 8-bit field for marking, the Type of Service (ToS) field for IPv4 and the Traffic Class field for IPv6.

These fields are used to carry the packet marking as assigned by the QoS classification tools. The field is then referred to by receiving devices to forward the packets based on the appropriate assigned QoS policy.

Figure 2 displays the contents of the 8-bit field. In RFC 791, the original IP standard specified the IP Preference (IPP) field to be used for QoS markings. However, in practice, these three bits did not provide enough granularity to implement QoS.

RFC 2474 supersedes RFC 791 and redefines the ToS field by renaming and extending the IPP field. The new field, as shown in Figure 2, has 6-bits allocated for QoS. Called the Differentiated Services Code Point (DSCP) field, these six bits offer a maximum of 64 possible classes of service. The remaining two IP Extended Congestion Notification (ECN) bits can be used by ECN-aware routers to mark packets instead of dropping them. The ECN marking informs downstream routers that there is congestion in the packet flow.

The 64 DSCP values are organized into three categories:

- **Best-Effort (BE)** - This is the default for all IP packets. The DSCP value is 0. The per-hop behavior is normal routing. When a router experiences congestion, these packets will be dropped. No QoS plan is implemented.

- **Expedited Forwarding (EF)** - RFC 3246 defines EF as the DSCP decimal value 46 (binary **101**110). The first 3 bits (101) map directly to the Layer 2 CoS value 5 used for voice traffic. At Layer 3, Cisco recommends that EF only be used to mark voice packets.

- **Assured Forwarding (AF)** - RFC 2597 defines AF to use the 5 most significant DSCP bits to indicate queues and drop preference. As shown in Figure 3, the first 3 most significant bits are used to designate the class. Class 4 is the best queue and Class 1 is the worst queue. The 4th and 5th most significant bits are used to designate the drop preference. The 6th most significant bit is set to zero. The AFxy formula shows how the AF values are calculated. For example, AF32 belongs to class 3 (binary 011) and has a medium drop preference (binary 10). The full DSCP value is 28 because you include the 6th 0 bit (binary 011100).

Because the first 3 most significant bits of the DSCP field indicate the class, these bits are also called the Class Selector (CS) bits. As shown in Figure 4, these 3 bits map directly to the 3 bits of the CoS field and the IPP field to maintain compatibility with 802.1p and RFC 791.

The table in Figure 5 shows how the CoS values map to the Class Selectors and the corresponding DSCP 6-bit value. This same table can be used to map IPP values to the Class Selectors.

Refer to
Online Course
for Illustration

6.2.2.7 Trust Boundaries

Where should markings occur? Traffic should be classified and marked as close to its source as technically and administratively feasible. This defines the trust boundary as shown in the figure.

- Trusted endpoints have the capabilities and intelligence to mark application traffic to the appropriate Layer 2 CoS and/or Layer 3 DSCP values. Examples of trusted endpoints include IP phones, wireless access points, videoconferencing gateways and systems, IP conferencing stations, and more.

- Secure endpoints can have traffic marked at the Layer 2 switch.

- Traffic can also be marked at Layer 3 switches / routers.

Re-marking of traffic is typically necessary. For example, re-marking CoS values to IP Precedent or DSCP values.

Refer to **Online Course** for Illustration

6.2.2.8   Congestion Avoidance

Congestion management includes queuing and scheduling methods where excess traffic is buffered or queued (and sometimes dropped) while it waits to be sent on an egress interface. Congestion avoidance tools are simpler. They monitor network traffic loads in an effort to anticipate and avoid congestion at common network and internetwork bottlenecks before congestion becomes a problem. These tools can monitor the average depth of the queue, as represented in the figure. When the queue is below the minimum threshold, there are no drops. As the queue fills up to the maximum threshold, a small percentage of packets are dropped. When the maximum threshold is passed, all packets are dropped.

Some congestion avoidance techniques provide preferential treatment for which packets will get dropped. For example, Cisco IOS QoS includes weighted random early detection (WRED) as a possible congestion avoidance solution. The WRED algorithm allows for congestion avoidance on network interfaces by providing buffer management and allowing TCP traffic to decrease, or throttle back, before buffers are exhausted. Using WRED helps avoid tail drops and maximizes network use and TCP-based application performance. There is no congestion avoidance for User Datagram Protocol (UDP)-based traffic, such as voice traffic. In case of UDP-based traffic, methods such as queuing and compression techniques help to reduce and even prevent UDP packet loss.

Refer to **Interactive Graphic** in online course

6.2.2.9   Shaping and Policing

Traffic shaping and traffic policing are two mechanisms provided by Cisco IOS QoS software to prevent congestion.

Traffic shaping retains excess packets in a queue and then schedules the excess for later transmission over increments of time. The result of traffic shaping is a smoothed packet output rate, as shown in Figure 1.

Shaping implies the existence of a queue and of sufficient memory to buffer delayed packets, while policing does not.

Ensure that you have sufficient memory when enabling shaping. In addition, shaping requires a scheduling function for later transmission of any delayed packets. This scheduling function allows you to organize the shaping queue into different queues. Examples of scheduling functions are CBWFQ and LLQ.

Shaping is an outbound concept; packets going out an interface get queued and can be shaped. In contrast, policing is applied to inbound traffic on an interface. When the traffic rate reaches the configured maximum rate, excess traffic is dropped (or remarked).

Policing is commonly implemented by service providers to enforce a contracted customer information rate (CIR). However, the service provider may also allow bursting over the CIR if the service provider's network is not currently experiencing congestion.

Refer to
Interactive Graphic
in online course

6.2.2.10   Activity - Identify QoS Mechanism Terminology

6.3   Summary

Refer to
Online Course
for Illustration

6.3.1.1   Chapter 6: Quality of Service

The quality of network transmission is impacted by the bandwidth of the links between the source and destination, the sources of delay as packets are routed to the destination, and jitter or the variation in delay of the received packets. Without QoS mechanisms in place, packets are processed in the order in which they are received. When congestion occurs, time-sensitive packets will be dropped with the same frequency as packets that are not time-sensitive.

Voice packets require latency of no more than 150 milliseconds (ms). Jitter should be no more than 30 ms, and voice packet loss should be no more than 1%. Voice traffic requires at least 30 Kb/s of bandwidth.

Video packets require latency no more than 400 milliseconds (ms). Jitter should be no more than 50 ms, and video packet loss should be no more than 1%. Video traffic requires at least 384 Kb/s of bandwidth.

For data packets, two factors impact the Quality of Experience (QoE) for end users:

- Does the data come from an interactive application?

- Is the data mission critical?

The four queuing algorithms discussed in this chapter are as follows:

- **First in First Out (FIFO)** - Packets are forwarded in the order in which they are received.

- **Weighted Fair Queuing (WFQ)** - Packets are classified into different flows based on header information including the ToS value.

- **Class-Based Weighted Fair Queuing (CBWFQ)** - Packets are assigned to user-defined classes based on matches to criteria such as protocols, ACLs, and input interfaces. The network administrator can assign bandwidth, weight, and maximum packet limit to each class.

- **Low Latency Queuing (LLQ)** - Delay-sensitive data such as voice is added to a priority queue so that it can be sent first (before packets in other queues).

The three queuing models discussed in the chapter are as follows:

- **Best-Effort** - This is the default queuing model for interfaces. All packets are treated in the same way. There is no QoS.

- **Integrated Services (IntServ)** - IntServ provides a way to deliver the end-to-end QoS that real-time applications require by explicitly managing network resources to provide QoS to specific user packet streams, sometimes called microflows.

- **Differentiated Services (DiffServ)** - DiffServ uses a soft QoS approach that depends on network devices that are set up to service multiple classes of traffic each with varying QoS requirements. Although there is no QoS guarantee, the DiffServ model is more cost-effective and scalable than IntServ.

QoS tools include the following:

- **Classification and Marking** - Classification determines the class of traffic to which packets or frames belong. Marking means that we are adding a value to the packet header. Devices receiving the packet look at this field to see if it matches a defined policy.

- **Congestion Avoidance** - Congestion avoidance tools monitor network traffic loads in an effort to anticipate and avoid congestion. As queues fill up to the maximum threshold, a small percentage of packets are dropped. Once the maximum threshold is passed, all packets are dropped.

- **Shaping and Policing** - Shaping retains excess packets in a queue and then schedules the excess for later transmission over increments of time. Shaping is used on outbound traffic. Policing either drops or remarks excess traffic. Policing is often applied to inbound traffic.

Go to the online course to take the quiz and exam.

Chapter 6 Quiz

This quiz is designed to provide an additional opportunity to practice the skills and knowledge presented in the chapter and to prepare for the chapter exam. You will be allowed multiple attempts and the grade does not appear in the gradebook.

Chapter 6 Exam

The chapter exam assesses your knowledge of the chapter content.

Your Chapter Notes

Network Evolution

7.0 Introduction

Refer to
Online Course
for Illustration

7.0.1.1 Chapter 7: Network Evolution

Technology is constantly changing. Networks are always evolving.

The Internet of Things (IoT) is a phrase that denotes the billions of electronic devices that are now able to connect to our data networks and the Internet.

Cloud computing and virtualization is enabling individuals and organizations to store and access large amounts of data without worrying about the physical components.

Software-defined networking (SDN) is redefining how network administrators think about the architecture of their networks.

This chapter introduces you to these emerging trends in today's networks.

7.1 Internet of Things

7.1.1 IoT Elements

Refer to
Online Course
for Illustration

7.1.1.1 What is the IoT?

In a very short time, the Internet has dramatically changed how we work, live, play, and learn. Yet, we have barely scratched the surface. Using existing and new technologies, we are connecting the physical world to the Internet. It is by connecting the unconnected that we transition from the Internet to the Internet of Things (IoT).

From its humble beginning as the Advanced Research Projects Agency Network (ARPANET) in 1969, when it interconnected a few sites, it is now predicted that the Internet will interconnect 50 billion things by 2020. The IoT refers to the network of these physical objects accessible through the Internet.

Fifty billion things provide trillions of gigabytes of data. How can they work together to enhance our decision-making and interactions to improve our lives and our businesses? Enabling these connections are the networks that we use daily.

Refer to
Online Course
for Illustration

7.1.1.2 The Converged Network and Things

Cisco estimates that 99 percent of things in the physical world are currently unconnected. Therefore, the IoT will experience tremendous growth as we connect more of the unconnected.

Many things are currently connected using a loose collection of independent, use-specific networks, as shown in the figure. For example, today's cars have multiple proprietary networks to control engine function, safety features, and communications systems. Converging these systems alone onto a common network would save over 50 lbs. (23 kg) of cable in a modern full-size sedan. Other examples include commercial and residential buildings, which have various control systems and networks for heating, ventilation, and air conditioning (HVAC), telephone service, security, and lighting.

These dissimilar networks are converging to share the same infrastructure. This infrastructure includes comprehensive security, analytics, and management capabilities. The connection of the components into a converged network that uses IoT technologies increases the power of the network to help people improve their daily lives.

7.1.1.3   Challenges to Connecting Things

Refer to **Online Course** for Illustration

The IoT connects smart objects to the Internet. It connects traditional computer devices as well as untraditional devices. Within the IoT, the communication is Machine-to-Machine (M2M), enabling communication between machines without human intervention. For example, M2M occurs in cars with temperature and oil sensors communicating with an onboard computer.

Click Play in the figure to see how Cisco is developing digitization solutions for all types of industries. Digitization means connecting people and things, and making sense of the data in a meaningful and secure way.

7.1.1.4   The Six Pillars of the Cisco IoT System

Refer to **Online Course** for Illustration

The challenge for IoT is to securely integrate millions of new things from multiple vendors into existing networks. To help address these challenges, Cisco introduced the Cisco IoT System to help organizations and industries adopt IoT solutions. Specifically, the Cisco IoT System reduces the complexities of digitization for manufacturing, utilities, oil and gas, transportation, mining, and public sector organizations.

The IoT system provides an infrastructure designed to manage large scale systems of very different endpoints and platforms, and the huge amount of data that they create. The Cisco IoT System uses a set of new and existing products and technologies to help reduce the complexity of digitization.

The Cisco IoT System uses the concept of pillars to identify foundational elements. Specifically, the IoT System identifies the six technology pillars displayed in the figure.

7.1.2   IoT Pillars

7.1.2.1   The Network Connectivity Pillar

Refer to **Online Course** for Illustration

There are many different types of networks: home networks, public Wi-Fi networks, small business networks, enterprise networks, service provider networks, data center networks, cloud networks, and IoT networks. Regardless of network type, they all need devices to provide network connectivity. However, network connectivity equipment varies depending on the type of network. For example, home networks typically consist of a wireless broadband router, while business networks will have multiple switches, APs, a firewall or firewalls, routers, and more.

The Cisco IoT network connectivity pillar identifies devices that can be used to provide IoT connectivity to many diverse industries and applications.

Click Play in the figure to see a video of how businesses can use the network to create ideal indoor environments. Using Cisco's Digital Ceiling, the network can manage lighting and air temperature seamlessly, based on the preferences of the occupants.

Refer to
Interactive Graphic
in online course

7.1.2.2   The Fog Computing Pillar

Networking models describe how data flows within a network. Networking models include:

- **Client-Server model** - (Figure 1) This is the most common model used in networks. Client devices request services of servers.

- **Cloud computing model** - (Figure 2) This is a newer model where servers and services are dispersed globally in distributed data centers. Cloud computing is discussed in more detail later in the chapter.

- **Fog computing** - (Figure 3) This IoT network model identifies a distributed computing infrastructure closer to the network edge. It enables edge devices to run applications locally and make immediate decisions. This reduces the data burden on networks as raw data does not need to be sent over network connections. It enhances resiliency by allowing IoT devices to operate when network connections are lost. It also enhances security by keeping sensitive data from being transported beyond the edge where it is needed.

These models are not mutually exclusive. Network administrators can use any combination of the three models to address the needs of the network users. The Fog computing pillar basically extends cloud connectivity closer to the edge. It enables end devices, such as smart meters, industrial sensors, robotic machines, and others, to connect to a local integrated computing, networking, and storage system.

Applications that use Fog computing can monitor or analyze real-time data from network-connected things and then take action such as locking a door, changing equipment settings, applying the brakes on a train, and more. For example, a traffic light can interact locally with a number of sensors that can detect the presence of pedestrians and bikers, and measure the distance and speed of approaching vehicles. The traffic light also interacts with neighboring lights providing a coordinated effort. Based on this information, the smart light sends warning signals to approaching vehicles and modifies its own cycle to prevent accidents. The data collected by the smart traffic light system is processed locally to do real-time analytics. Coordinating with neighboring smart traffic light systems in the Fog allows for any modification of the cycle. For example, it can change the timing of the cycles in response to road conditions or traffic patterns. The data from clusters of smart traffic light systems is sent to the cloud to analyze long-term traffic patterns.

Cisco predicts that 40% of IoT-created data will be processed in the Fog by 2018.

Refer to
Interactive Graphic
in online course

7.1.2.3   The Security Pillar

All networks need to be secured. However, the IoT introduces new attack vectors not typically encountered with normal enterprise networks. The Cisco IoT security pillar offers scalable cybersecurity solutions, enabling an organization to quickly and effectively discover, contain, and remediate an attack to minimize damage.

These cybersecurity solutions include:

- **Operational Technology (OT) specific security** - OT is the hardware and software that keeps power plants running and manages factory process lines. OT security includes the ISA 3000 industrial security appliance (Figure 1) and Fog data services.

- **IoT Network security** - Includes network and perimeter security devices such as switches, routers, ASA Firewall devices, and Cisco FirePOWER Next-Generation Intrusion Prevention Services (NGIPS) (Figure 2).

- **IoT Physical security** - Cisco Video Surveillance IP Cameras (Figure 3) are feature-rich digital cameras that enable surveillance in a wide variety of environments. Available in standard and high definition, box and dome, wired and wireless, and stationery and pan-tilt-zoom (PTZ) versions, the cameras support MPEG-4 and H.264, and offer efficient network utilization while providing high-quality video.

Refer to **Video** in online course

7.1.2.4   Data Analytics Pillar

The IoT can connect billions of devices capable of creating exabytes of data every day. To provide value, this data must be rapidly processed and transformed into actionable intelligence.

The Cisco IoT analytics infrastructure consists of distributed network infrastructure components and IoT-specific, application programming interfaces (APIs).

Click Play in the figure to see a video about Cisco data analytics solutions.

Refer to **Online Course** for Illustration

7.1.2.5   Management and Automation Pillar

The IoT greatly expands the size and diversity of the network to include the billions of smart objects that sense, monitor, control, and react. While networking these previously unconnected devices can deliver unparalleled levels of business and operational intelligence, it is essential to understand that operational environments are made up of multiple, disparate functional areas. Each of these areas also has distinctive requirements, including the need to track specific metrics. Operational technology systems can vary widely by industry, as well as by function in a given industry.

Cisco delivers a broad range of IoT management and automation capabilities throughout the extended network. Cisco management and automation products can be customized for specific industries to provide enhanced security and control and support.

The Cisco IoT System management and automation portfolio includes management tools such as the Cisco IoT Field Network Director shown in the figure. Other management tools include Cisco Prime, Cisco Video Surveillance Manager, and more.

Refer to **Video** in online course

7.1.2.6   Application Enablement Platform Pillar

The Application Enablement Platform pillar provides the infrastructure for application hosting and application mobility between cloud and Fog computing. The Fog environment allows for multiple instances of the application across different end devices and sensors. These instances can communicate with each other for redundancy and data-sharing purposes to create business models such pay-as-you-go consumption for objects, machines, and products.

For example, Cisco IOx which is a combination of Cisco IOS and Linux, allows routers to host applications close to the objects they need to monitor, control, analyze, and optimize. Cisco IOx services are offered on multiple hardware devices that are customized for various industry needs and can therefore support applications specific to those industries.

Click Play in the figure to see a light-hearted interview about Cisco IOx.

Refer to
Interactive Graphic
in online course

7.1.2.7   Activity - Identify the IoT Pillars

7.2   Cloud and Virtualization

7.2.1   Cloud Computing

Refer to **Video**
in online course

7.2.1.1   Video Tutorial – Cloud and Virtualization

Click Play for an overview of Cloud computing and virtualization.

Click here to download a transcript of the video.

Refer to
Online Course
for Illustration

7.2.1.2   Cloud Overview

Cloud computing involves large numbers of computers connected through a network that can be physically located anywhere. Providers rely heavily on virtualization to deliver their cloud computing services. Cloud computing can reduce operational costs by using resources more efficiently. Cloud computing supports a variety of data management issues:

- Enables access to organizational data anywhere and at any time

- Streamlines the organization's IT operations by subscribing only to needed services

- Eliminates or reduces the need for onsite IT equipment, maintenance, and management

- Reduces cost for equipment, energy, physical plant requirements, and personnel training needs

- Enables rapid responses to increasing data volume requirements

Cloud computing, with its "pay-as-you-go" model, allows organizations to treat computing and storage expenses more as a utility rather than investing in infrastructure. Capital expenditures are transformed into operating expenditures.

Refer to
Interactive Graphic
in online course

7.2.1.3   Cloud Services

Cloud services are available in a variety of options, tailored to meet customer requirements. The three main cloud computing services defined by the National Institute of Standards and Technology (NIST) in their Special Publication 800-145 are as follows:

- **Software as a Service (SaaS):** The cloud provider is responsible for access to services, such as email, communication, and Office 365 that are delivered over the Internet. The user is only needs to provide their data.

- **Platform as a Service (PaaS):** The cloud provider is responsible for access to the development tools and services used to deliver the applications.

- **Infrastructure as a Service (IaaS):** The cloud provider is responsible for access to the network equipment, virtualized network services, and supporting network infrastructure.

As shown in the figure, cloud service providers have extended this model to also provide IT support for each of the cloud computing services (ITaaS).

For businesses, ITaaS can extend the capability of IT without requiring investment in new infrastructure, training new personnel, or licensing new software. These services are available on demand and delivered economically to any device anywhere in the world without compromising security or function.

Refer to **Online Course** for Illustration

7.2.1.4 Cloud Models

There are four primary cloud modes, as shown in the figure.

- **Public clouds:** Cloud-based applications and services offered in a public cloud are made available to the general population. Services may be free or are offered on a pay-per-use model, such as paying for online storage. The public cloud uses the Internet to provide services.

- **Private clouds:** Cloud-based applications and services offered in a private cloud are intended for a specific organization or entity, such as the government. A private cloud can be set up using the organization's private network, though this can be expensive to build and maintain. A private cloud can also be managed by an outside organization with strict access security.

- **Hybrid clouds:** A hybrid cloud is made up of two or more clouds (example: part custom, part public), where each part remains a distinctive object, but both are connected using a single architecture. Individuals on a hybrid cloud would be able to have degrees of access to various services based on user access rights.

- **Community clouds:** A community cloud is created for exclusive use by a specific community. The differences between public clouds and community clouds are the functional needs that have been customized for the community. For example, healthcare organizations must remain compliant with policies and laws (e.g., HIPAA) that require special authentication and confidentiality.

Refer to **Online Course** for Illustration

7.2.1.5 Cloud Computing versus Data Center

The terms data center and cloud computing are often incorrectly used. These are the correct definitions of data center and cloud computing:

- **Data center:** Typically a data storage and processing facility run by an in-house IT department or leased offsite.

- **Cloud computing:** Typically an off-premise service that offers on-demand access to a shared pool of configurable computing resources. These resources can be rapidly provisioned and released with minimal management effort.

Cloud computing is possible because of data centers. A data center is a facility used to house computer systems and associated components. A data center can occupy one room of a building, one or more floors, or an entire building. Data centers are typically very expensive to build and maintain. For this reason, only large organizations use privately built data centers to house their data and provide services to users. Smaller organizations that cannot afford to maintain their own private data center can reduce the overall cost of ownership by leasing server and storage services from a larger data center organization in the cloud.

Cloud computing is often a service provided by data centers, as shown in the figure. Cloud service providers use data centers to host their cloud services and cloud-based resources. To ensure availability of data services and resources, providers often maintain space in several remote data centers.

Refer to **Interactive Graphic** in online course

7.2.1.6   Activity - Identify Cloud Computing Terminology

7.2.2   Virtualization

Refer to **Online Course** for Illustration

7.2.2.1   Cloud Computing and Virtualization

The terms "cloud computing" and "virtualization" are often used interchangeably; however, they mean different things. Virtualization is the foundation of cloud computing. Without it, cloud computing, as it is most-widely implemented, would not be possible.

Cloud computing separates the application from the hardware. Virtualization separates the OS from the hardware. Various providers offer virtual cloud services that can dynamically provision servers as required. For example, Amazon Elastic Compute cloud (Amazon EC2) web service provides a simple way for customers to dynamically provision the compute resources they need. These virtualized instances of servers are created on demand in Amazon's EC2.

Refer to **Online Course** for Illustration

7.2.2.2   Dedicated Servers

To fully appreciate virtualization, it is first necessary to understand some of the history of server technology. Historically, enterprise servers consisted of a server operating system (OS), such as Windows Server or Linux Server, installed on specific hardware, as shown in the figure. All of a server's RAM, processing power, and hard drive space were dedicated to the service provided (e.g., Web, email services, etc.)

The major problem with this configuration is that when a component fails, the service that is provided by this server becomes unavailable. This is known as a single point of failure. Another problem was that dedicated servers were underused. Dedicated servers often sat idle for long periods of time, waiting until there was a need to deliver the specific service they provide. These servers wasted energy and took up more space than was warranted by their amount of service. This is known as server sprawl.

Refer to **Online Course** for Illustration

7.2.2.3   Server Virtualization

Server virtualization takes advantage of idle resources and consolidates the number of required servers. This also allows for multiple operating systems to exist on a single hardware platform.

For example, in the figure, the previous eight dedicated servers have been consolidated into two servers using hypervisors to support multiple virtual instances of the operating systems.

The hypervisor is a program, firmware, or hardware that adds an abstraction layer on top of the real physical hardware. The abstraction layer is used to create virtual machines which have access to all the hardware of the physical machine such as CPUs, memory, disk controllers, and NICs. Each of these virtual machines runs a complete and separate operating system. With virtualization, enterprises can now consolidate the number of servers they require. For example, it is not uncommon for 100 physical servers to be consolidated as virtual machines on top of 10 physical servers that are using hypervisors.

The use of virtualization normally includes redundancy to protect from a single point of failure. Redundancy can be implemented in different ways. If the hypervisor fails, the VM can be restarted on another hypervisor. Also, the same VM can be run on two hypervisors concurrently, copying the RAM and CPU instructions between them. If one hypervisor fails, the VM continues running on the other hypervisor. The services running on the VMs are also virtual and can be dynamically installed or uninstalled, as needed.

Refer to **Online Course** for Illustration

7.2.2.4   Advantages of Virtualization

One major advantage of virtualization is overall reduced cost:

- **Less equipment is required** - Virtualization enables server consolidation, which requires fewer physical servers, fewer networking devices, and less supporting infrastructure. It also means lower maintenance costs.

- **Less energy is consumed** - Consolidating servers lowers the monthly power and cooling costs. Reduced consumption helps enterprises to achieve a smaller carbon footprint.

- **Less space is required** - Server consolidation with virtualization reduces the overall footprint of the data center. Fewer servers, network devices, and racks reduce the amount of required floor space.

These are additional benefits of virtualization:

- **Easier prototyping** - Self-contained labs, operating on isolated networks, can be rapidly created for testing and prototyping network deployments. If a mistake is made, an administrator can simply revert to a previous version. The testing environments can be online, but isolated from end users. When testing is completed, the servers and systems can be deployed to end users.

- **Faster server provisioning** - Creating a virtual server is far faster than provisioning a physical server.

- **Increased server uptime** - Most server virtualization platforms now offer advanced redundant fault tolerance features, such as live migration, storage migration, high availability, and distributed resource scheduling.

- **Improved disaster recovery** - Virtualization offers advanced business continuity solutions. It provides hardware abstraction capability so that the recovery site no longer needs to have hardware that is identical to the hardware in the production environment. Most enterprise server virtualization platforms also have software that can help test and automate the failover before a disaster does happen.

- **Legacy Support** - Virtualization can extend the life of OSs and applications providing more time for organizations to migrate to newer solutions.

Refer to
Interactive Graphic
in online course

7.2.2.5   Abstraction Layers

To help explain how virtualization works, it is useful to use layers of abstraction in computer architectures. A computer system consists of the following abstraction layers, as illustrated in Figure 1:

- Services

- OS

- Firmware

- Hardware

At each of these layers of abstraction, some type of programming code is used as an interface between the layer below and the layer above. For example, the C programming language is often used to program the firmware that accesses the hardware.

An example of virtualization is shown in Figure 2. A hypervisor is installed between the firmware and the OS. The hypervisor can support multiple instances of OSs.

Refer to
Online Course
for Illustration

7.2.2.6   Type 2 Hypervisors

A hypervisor is software that creates and runs VM instances. The computer, on which a hypervisor is supporting one or more VMs, is a host machine. Type 2 hypervisors are also called hosted hypervisors. This is because the hypervisor is installed on top of the existing OS, such as Mac OS X, Windows, or Linux. Then, one or more additional OS instances are installed on top of the hypervisor, as shown in the figure.

A big advantage of Type 2 hypervisors is that management console software is not required.

Type 2 hypervisors are very popular with consumers and for organizations experimenting with virtualization. Common Type 2 hypervisors include:

- Virtual PC

- VMware Workstation

- Oracle VM VirtualBox

- VMware Fusion

- Mac OS X Parallels

Many of these Type 2 hypervisors are free. Some offer more advanced features for a fee.

Note   It is important to make sure that the host machine is robust enough to install and run the VMs, so that it does not run out of resources.

Refer to
Interactive Graphic
in online course

7.2.2.7   Activity - Identify Virtualization Terminology

7.2.3   Virtual Network Infrastructure

Refer to
Online Course
for Illustration

7.2.3.1   Type 1 Hypervisors

Type 1 hypervisors are also called the "bare metal" approach because the hypervisor is installed directly on the hardware. Type 1 hypervisors are usually used on enterprise servers and data center networking devices.

With Type 1 hypervisors, the hypervisor is installed directly on the server or networking hardware. Then, instances of an OS are installed on the hypervisor, as shown in the figure. Type 1 hypervisors have direct access to the hardware resources; therefore, they are more efficient than hosted architectures. Type 1 hypervisors improve scalability, performance, and robustness.

Refer to
Interactive Graphic
in online course

7.2.3.2   Installing a VM on a Hypervisor

When a Type 1 hypervisor is installed, and the server is rebooted, only basic information is displayed, such as the OS version, the amount of RAM, and the IP address. An OS instance cannot be created from this screen. Type 1 hypervisors require a "management console" to manage the hypervisor. Management software is used to manage multiple servers using the same hypervisor. The management console can automatically consolidate servers and power on or off servers as required.

For example, assume that Server1 in the figure becomes low on resources. To make more resources available, the management console moves the Windows instance to the hypervisor on Server2.

The management console provides recovery from hardware failure. If a server component fails, the management console automatically and seamlessly moves the VM to another server. The management console for the Cisco Unified Computing System (UCS) is shown in Figure 2. Cisco UCS Manager provides management for all software and hardware components in the Cisco UCS. It controls multiple servers and manages resources for thousands of VMs.

Some management consoles also allow over allocation. Over allocation is when multiple OS instances are installed, but their memory allocation exceeds the total amount of memory that a server has. For example, a server has 16 GB of RAM, but the administrator creates four OS instances with 10 GB of RAM allocated to each. This type of over allocation is a common practice because all four OS instances rarely require the full 10 GB of RAM at any one moment.

Refer to
Online Course
for Illustration

7.2.3.3   Network Virtualization

Server virtualization hides server resources (for example, the number and identity of physical servers, processors, and OSs) from server users. This practice can create problems if the data center is using traditional network architectures.

For example, Virtual LANs (VLANs) used by VMs must be assigned to the same switch port as the physical server running the hypervisor. However, VMs are movable, and the network administrator must be able to add, drop, and change network resources and profiles. This process is difficult to do with traditional network switches.

Another problem is that traffic flows differ substantially from the traditional client-server model. Typically, a data center has a considerable amount of traffic being exchanged between virtual servers (referred to as East-West traffic). These flows change in location and intensity over time, requiring a flexible approach to network resource management.

Existing network infrastructures can respond to changing requirements related to the management of traffic flows by using Quality of Service (QoS) and security level configurations for individual flows. However, in large enterprises using multivendor equipment, each time a new VM is enabled, the necessary reconfiguration can be very time-consuming.

Could the network infrastructure also benefit from virtualization? If so, then how?

The answer is found in how a networking device operates using a data plane and a control plane, as discussed later in the chapter.

Refer to **Interactive Graphic** in online course

7.2.3.4   Activity - Identify Hypervisor Terminology

7.3   Network Programming

7.3.1   Software-Defined Networking

Refer to **Video** in online course

7.3.1.1   Video Tutorial - Network Programming, SDN, and Controllers

Click Play for a tutorial on network programming, SDN, and controllers.

Click here to download a transcript of the video.

Refer to **Interactive Graphic** in online course

7.3.1.2   Control Plane and Data Plane

A network device contains the following planes:

- **Control plane** - This is typically regarded as the brains of a device. It is used to make forwarding decisions. The control plane contains Layer 2 and Layer 3 route forwarding mechanisms, such as routing protocol neighbor tables and topology tables, IPv4 and IPv6 routing tables, STP, and the ARP table. Information sent to the control plane is processed by the CPU.

- **Data plane** - Also called the forwarding plane, this plane is typically the switch fabric connecting the various network ports on a device. The data plane of each device is used to forward traffic flows. Routers and switches use information from the control plane to forward incoming traffic out the appropriate egress interface. Information in the data plane is typically processed by a special data plane processor, such as a digital signal processor (DSP), without the CPU getting involved.

The example in Figure 1 illustrates how Cisco Express Forwarding (CEF) uses the control plane and data plane to process packets.

CEF is an advanced, Layer 3 IP switching technology that enables forwarding of packets to occur at the data plane without consulting the control plane. In CEF, the control plane's routing table pre-populates the CEF Forwarding Information Base (FIB) table in the data plane. The control plane's ARP table pre-populates the adjacency table. Packets are then forwarded directly by the data plane based on the information contained in the FIB and adjacency table, without needing to consult the information in the control plane.

To virtualize the network, the control plane function is removed from each device and is performed by a centralized controller, as shown in Figure 2. The centralized controller communicates control plane functions to each device. Each device can now focus on forwarding data while the centralized controller manages data flow, increases security, and provides other services.

Refer to
Online Course
for Illustration

7.3.1.3   Virtualizing the Network

Over a decade ago, VMware developed a virtualizing technology that enabled a host OS to support one or more client OSs. Most virtualization technologies are now based on this technology. The transformation of dedicated servers to virtualized servers has been embraced and is rapidly being implemented in data center and enterprise networks.

Two major network architectures have been developed to support network virtualization:

- **Software Defined Networking (SDN)** - A network architecture that virtualizes the network.

- **Cisco Application Centric Infrastructure (ACI)** - A purpose-built hardware solution for integrating cloud computing and data center management.

These are some other network virtualization technologies, some of which are included as components in SDN and ACI:

- **OpenFlow** - This approach was developed at Stanford University to manage traffic between routers, switches, wireless access points, and a controller. The OpenFlow protocol is a basic element in building SDN solutions. Click here to learn more about OpenFlow.

- **OpenStack** - This approach is a virtualization and orchestration platform available to build scalable cloud environments and provide an infrastructure as a service (IaaS) solution. OpenStack is often used with Cisco ACI. Orchestration in networking is the process of automating the provisioning of network components such as servers, storage, switches, routers, and applications. Click here to learn more about OpenStack.

- **Other components** - Other components include Interface to the Routing System (I2RS), Transparent Interconnection of Lots of Links (TRILL), Cisco FabricPath (FP), and IEEE 802.1aq Shortest Path Bridging (SPB).

Refer to
Interactive Graphic
in online course

7.3.1.4   SDN Architecture

In a traditional router or switch architecture, the control plane and data plane functions occur in the same device. Routing decisions and packet forwarding are the responsibility of the device operating system.

Software defined networking (SDN) is a network architecture that has been developed to virtualize the network. For example, SDN can virtualize the control plane. Also known as controller-based SDN, SDN moves the control plane from each network device to a central network intelligence and policy-making entity called the SDN controller. The two architectures are shown in Figure 1.

The SDN controller is a logical entity that enables network administrators to manage and dictate how the data plane of virtual switches and routers should handle network traffic. It orchestrates, mediates, and facilitates communication between applications and network elements.

The SDN framework is illustrated in Figure 2. Note the use of Application Programming Interfaces (APIs) within the SDN framework. An API is a set of standardized requests that define the proper way for an application to request services from another application. The SDN controller uses northbound APIs to communicate with the upstream applications. These APIs help network administrators shape traffic and deploy services. The SDN controller also uses southbound APIs to define the behavior of the downstream virtual switches and routers. OpenFlow is the original and widely implemented southbound API. The Open Networking Foundation is responsible for maintaining the OpenFlow standard.

Note   Traffic in a modern data center is described as North-South (going between external data center users and the data center servers) and East-West (going between data center servers).

Visit this website to learn more about SDN, OpenFlow, and the Open Networking Foundation: https://www.opennetworking.org/sdn-resources/sdn-definition

Refer to
Interactive Graphic
in online course

7.3.1.5   Activity - Identify Control Plane and Data Plane Characteristics

7.3.2   Controllers

Refer to
Interactive Graphic
in online course

7.3.2.1   SDN Controller and Operations

The SDN controller defines the data flows that occur in the SDN Data Plane. A flow is a sequence of packets traversing a network that share a set of header field values. For example, a flow could consist of all packets with the same source and destination IP addresses, or all packets with the same VLAN identifier.

Each flow traveling through the network must first get permission from the SDN controller, which verifies that the communication is permissible according to the network policy. If the controller allows a flow, it computes a route for the flow to take and adds an entry for that flow in each of the switches along the path.

All complex functions are performed by the controller. The controller populates flow tables. Switches manage the flow tables. In the figure, an SDN controller communicates with OpenFlow-compatible switches using the OpenFlow protocol. This protocol uses Transport Layer Security (TLS) to securely send control plane communications over the network. Each OpenFlow switch connects to other OpenFlow switches. They can also connect to end-user devices that are part of a packet flow.

Within each switch, a series of tables implemented in hardware or firmware are used to manage the flows of packets through the switch. To the switch, a flow is a sequence of packets that matches a specific entry in a flow table.

Refer to **Video**
in online course

7.3.2.2   Cisco Application Centric Infrastructure

Very few organizations actually have the desire or skill to program the network using SDN tools. However, the majority of organizations want to automate the network, accelerate application deployments, and align their IT infrastructures to better meet business requirements. Cisco developed the Application Centric Infrastructure (ACI) to meet these objectives in more advanced and innovative ways than earlier SDN approaches.

ACI is a data center network architecture that was developed by Insieme and acquired by Cisco in 2013. Cisco ACI is a purpose-built hardware solution for integrating cloud computing and data center management. At a high level, the policy element of the network is removed from the data plane. This simplifies the way data center networks are created.

To learn more about the differences between SDN and ACI: http://blogs.cisco.com/datacenter/is-aci-really-sdn-one-point-of-view-to-clarify-the-conversation

Click Play in the figure to see an overview of the fundamentals of ACI.

Refer to
Online Course
for Illustration

7.3.2.3   Core Components of ACI

These are the three core components of the ACI architecture:

- **Application Network Profile (ANP)** - An ANP is a collection of end-point groups (EPG), their connections, and the policies that define those connections. The EPGs shown in the figure, such as VLANs, Web services, and applications, are just examples. An ANP is often much more complex.

- **Application Policy Infrastructure Controller (APIC)** - The APIC is considered to be the brains of the ACI architecture. APIC is a centralized software controller that manages and operates a scalable ACI clustered fabric. It is designed for programmability and centralized management. It translates application policies into network programming.

- **Cisco Nexus 9000 Series switches** - These switches provide an application-aware switching fabric and work with an APIC to manage the virtual and physical network infrastructure.

As shown in the figure, the APIC is positioned between the APN and the ACI-enabled network infrastructure. The APIC translates the application requirements into a network configuration to meet those needs.

Refer to
Online Course
for Illustration

7.3.2.4   Spine–Leaf Topology

The Cisco ACI fabric is composed of the APIC and the Cisco Nexus 9000 series switches using two-tier spine-leaf topology, as shown in the figure. The leaf switches always attach to the spines, but they never attach to each other. Similarly, the spine switches only attach to the leaf and core switches (not shown). In this two-tier topology, everything is one hop from everything else.

The Cisco APICs and all other devices in the network physically attach to leaf switches.

When compared to SDN, the APIC controller does not manipulate the data path directly. Instead, the APIC centralizes the policy definition and programs the leaf switches to forward traffic based on the defined policies.

For virtualization, ACI supports multivendor hypervisor environments that would connect to the leaf switches, including the following:

- Microsoft (Hyper-V/SCVMM/Azure Pack)

- Red Hat Enterprise Linux OS (KVM OVS/OpenStack)

- VMware (ESX/vCenter/vShield)

Refer to
Interactive Graphic
in online course

7.3.2.5   SDN Types

The Cisco Application Policy Infrastructure Controller - Enterprise Module (APIC-EM)
extends ACI aimed at enterprise and campus deployments. To better understand APIC-EM,
it is helpful to take a broader look at the three types of SDN:

- **Device-based SDN** - In this type of SDN, the devices are programmable by applications running on the device itself or on a server in the network, as shown in Figure 1. Cisco OnePK is an example of a device-based SDN. It enables programmers to build applications using C, and Java with Python, to integrate and interact with Cisco devices.

- **Controller-based SDN** - This type of SDN uses a centralized controller that has knowledge of all devices in the network, as shown in Figure 2. The applications can interface with the controller responsible for managing devices and manipulating traffic flows throughout the network. The Cisco Open SDN Controller is a commercial distribution of OpenDaylight.

- **Policy-based SDN** - This type of SDN is similar to controller-based SDN where a centralized controller has a view of all devices in the network, as shown in Figure 3. Policy-based SDN includes an additional Policy layer that operates at a higher level of abstraction. It uses built-in applications that automate advanced configuration tasks via a guided workflow and user-friendly GUI. No programming skills are required. Cisco APIC-EM is an example of this type of SDN.

Refer to
Interactive Graphic
in online course

7.3.2.6   APIC–EM Features

Each type of SDN has its own features and advantages. Policy-based SDN is the most
robust, providing for a simple mechanism to control and manage policies across the entire
network. Cisco APIC-EM provides the following features:

- **Discovery** - Supports a discovery functionality that is used to populate the controller's device and host inventory database.

- **Device Inventory** - Collects detailed information from devices within the network including device name, device status, MAC address, IPv4/IPv6 addresses, IOS/Firmware, platform, up time, and configuration.

- **Host Inventory** - Collects detailed information from hosts with the network including host name, user ID, MAC address, IPv4/IPv6 addresses, and network attachment point.

- **Topology** - Supports a graphical view of the network (topology view). The Cisco APIC-EM automatically discovers and maps devices to a physical topology with detailed device level data. In addition, auto-visualization of Layer 2 and 3 topologies on top of the physical topology provides a granular view for design planning and simplified troubleshooting. The figure shows an example of a topology view generated by the Cisco APIC-EM.

- **Policy** - Ability to view and control policies across the entire network including QoS.

- **Policy Analysis** - Inspection and analysis of network access control policies. Ability to trace application specific paths between end devices to quickly identify ACLs in use and problem areas. Enables ACL change management with easy identification of redundancy, conflicts and incorrect ordering of access control entries. Incorrect ACL entries are known as shadows.

Click here to learn more about the fundamentals of Cisco APIC-EM.

Refer to
Interactive Graphic
in online course

7.3.2.7 APIC-EM ACL Analysis

One of the most important features of the APIC-EM controller is the ability to manage policies across the entire network. Policies operate at a higher level of abstraction. Traditional device configuration applies to one device at a time, whereas SDN policies apply to the entire network.

APIC-EM ACL Analysis and Path Trace provide tools to allow the administrator to analyze and understand ACL policies and configurations. Creating new ACLs or editing existing ACLs across a network to implement a new security policy can be challenging. Administrators are hesitant of changing ACLs for fear of breaking them and causing new problems. ACL Analysis and Path Trace allows the administrator to easily visualize traffic flows and discover any conflicting, duplicate, or shadowed ACL entries.

APIC-EM provides the following tools to troubleshoot ACL entries:

- **ACL Analysis** - This tool examines ACLs on devices, searching for redundant, conflicting, or shadowed entries. ACL Analysis enables ACL inspection and interrogation across the entire network, exposing any problems and conflicts. An example screenshot of this tool is shown in Figure 1.

- **ACL Path Trace** - This tool examines specific ACLs on the path between two end nodes, displaying any potential issues. An example screenshot of this tool is shown in Figure 2.

To learn more about ACL Analysis and ACL Path Trace view the following video: https://www.youtube.com/watch?v=-acUj5PVFLU

Refer to
Interactive Graphic
in online course

7.3.2.8 Activity - Identify SDN Types

7.4 Summary

Refer to
Online Course
for Illustration

7.4.1.1 Chapter 7: Network Evolution

The IoT refers to the network of billons of physical objects accessible through the Internet as we continue to connect the unconnected. The challenge for IoT is to securely integrate new things from multiple vendors into existing networks. The six pillars of IoT are:

- Network Connectivity
- Fog Computing
- Security
- Data Analytics
- Management and Automation
- Application Enablement Platform

Cloud computing involves large numbers of computers connected through a network that can be physically located anywhere. Cloud computing, with its "pay-as-you-go" model, allows organizations to treat computing and storage expenses more as a utility rather than investing in infrastructure. Cloud computing services include:

- Software as a Service (SaaS)

- Platform as a Service (PaaS)

- Infrastructure as a Service (IaaS)

- IT as a Service (ITaaS)

Cloud models include:

- Public clouds

- Private clouds

- Hybrid clouds

- Community clouds

Cloud computing is possible because of data centers. A data center is a facility used to house computer systems and associated components. Data centers rely heavily on virtualization to provide cloud computing services. Cloud computing separates the application from the hardware. Virtualization separates the OS from the hardware. This allows cloud computing customers to dynamically provision the compute resources they need when they need them.

Virtualized server hardware is managed through a hypervisor. Type 1 hypervisors are installed directly on the hardware. Then any OSs and VMs can be installed. Type 2 hypervisors, such as Mac OS X Parallels or Oracle VM VirtualBox, are installed on top of any existing OS.

SDN is a network architecture that has been developed to virtualize the network. For example, SDN can virtualize the control plane. Also known as controller-based SDN, SDN moves the control plane from each network device to a central network intelligence and policy-making entity called the SDN controller. The SDN controller defines the data flows that occur in the SDN data plane.

The three types of SDN are:

- Device-based SDN

- Controller-based SDN

- Policy-based SDN

Policy-based SDN, such as Cisco's APIC-EM, is the most robust, providing for a simple mechanism to control and manage policies across the entire network. One of the most important features of the APIC-EM controller is the ability to manage policies across the entire network.

Go to the online course to take the quiz and exam.

Chapter 7 Quiz

This quiz is designed to provide an additional opportunity to practice the skills and knowledge presented in the chapter and to prepare for the chapter exam. You will be allowed multiple attempts and the grade does not appear in the gradebook.

Chapter 7 Exam

The chapter exam assesses your knowledge of the chapter content.

Your Chapter Notes

Network Troubleshooting

8.0 Introduction

Refer to
Online Course
for Illustration

8.0.1.1 Introduction

If a network or a portion of a network goes down, it can have a severe negative impact on the business. Network administrators must use a systematic approach to troubleshooting when network problems occur to bring the network back to full production as quickly as possible.

The ability for a network administrator to be able to resolve network problems quickly and efficiently is one of the most sought after skills in IT. Enterprises need individuals with strong network troubleshooting skills and the only way to gain these skills is through hands-on experience and by using systematic troubleshooting approaches.

This chapter describes general troubleshooting procedures, methods, tools, and the network documentation that should be maintained. Typical symptoms and causes at several layers of the OSI model are also discussed.

Refer to
Online Course
for Illustration

8.0.1.2 Class Activity - Network Breakdown

Network Breakdown

You have just moved into your new office, and your network is very small. After a long weekend of setting up the new network, you discover that it is not working correctly.

Some of the devices cannot access each other and some cannot access the router which connects to the ISP.

It is your responsibility to troubleshoot and fix the problems. You decide to start with basic commands to identify possible troubleshooting areas.

8.1 Troubleshooting Methodology

8.1.1 Network Documentation

Refer to
Interactive Graphic
in online course

8.1.1.1 Documenting the Network

For network administrators to be able to monitor and troubleshoot a network, they must have a complete set of accurate and current network documentation. This documentation includes:

- Configuration files, including network configuration files and end-system configuration files
- Physical and logical topology diagrams
- A baseline performance levels

Network documentation allows network administrators to efficiently diagnose and correct network problems, based on the network design and the expected performance of the network under normal operating conditions. All network documentation information should be kept in a single location either as hard copy or on the network on a protected server. Backup documentation should be maintained and kept in a separate location.

Network Configuration Files

Network configuration files contain accurate, up-to-date records of the hardware and software used in a network. Within the network configuration files a table should exist for each network device used on the network, containing all relevant information about that device.

For example, Figure 1 displays a sample network configuration table for two routers while Figure 2 displays a similar table for a LAN switch.

Information that could be captured within a device table includes:

- Type of device, model designation
- IOS image name
- Device network hostname
- Location of the device (building, floor, room, rack, panel)
- If modular, include each module type and slot number
- Data link layer addresses
- Network layer addresses
- Any additional important information about physical aspects of the device

End-system Configuration Files

End-system configuration files focus on the hardware and software used in end-system devices, such as servers, network management consoles, and user workstations. An incorrectly configured end system can have a negative impact on the overall performance of a network. For this reason, having a sample baseline record of the hardware and software used on devices, and recorded in end-system documentation as shown in Figure 3 can be very useful when troubleshooting.

For troubleshooting purposes, the following information could be documented within the end-system configuration table:

- Device name (purpose)
- Operating system and version
- IPv4 and IPv6 addresses
- Subnet mask and prefix length
- Default gateway and DNS server
- Any high-bandwidth network applications used on the end system

Refer to
Interactive Graphic
in online course

8.1.1.2   Network Topology Diagrams

Network Topology Diagrams

Network topology diagrams keep track of the location, function, and status of devices on the network. There are two types of network topology diagrams: the physical topology and the logical topology.

Physical Topology

A physical network topology shows the physical layout of the devices connected to the network. It is necessary to know how devices are physically connected to troubleshoot physical layer problems. Information recorded on the diagram typically includes:

- Device type
- Model and manufacturer
- Operating system version
- Cable type and identifier
- Cable specification
- Connector type
- Cabling endpoints

Figure 1 shows a sample physical network topology diagram.

Logical Topology

A logical network topology illustrates how devices are logically connected to the network, meaning how devices actually transfer data across the network when communicating with other devices. Symbols are used to represent network elements, such as routers, servers, hosts, VPN concentrators, and security devices. Additionally, connections between multiple sites may be shown, but do not represent actual physical locations. Information recorded on a logical network diagram may include:

- Device identifiers
- IP address and prefix lengths
- Interface identifiers
- Connection type
- Frame Relay DLCI for virtual circuits (if applicable)
- Site-to-site VPNs
- Routing protocols
- Static routes
- Data-link protocols
- WAN technologies used

Figure 2 shows a sample logical IPv4 network topology. Although IPv6 addresses could also be displayed in the same topology, it may be clearer to create a separate logical IPv6 network topology diagram.

Refer to
Online Course
for Illustration

8.1.1.3   Establishing a Network Baseline

The purpose of network monitoring is to watch network performance in comparison to a predetermined baseline. A baseline is used to establish normal network or system performance. Establishing a network performance baseline requires collecting performance data from the ports and devices that are essential to network operation. The figure shows several questions that a baseline should answer.

Measuring the initial performance and availability of critical network devices and links allows a network administrator to determine the difference between abnormal behavior and proper network performance as the network grows or traffic patterns change. The baseline also provides insight into whether the current network design can meet business requirements. Without a baseline, no standard exists to measure the optimum nature of network traffic and congestion levels.

Analysis after an initial baseline also tends to reveal hidden problems. The collected data shows the true nature of congestion or potential congestion in a network. It may also reveal areas in the network that are underutilized and quite often can lead to network redesign efforts, based on quality and capacity observations.

Refer to
Interactive Graphic
in online course

8.1.1.4   Steps to Establish a Network Baseline

The initial network performance baseline sets the stage for measuring the effects of network changes and subsequent troubleshooting efforts. Therefore it is important to plan for it carefully.

To establish and capture an initial network baseline, perform the following steps:

Step 1.   Determine what types of data to collect.

When conducting the initial baseline, start by selecting a few variables that represent the defined policies. If too many data points are selected, the amount of data can be overwhelming, making analysis of the collected data difficult. Start out simply and fine-tune along the way. Some good starting measures are interface utilization and CPU utilization.

Step 2.   Identify devices and ports of interest.

Use the network topology to identify those devices and ports for which performance data should be measured. Devices and ports of interest include:

- Network device ports that connect to other network devices
- Servers
- Key users
- Anything else considered critical to operations

A logical network topology diagram can be useful in identifying key devices and ports to monitor. For example, in Figure 1 the network administrator has highlighted the devices and ports of interest to monitor during the baseline test. The devices of interest include PC1 (the Admin terminal), and SRV1 (the Web/TFTP server). The ports of interest include those ports on R1, R2, and R3 that connect to the other routers or to switches, and on R2, the port that connects to SRV1 (G0/0).

By shortening the list of ports that are polled, the results are concise, and the network management load is minimized. Remember that an interface on a router or switch can be a virtual interface, such as a switch virtual interface (SVI).

Step 3. Determine the baseline duration.

The length of time and the baseline information being gathered must be sufficient for establishing a typical picture of the network. It is important that daily trends of network traffic are monitored. It is also important to monitor for trends that occur over a longer period of time, such as weekly or monthly. For this reason, when capturing data for analysis, the period specified should be, at a minimum, seven days long.

Figure 2 shows examples of several screenshots of CPU utilization trends captured over a daily, weekly, monthly, and yearly period. In this example, notice that the work week trends are too short to reveal the recurring utilization surge every weekend on Saturday evening, when a database backup operation consumes network bandwidth. This recurring pattern is revealed in the monthly trend. A yearly trend as shown in the example may be too long of a duration to provide meaningful baseline performance details. However, it may help identify long term patterns which should be analyzed further. Typically, a baseline needs to last no more than six weeks, unless specific long-term trends need to be measured. Generally, a two-to-four-week baseline is adequate.

Baseline measurements should not be performed during times of unique traffic patterns, because the data would provide an inaccurate picture of normal network operations. Baseline analysis of the network should be conducted on a regular basis. Perform an annual analysis of the entire network or baseline different sections of the network on a rotating basis. Analysis must be conducted regularly to understand how the network is affected by growth and other changes.

Refer to
Interactive Graphic
in online course

8.1.1.5 Measuring Data

When documenting the network, it is often necessary to gather information directly from routers and switches. Obvious useful network documentation commands include **ping**, **traceroute**, and **telnet** as well as the following **show** commands:

- The **show ip interface brief** and **show ipv6 interface brief** commands are used to display the up or down status and IP address of all interfaces on a device.

- The **show ip route** and **show ipv6 route** commands are used to display the routing table in a router to learn the directly connected neighbors, more remote devices (through learned routes), and the routing protocols that have been configured.

- The **show cdp neighbors detail** command is used to obtain detailed information about directly connected Cisco neighbor devices.

The figure lists some of the most common Cisco IOS commands used for data collection.

Manual data collection using **show** commands on individual network devices is extremely time consuming and is not a scalable solution. Manual collection of data should be reserved for smaller networks or limited to mission-critical network devices. For simpler network designs, baseline tasks typically use a combination of manual data collection and simple network protocol inspectors.

Sophisticated network management software is typically used to baseline large and complex networks. These software packages enable administrators to automatically create and review reports, compare current performance levels with historical observations, automatically identify performance problems, and create alerts for applications that do not provide expected levels of service.

Establishing an initial baseline or conducting a performance-monitoring analysis may require many hours or days to accurately reflect network performance. Network management software or protocol inspectors and sniffers often run continuously over the course of the data collection process.

Refer to **Interactive Graphic** in online course

8.1.1.6   Activity - Identify Benefits for Establishing a Network Baseline

Refer to **Interactive Graphic** in online course

8.1.1.7   Activity - Identify Commands Used for Measuring Data

Refer to **Packet Tracer Activity** for this chapter

8.1.1.8   Packet Tracer - Troubleshooting Challenge - Documenting the Network

Background/Scenario

This activity covers the steps to take to discover a network using primarily the **telnet**, **show cdp neighbors detail**, and **show ip route** commands. This is Part I of a two-part activity. Part II is Packet Tracer - Troubleshooting Challenge - Using Documentation to Solve Issues, which comes later in the chapter.

The topology you see when you open the Packet Tracer activity does not reveal all of the details of the network. The details have been hidden using the cluster function of Packet Tracer. The network infrastructure has been collapsed, and the topology in the file shows only the end devices. Your task is to use your knowledge of networking and discovery commands to learn about the full network topology and document it.

8.1.2   Troubleshooting Process

Refer to **Interactive Graphic** in online course

8.1.2.1   General Troubleshooting Procedures

Troubleshooting takes a large portion of network administrators' and support personnel's time. Using efficient troubleshooting techniques shortens overall troubleshooting time when working in a production environment.

There are three major stages to the troubleshooting process:

Stage 1.   Gather symptoms - Troubleshooting begins with gathering and documenting symptoms from the network, end systems, and users (Figure 1). In addition, the network administrator determines which network components have been affected and how the functionality of the network has changed compared to the baseline. Symptoms may appear in many different forms, including alerts from the network management system, console messages, and user complaints. While gathering symptoms, it is important that the network administrator ask questions and investigate the issue in order to localize the problem to a smaller range of possibilities. For example, is the problem restricted to a single device, a group of devices, or an entire subnet or network of devices?

Stage 2. **Isolate the problem** - Isolating is the process of eliminating variables until a single problem, or a set of related problems has been identified as the cause (Figure 2). To do this, the network administrator examines the characteristics of the problems at the logical layers of the network so that the most likely cause can be selected. At this stage, the network administrator may gather and document more symptoms, depending on the characteristics that are identified.

Stage 3. **Implement corrective action** - Having identified the cause of the problem, the network administrator works to correct the problem by implementing, testing, and documenting possible solutions (Figure 3). After finding the problem and determining a solution, the network administrator may need to decide if the solution can be implemented immediately or if it must be postponed. This depends on the impact of the changes on the users and the network. The severity of the problem should be weighed against the impact of the solution. For example, if a critical server or router must be offline for a significant amount of time, it may be better to wait until the end of the workday to implement the fix. Sometimes, a workaround can be created until the actual problem is resolved. This is typically part of a company's change control procedures.

If the corrective action creates another problem or does not solve the problem, the attempted solution is documented, the changes are removed, and the network administrator returns to gathering symptoms and isolating the issue.

These stages are not mutually exclusive. At any point in the process, it may be necessary to return to previous stages. For instance, the network administrator may need to gather more symptoms while isolating a problem. Additionally, when attempting to correct a problem, another problem could be created. In this instance, remove changes and begin troubleshooting again.

A troubleshooting policy, including change control procedures which documents the change made and who made the change, should be established for each stage. A policy provides a consistent manner in which to perform each stage. Part of the policy should include documenting every important piece of information.

Communicate to the users and anyone involved in the troubleshooting process that the problem has been resolved. Other IT team members should be informed of the solution. Appropriate documentation of the cause and the fix will assist other support technicians in preventing and solving similar problems in the future.

Refer to
Interactive Graphic
in online course

8.1.2.2   Gathering Symptoms

When gathering symptoms, it is important that the administrator gather facts and evidence to progressively eliminate possible causes, and eventually identify the root cause of the issue. By analyzing the information, the network administrator formulates a hypothesis to propose possible causes and solutions, while eliminating others.

As shown in Figure 1, there are five information gathering steps.

Step 1. **Gather information** - Gather information from the trouble ticket, users, or end systems affected by the problem to form a definition of the problem.

Step 2. **Determine ownership** - If the problem is within the control of the organization, move onto the next stage. If the problem is outside the boundary of the organization's control (for example, lost Internet connectivity outside of the autonomous system), contact an administrator for the external system before gathering additional network symptoms.

Step 3. **Narrow the scope** - Determine if the problem is at the core, distribution, or access layer of the network. At the identified layer, analyze the existing symptoms and use your knowledge of the network topology to determine which piece of equipment is the most likely cause.

Step 4. **Gather symptoms from suspect devices** - Using a layered troubleshooting approach, gather hardware and software symptoms from the suspect devices. Start with the most likely possibility and use knowledge and experience to determine if the problem is more likely a hardware or software configuration problem.

Step 5. **Document symptoms** - Sometimes the problem can be solved using the documented symptoms. If not, begin the isolating stage of the general troubleshooting process.

To gather symptoms from suspected networking device, use Cisco IOS commands and other tools including:

- **ping, traceroute,** and **telnet** commands
- **show** and **debug** commands
- packet captures
- device logs

The table in Figure 2 describes common Cisco IOS commands used to gather the symptoms of a network problem.

Note Although the **debug** command is an important tool for gathering symptoms, it generates a large amount of console message traffic and the performance of a network device can be noticeably affected. If the **debug** must be performed during normal working hours, warn network users that a troubleshooting effort is underway and that network performance may be affected. Remember to disable debugging when you are done.

Refer to
Online Course
for Illustration

8.1.2.3 Questioning End Users

In many cases the problem is reported by an end user. The information may often be vague or misleading, such as, "The network is down" or "I cannot access my email". In these cases, the problem must be better defined. This may require asking questions of the end users.

Use effective questioning techniques when asking the end users about a network problem they may be experiencing. This will help you to get the information required to document the symptoms of a problem.

The table in the figure provides some guidelines and sample end-user questions.

Refer to
Interactive Graphic
in online course

8.1.2.4   Activity - Identify Commands for Gathering Symptoms

8.1.3   Isolating the Issue Using Layered Models

Refer to
Interactive Graphic
in online course

8.1.3.1   Using Layered Models for Troubleshooting

After all symptoms are gathered, if no solution is identified, the network administrator compares the characteristics of the problem to the logical layers of the network to isolate and solve the issue.

Logical networking models, such as the OSI and TCP/IP models, separate network functionality into modular layers. These layered models can be applied to the physical network to isolate network problems when troubleshooting. For example, if the symptoms suggest a physical connection problem, the network technician can focus on troubleshooting the circuit that operates at the physical layer. If that circuit functions as expected, the technician looks at areas within another layer that could be causing the problem.

OSI Reference Model

The OSI reference model provides a common language for network administrators and is commonly used in troubleshooting networks. Problems are typically described in terms of a given OSI model layer.

The OSI reference model describes how information from a software application in one computer moves through a network medium to a software application in another computer.

The upper layers (5 to 7) of the OSI model deal with application issues and generally are implemented only in software. The application layer is closest to the end user. Both users and application layer processes interact with software applications that contain a communications component.

The lower layers (1 to 4) of the OSI model handle data-transport issues. Layers 3 and 4 are generally implemented only in software. The physical layer (Layer 1) and data link layer (Layer 2) are implemented in hardware and software. The physical layer is closest to the physical network medium, such as the network cabling, and is responsible for actually placing information on the medium.

Figure 1 shows some common devices and the OSI layers that must be examined during the troubleshooting process for that device. Notice that routers and multilayer switches are shown at Layer 4, the transport layer. Although routers and multilayer switches usually make forwarding decisions at Layer 3, ACLs on these devices can be used to make filtering decisions using Layer 4 information.

TCP/IP Model

Similar to the OSI networking model, the TCP/IP networking model also divides networking architecture into modular layers. Figure 2 shows how the TCP/IP networking model maps to the layers of the OSI networking model. It is this close mapping that allows the TCP/IP suite of protocols to successfully communicate with so many networking technologies.

The application layer in the TCP/IP suite actually combines the functions of the three OSI model layers: session, presentation, and application. The application layer provides communication between applications, such as FTP, HTTP, and SMTP on separate hosts.

The transport layers of TCP/IP and OSI directly correspond in function. The transport layer is responsible for exchanging segments between devices on a TCP/IP network.

The TCP/IP Internet layer relates to the OSI network layer. The Internet layer is responsible for addressing used for data transfer from source to destination.

The TCP/IP network access layer corresponds to the OSI physical and data link layers. The network access layer communicates directly with the network media and provides an interface between the architecture of the network and the Internet layer.

Refer to
Interactive Graphic
in online course

8.1.3.2   Troubleshooting Methods

Using the layered models, there are three primary methods for troubleshooting networks:

- Bottom-up
- Top-down
- Divide-and-conquer

Each approach has its advantages and disadvantages. This topic describes the three methods and provides guidelines for choosing the best method for a specific situation.

Bottom-Up Troubleshooting Method

In bottom-up troubleshooting, you start with the physical components of the network and move up through the layers of the OSI model until the cause of the problem is identified, as shown in Figure 1. Bottom-up troubleshooting is a good approach to use when the problem is suspected to be a physical one. Most networking problems reside at the lower levels, so implementing the bottom-up approach is often effective.

The disadvantage with the bottom-up troubleshooting approach is it requires that you check every device and interface on the network until the possible cause of the problem is found. Remember that each conclusion and possibility must be documented so there can be a lot of paper work associated with this approach. A further challenge is to determine which devices to start examining first.

Top-Down Troubleshooting Method

In Figure 2, top-down troubleshooting starts with the end-user applications and moves down through the layers of the OSI model until the cause of the problem has been identified. End-user applications of an end system are tested before tackling the more specific networking pieces. Use this approach for simpler problems, or when you think the problem is with a piece of software.

The disadvantage with the top-down approach is it requires checking every network application until the possible cause of the problem is found. Each conclusion and possibility must be documented. The challenge is to determine which application to start examining first.

Divide-and-Conquer Troubleshooting Method

Figure 3 shows the divide-and-conquer approach to troubleshooting a networking problem. The network administrator selects a layer and tests in both directions from that layer.

In divide-and-conquer troubleshooting, you start by collecting user experiences of the problem, document the symptoms and then, using that information, make an informed guess as to which OSI layer to start your investigation. When a layer is verified to be functioning properly, it can be assumed that the layers below it are functioning. The administrator can work up the OSI layers. If an OSI layer is not functioning properly, the administrator can work down the OSI layer model.

For example, if users cannot access the web server, but they can ping the server, then the problem is above Layer 3. If pinging the server is unsuccessful, then the problem is likely at a lower OSI layer.

Refer to
Online Course
for Illustration

8.1.3.3   Other Troubleshooting Methods

In addition to the systematic, layered approach to troubleshooting, there are also, less-structured troubleshooting approaches.

One troubleshooting approach is based on an educated guess by the network administrator, based on the symptoms of the problem. This method is more successfully implemented by seasoned network administrators, because seasoned network administrators rely on their extensive knowledge and experience to decisively isolate and solve network issues. With a less-experienced network administrator, this troubleshooting method may be more like random troubleshooting.

Another approach involves comparing a working and non-working situation, and spotting significant differences, including:

- Configurations
- Software versions
- Hardware and other device properties

Using this method may lead to a working solution, but without clearly revealing the cause of the problem. This method can be helpful when the network administrator is lacking an area of expertise, or when the problem needs to be resolved quickly. After the fix has been implemented, the network administrator can do further research on the actual cause of the problem.

Substitution is another quick troubleshooting methodology. It involves swapping the problematic device with a known, working one. If the problem is fixed, that the network administrator knows the problem is with the removed device. If the problem remains, then the cause may be elsewhere. In specific situations, this can be an ideal method for quick problem resolution, such as when a critical single point of failure, like a border router, goes down. It may be more beneficial to simply replace the device and restore service, rather than troubleshoot the issue.

Refer to
Online Course
for Illustration

8.1.3.4   Guidelines for Selecting a Troubleshooting Method

To quickly resolve network problems, take the time to select the most effective network troubleshooting method. The figure illustrates this process.

The following is an example of how to choose a troubleshooting method based on a specific problem:

Two IP routers are not exchanging routing information. The last time this type of problem occurred it was a protocol issue. Therefore, choose the divide-and-conquer troubleshooting method. Analysis reveals that there is connectivity between the routers. Start the troubleshooting process at the physical or data link layer. Confirm connectivity and begin testing the TCP/IP-related functions at the next layer up in the OSI model, the network layer.

Refer to
Interactive Graphic
in online course

8.1.3.5   Activity - Troubleshooting Methods

8.2   Troubleshooting Scenarios

8.2.1   Using IP SLA

Refer to
Online Course
for Illustration

8.2.1.1   IP SLA Concepts

Network administrators must be proactive and continually monitor and test the network. The goal is to discover a network failure as early as possible. A useful tool for this task is the Cisco IOS IP Service Level Agreement (SLA).

IP SLAs use generated traffic to measure network performance between two networking devices, multiple network locations, or across multiple network paths. In the example in the figure, R1 is the IP SLA source that monitors the connection to the DNS server by periodically sending ICMP requests to the server.

Network engineers use IP SLAs to simulate network data and IP services to collect network performance information in real time. Performance monitoring can be done anytime, anywhere, without deploying a physical probe.

Note   Ping and traceroute are probe tools. A physical probe is different. It is a device that can be inserted somewhere in the network to collect and monitor traffic. The use of physical probes is beyond the scope of this course.

Measurements provided by the various IP SLA operations can be used for troubleshooting networks by providing consistent, reliable measurements that immediately identify problems and save troubleshooting time.

There are additional benefits for using IP SLAs:

- Service-level agreement monitoring, measurement, and verification

- Network performance monitoring to provide continuous, reliable, and predictable measurements to measure the jitter, latency, or packet loss in the network

- IP service network health assessment to verify that the existing QoS is sufficient for new IP services

- Edge-to-edge network availability monitoring for proactive connectivity verification of network resources

Multiple IP SLA operations can be running on the network, or on a device, at any time. IP SLA information can be displayed using CLI commands or through SNMP.

Note   SNMP notifications based on the data gathered by an IP SLA operation is beyond the scope of this course.

Refer to
Online Course
for Illustration

8.2.1.2 IP SLA Configuration

Instead of using **ping** manually, a network engineer can use the IP SLA ICMP Echo operation to test the availability of network devices. A network device can be any device with IP capabilities (router, switch, PC, server, etc.). The IP SLA ICMP Echo operation provides the following measurements:

- Availability monitoring (packet loss statistics)

- Performance monitoring (latency and response time)

- Network operation (end-to-end connectivity)

To verify that the desired IP SLA operation is supported on the source device, use the **show ip sla application** privileged EXEC mode command. The output generated in the figure confirms that R1 is capable of supporting IP SLA. However, there are currently no sessions configured.

To create an IP SLA operation and enter IP SLA configuration mode, use the **ip sla** *operation-number* global configuration command. The operation number is a unique number used to identify the operation being configured.

From IP SLA configuration mode, you can configure the IP SLA operation as an ICMP Echo operation and enter ICMP echo configuration mode using the following command:

```
Router(config-ip-sla)# icmp-echo { dest-ip-address | dest-hostname }
[ source-ip { ip-address | hostname } | source-interface interface-id ]
```

Next, set the rate at which a specified IP SLA operation repeats using the **frequency** *seconds* command. The range is from 1 to 604800 seconds and the default is 60 seconds.

To schedule the IP SLA operation, use the following global configuration command:

```
Router(config)# ip sla schedule operation-number [ life { forever |
seconds }] [ start-time { hh : mm [: ss ] [ month day | day month ] |
pending | now | after hh:mm:ss ] [ ageout seconds ] [ recurring ]
```

Refer to
Interactive Graphic
in online course

8.2.1.3 Sample IP SLA Configuration

To help understand how to configure a simple IP SLA, refer to the topology in Figure 1.

The configuration in Figure 2 configures an IP SLA operation with an operation number of 1. Multiple IP SLA operations may be configured on a device. Each operation can be referred to by its operation-number. The **icmp-echo** command identifies the destination address to be monitored. In the example, it is set to monitor R3's S1 interface. The **frequency** command is setting the IP SLA rate to 30 second intervals.

The **ip sla schedule** command is scheduling the IP SLA operation number 1 to start immediately (now) and continue until manually cancelled (forever).

Note   Use the **no ip sla schedule** *operation-number* command to cancel the SLA operation. The SLA operation configuration is preserved and can be rescheduled when needed.

Refer to
Interactive Graphic
in online course

8.2.1.4 Verifying an IP SLA Configuration

Use the **show ip sla configuration** *operation-number* command to display configuration values including all defaults for IP SLA operations or for a specific operation.

In Figure 1, the **show ip sla configuration** command displays the IP SLA ICMP Echo configuration.

Use the **show ip sla statistics** [*operation-number*] command to display the IP SLA operation monitoring statistics, as shown in Figure 2.

Refer to
Lab Activity
for this chapter

8.2.1.5 Lab – Configure IP SLA ICMP Echo

In this lab, you will complete the following objectives:

- Build the Network and Verify Connectivity
- Configure IP SLA ICMP Echo on R1
- Test and Monitor the IP SLA Operation

8.2.2 Troubleshooting Tools

Refer to
Interactive Graphic
in online course

8.2.2.1 Software Troubleshooting Tools

A wide variety of software and hardware tools are available to make troubleshooting easier. These tools may be used to gather and analyze symptoms of network problems. They often provide monitoring and reporting functions that can be used to establish the network baseline.

Common software troubleshooting tools include:

Network Management System Tools

Network management system (NMS) tools include device-level monitoring, configuration, and fault-management tools. Figure 1 shows an example display from the WhatsUp Gold NMS software. These tools can be used to investigate and correct network problems. Network monitoring software graphically displays a physical view of network devices, allowing network managers to monitor remote devices continuously and automatically. Device management software provides dynamic device status, statistics, and configuration information for key network devices.

Knowledge Bases

On-line network device vendor knowledge bases have become indispensable sources of information. When vendor-based knowledge bases are combined with Internet search engines like Google, a network administrator has access to a vast pool of experience-based information.

Figure 2 shows the Cisco **Tools & Resources** page found at http://www.cisco.com. This page provides information on Cisco-related hardware and software. It contains troubleshooting procedures, implementation guides, and original white papers on most aspects of networking technology.

Baselining Tools

Many tools for automating the network documentation and baselining process are available. Figure 3 shows a screen capture of the SolarWinds Network Performance Monitor 12 baseline view. Baselining tools help with common documentation tasks. For example, they can draw network diagrams, help keep network software and hardware documentation up-to-date, and help to cost-effectively measure baseline network bandwidth use.

Refer to **Online Course** for Illustration

8.2.2.2   Protocol Analyzers

Protocol analyzers are useful to investigate packet content while flowing through the network. A protocol analyzer decodes the various protocol layers in a recorded frame and presents this information in a relatively easy to use format. The figure shows a screen capture of the Wireshark protocol analyzer.

The information displayed by a protocol analyzer includes the physical, data link, protocol, and descriptions for each frame. Most protocol analyzers can filter traffic that meets certain criteria so that, for example, all traffic to and from a particular device can be captured. Protocol analyzers such as Wireshark can help troubleshoot network performance problems. It is important to have both a good understanding of TCP/IP and how to use a protocol analyzer to inspect information at each TCP/IP layer.

Note   To become more knowledgeable and skillful using Wireshark, an excellent resource is http://www.wiresharkbook.com.

Refer to **Interactive Graphic** in online course

8.2.2.3   Hardware Troubleshooting Tools

There are multiple types of hardware troubleshooting tools.

Common hardware troubleshooting tools include:

- **Digital Multimeters** - Digital multimeters (DMMs), such as the Fluke 179 shown in Figure 1, are test instruments that are used to directly measure electrical values of voltage, current, and resistance. In network troubleshooting, most tests that would need a multimeter involve checking power supply voltage levels and verifying that network devices are receiving power.

- **Cable Testers** - Cable testers are specialized, handheld devices designed for testing the various types of data communication cabling. Figure 2 displays the Fluke LinkRunner AT Network Auto-Tester. Cable testers can be used to detect broken wires, crossed-over wiring, shorted connections, and improperly paired connections. These devices can be inexpensive continuity testers, moderately priced data cabling testers, or expensive time-domain reflectometers (TDRs). TDRs are used to pinpoint the distance to a break in a cable. These devices send signals along the cable and wait for them to be reflected. The time between sending the signal and receiving it back is converted into a distance measurement. The TDR function is normally packaged with data cabling testers. TDRs used to test fiber optic cables are known as optical time-domain reflectometers (OTDRs).

- **Cable Analyzers** - Cable analyzers, such as the Fluke DTX Cable Analyzer in Figure 3, are multifunctional handheld devices that are used to test and certify copper and fiber cables for different services and standards. The more sophisticated tools include advanced troubleshooting diagnostics that measure the distance to a performance defect such as near-end crosstalk (NEXT) or return loss (RL), identify corrective actions, and graphically display crosstalk and impedance behavior. Cable analyzers also typically include PC-based software. After field data is collected, the data from the handheld device can be uploaded so that the network administrator can create up-to-date reports.

- **Portable Network Analyzers** - Portable devices like the Fluke OptiView in Figure 4 are used for troubleshooting switched networks and VLANs. By plugging the network analyzer in anywhere on the network, a network engineer can see the switch port to which the device is connected, and the average and peak utilization. The analyzer can also be used to discover VLAN configuration, identify top network talkers, analyze network traffic, and view interface details. The device can typically output to a PC that has network monitoring software installed for further analysis and troubleshooting.

- **Network Analysis Module** - The Cisco NAM is a device or software as shown in Figure 5. It provides an embedded browser-based interface that generates reports on the traffic that consumes critical network resources. It displays a graphical representation of traffic from local and remote switches and routers such as seen in Figure 6. In addition, the NAM can capture and decode packets and track response times to pinpoint an application problem to a particular network or server.

Refer to **Interactive Graphic** in online course

8.2.2.4   Using a Syslog Server for Troubleshooting

Syslog is a simple protocol used by an IP device known as a syslog client, to send text-based log messages to another IP device, the syslog server. Syslog is currently defined in RFC 5424.

Implementing a logging facility is an important part of network security and for network troubleshooting. Cisco devices can log information regarding configuration changes, ACL violations, interface status, and many other types of events. Cisco devices can send log messages to several different facilities. Event messages can be sent to one or more of the following:

- **Console** - Console logging is on by default. Messages log to the console and can be viewed when modifying or testing the router or switch using terminal emulation software while connected to the console port of the network device.

- **Terminal lines** - Enabled EXEC sessions can be configured to receive log messages on any terminal lines. Similar to console logging, this type of logging is not stored by the network device and, therefore, is only valuable to the user on that line.

- **Buffered logging** - Buffered logging is a little more useful as a troubleshooting tool because log messages are stored in memory for a time. However, log messages are cleared when the device is rebooted.

- **SNMP traps** - Certain thresholds can be preconfigured on routers and other devices. Router events, such as exceeding a threshold, can be processed by the router and forwarded as SNMP traps to an external SNMP network management station. SNMP traps are a viable security logging facility, but require the configuration and maintenance of an SNMP system.

- **Syslog** - Cisco routers and switches can be configured to forward log messages to an external syslog service. This service can reside on any number of servers or workstations, including Microsoft Windows and Linux-based systems. Syslog is the most popular message logging facility, because it provides long-term log storage capabilities and a central location for all router messages.

Cisco IOS log messages fall into one of eight levels, shown in Figure 1. The lower the level number, the higher the severity level. By default, all messages from level 0 to 7 are logged to the console. While the ability to view logs on a central syslog server is helpful in troubleshooting, sifting through a large amount of data can be an overwhelming task. The **logging trap** *level* command limits messages logged to the syslog server based on severity. The level is the name or number of the severity *level*. Only messages equal to or numerically lower than the specified *level* are logged.

In the example in Figure 2, system messages from level 0 (emergencies) to 5 (notifications) are sent to the syslog server at 209.165.200.225.

Refer to
Interactive Graphic
in online course

8.2.2.5 Activity - Identify Common Troubleshooting Tools

8.2.3 Symptoms and Causes of Network Troubleshooting

Refer to
Online Course
for Illustration

8.2.3.1 Physical Layer Troubleshooting

The physical layer transmits bits from one computer to another and regulates the transmission of a stream of bits over the physical medium. The physical layer is the only layer with physically tangible properties, such as wires, cards, and antennas.

Issues on a network often present as performance problems. Performance problems mean that there is a difference between the expected behavior and the observed behavior, and the system is not functioning as could be reasonably expected. Failures and suboptimal conditions at the physical layer not only inconvenience users but can impact the productivity of the entire company. Networks that experience these kinds of conditions usually shut down. Because the upper layers of the OSI model depend on the physical layer to function, a network administrator must have the ability to effectively isolate and correct problems at this layer.

Common symptoms of network problems at the physical layer include:

- **Performance lower than baseline** - The most common reasons for slow or poor performance include overloaded or underpowered servers, unsuitable switch or router configurations, traffic congestion on a low-capacity link, and chronic frame loss.

- **Loss of connectivity** - If a cable or device fails; the most obvious symptom is a loss of connectivity between the devices that communicate over that link or with the failed device or interface. This is indicated by a simple ping test. Intermittent loss of connectivity can indicate a loose or oxidized connection.

- **Network bottlenecks or congestion** - If a router, interface, or cable fails, routing protocols may redirect traffic to other routes that are not designed to carry the extra capacity. This can result in congestion or bottlenecks in those parts of the network.

- **High CPU utilization rates** - High CPU utilization rates are a symptom that a device, such as a router, switch, or server, is operating at or exceeding its design limits. If not addressed quickly, CPU overloading can cause a device to shut down or fail.

- **Console error messages** - Error messages reported on the device console could indicate a physical layer problem.

Issues that commonly cause network problems at the physical layer include:

- **Power-related** - Power-related issues are the most fundamental reason for network failure. Also, check the operation of the fans, and ensure that the chassis intake and exhaust vents are clear. If other nearby units have also powered down, suspect a power failure at the main power supply.

- **Hardware faults** - Faulty network interface cards (NICs) can be the cause of network transmission errors due to late collisions, short frames, and jabber. Jabber is often defined as the condition in which a network device continually transmits random, meaningless data onto the network. Other likely causes of jabber are faulty or corrupt NIC driver files, bad cabling, or grounding problems.

- **Cabling faults** - Many problems can be corrected by simply reseating cables that have become partially disconnected. When performing a physical inspection, look for damaged cables, improper cable types, and poorly crimped RJ-45 connectors. Suspect cables should be tested or exchanged with a known functioning cable.

- **Attenuation** - Attenuation can be caused if a cable length exceeds the design limit for the media, or when there is a poor connection resulting from a loose cable or dirty or oxidized contacts. If attenuation is severe, the receiving device cannot always successfully distinguish one bit in the data stream from another bit.

- **Noise** - Local electromagnetic interference (EMI) is commonly known as noise. Noise can be generated by many sources, such as FM radio stations, police radio, building security, and avionics for automated landing, crosstalk (noise induced by other cables in the same pathway or adjacent cables), nearby electric cables, devices with large electric motors, or anything that includes a transmitter more powerful than a cell phone.

- **Interface configuration errors** - Many things can be misconfigured on an interface to cause it to go down, such as incorrect clock rate, incorrect clock source, and interface not being turned on. This causes a loss of connectivity with attached network segments.

- **Exceeding design limits** - A component may be operating suboptimally at the physical layer because it is being utilized beyond specifications or configured capacity. When troubleshooting this type of problem, it becomes evident that resources for the device are operating at or near the maximum capacity and there is an increase in the number of interface errors.

- **CPU overload** - Symptoms include processes with high CPU utilization percentages, input queue drops, slow performance, SNMP timeouts, no remote access, or services such as DHCP, Telnet, and ping are slow or fail to respond. On a switch the following could occur: spanning tree reconvergence, EtherChannel links bounce, UDLD flapping, IP SLAs failures. For routers, there could be no routing updates, route flapping, or HSRP flapping. One of the causes of CPU overload in a router or switch is high traffic. If one or more interfaces are regularly overloaded with traffic, consider redesigning the traffic flow in the network or upgrading the hardware.

Refer to
Online Course
for Illustration

8.2.3.2   Data Link Layer Troubleshooting

Troubleshooting Layer 2 problems can be a challenging process. The configuration and operation of these protocols are critical to creating a functional, well-tuned network.

Layer 2 problems cause specific symptoms that, when recognized, will help identify the problem quickly.

Common symptoms of network problems at the data link layer include:

- **No functionality or connectivity at the network layer or above** - Some Layer 2 problems can stop the exchange of frames across a link, while others only cause network performance to degrade.

- **Network is operating below baseline performance levels** - There are two distinct types of suboptimal Layer 2 operation that can occur in a network. First, the frames take a suboptimal path to their destination but do arrive. In this case, the network might experience high-bandwidth usage on links that should not have that level of traffic. Second, some frames are dropped. These problems can be identified through error counter statistics and console error messages that appear on the switch or router. In an Ethernet environment, an extended or continuous ping also reveals if frames are being dropped.

- **Excessive broadcasts** - Operating systems use broadcasts and multicasts extensively to discover network services and other hosts. Generally, excessive broadcasts result from one of the following situations: poorly programmed or configured applications, large Layer 2 broadcast domains, or underlying network problems, such as STP loops or route flapping.

- **Console messages** - In some instances, a router recognizes that a Layer 2 problem has occurred and sends alert messages to the console. Typically, a router does this when it detects a problem with interpreting incoming frames (encapsulation or framing problems) or when keepalives are expected but do not arrive. The most common console message that indicates a Layer 2 problem is a line protocol down message.

Issues at the data link layer that commonly result in network connectivity or performance problems include:

- **Encapsulation errors** - An encapsulation error occurs because the bits placed in a particular field by the sender are not what the receiver expects to see. This condition occurs when the encapsulation at one end of a WAN link is configured differently from the encapsulation used at the other end.

- **Address mapping errors** - In topologies, such as point-to-multipoint or broadcast Ethernet, it is essential that an appropriate Layer 2 destination address be given to the frame. This ensures its arrival at the correct destination. To achieve this, the network device must match a destination Layer 3 address with the correct Layer 2 address using either static or dynamic maps. In a dynamic environment, the mapping of Layer 2 and Layer 3 information can fail because devices may have been specifically configured not to respond to ARP requests, the Layer 2 or Layer 3 information that is cached may have physically changed, or invalid ARP replies are received because of a misconfiguration or a security attack.

- **Framing errors** - Frames usually work in groups of 8-bit bytes. A framing error occurs when a frame does not end on an 8-bit byte boundary. When this happens, the receiver may have problems determining where one frame ends and another frame starts. Too many invalid frames may prevent valid keepalives from being exchanged. Framing errors can be caused by a noisy serial line, an improperly designed cable (too long or not properly shielded), faulty NIC, duplex mismatch, or an incorrectly configured channel service unit (CSU) line clock.

- **STP failures or loops** - The purpose of the Spanning Tree Protocol (STP) is to resolve a redundant physical topology into a tree-like topology by blocking redundant ports. Most STP problems are related to forwarding loops that occur when no ports in a redundant topology are blocked and traffic is forwarded in circles indefinitely, excessive flooding because of a high rate of STP topology changes. A topology change should be a rare event in a well-configured network. When a link between two switches goes up or down, there is eventually a topology change when the STP state of the port is changing to or from forwarding. However, when a port is flapping (oscillating between up and down states), this causes repetitive topology changes and flooding, or slow STP convergence or re-convergence. This can be caused by a mismatch between the real and documented topology, a configuration error, such as an inconsistent configuration of STP timers, an overloaded switch CPU during convergence, or a software defect.

Refer to
Online Course
for Illustration

8.2.3.3 Network Layer Troubleshooting

Network layer problems include any problem that involves a Layer 3 protocol, both routed protocols (such as IPv4 or IPv6) and routing protocols (such as EIGRP, OSPF, etc.).

Common symptoms of network problems at the network layer include:

- **Network failure** - Network failure is when the network is nearly or completely non-functional, affecting all users and applications on the network. These failures are usually noticed quickly by users and network administrators, and are obviously critical to the productivity of a company.

- **Suboptimal performance** - Network optimization problems usually involve a subset of users, applications, destinations, or a particular type of traffic. Optimization issues can be difficult to detect and even harder to isolate and diagnose. This is because they usually involve multiple layers, or even a single host computer. Determining that the problem is a network layer problem can take time.

In most networks, static routes are used in combination with dynamic routing protocols. Improper configuration of static routes can lead to less than optimal routing. In some cases, improperly configured static routes can create routing loops which make parts of the network unreachable.

Troubleshooting dynamic routing protocols requires a thorough understanding of how the specific routing protocol functions. Some problems are common to all routing protocols, while other problems are particular to the individual routing protocol.

There is no single template for solving Layer 3 problems. Routing problems are solved with a methodical process, using a series of commands to isolate and diagnose the problem.

Here are some areas to explore when diagnosing a possible problem involving routing protocols:

- **General network issues** - Often a change in the topology, such as a down link, may have effects on other areas of the network that might not be obvious at the time. This may include the installation of new routes, static or dynamic, or removal of other routes. Determine whether anything in the network has recently changed, and if there is anyone currently working on the network infrastructure.

- **Connectivity issues** - Check for any equipment and connectivity problems, including power problems such as outages and environmental problems (for example, overheating). Also check for Layer 1 problems, such as cabling problems, bad ports, and ISP problems.

- **Routing table** - Check the routing table for anything unexpected, such as missing routes or unexpected routes. Use **debug** commands to view routing updates and routing table maintenance.

- **Neighbor issues** - If the routing protocol establishes an adjacency with a neighbor, check to see if there are any problems with the routers forming neighbor adjacencies.

- **Topology database** - If the routing protocol uses a topology table or database, check the table for anything unexpected, such as missing entries or unexpected entries.

Refer to **Interactive Graphic** in online course

8.2.3.4   Transport Layer Troubleshooting - ACLs

Network problems can arise from transport layer problems on the router, particularly at the edge of the network where traffic is examined and modified. Two of the most commonly implemented transport layer technologies are access control lists (ACLs) and Network Address Translation (NAT), as shown in Figure 1.

The most common issues with ACLs are caused by improper configuration, as shown in Figure 2. Problems with ACLs may cause otherwise working systems to fail. There are several areas where misconfigurations commonly occur:

- **Selection of traffic flow** - Traffic is defined by both the router interface through which the traffic is traveling and the direction in which this traffic is traveling. An ACL must be applied to the correct interface, and the correct traffic direction must be selected to function properly.

- **Order of access control entries** - The entries in an ACL should be from specific to general. Although an ACL may have an entry to specifically permit a particular traffic flow, packets never match that entry if they are being denied by another entry earlier in the list. If the router is running both ACLs and NAT, the order in which each of these technologies is applied to a traffic flow is important. Inbound traffic is processed by the inbound ACL before being processed by outside-to-inside NAT. Outbound traffic is processed by the outbound ACL after being processed by inside-to-outside NAT.

- **Implicit deny any** - When high security is not required on the ACL, this implicit access control element can be the cause of an ACL misconfiguration.

- **Addresses and IPv4 wildcard masks** - Complex IPv4 wildcard masks provide significant improvements in efficiency, but are more subject to configuration errors. An example of a complex wildcard mask is using the IPv4 address 10.0.32.0 and wildcard mask 0.0.32.15 to select the first 15 host addresses in either the 10.0.0.0 network or the 10.0.32.0 network.

- **Selection of transport layer protocol** - When configuring ACLs, it is important that only the correct transport layer protocols be specified. Many network administrators, when unsure whether a particular traffic flow uses a TCP port or a UDP port, configure both. Specifying both opens a hole through the firewall, possibly giving intruders an avenue into the network. It also introduces an extra element into the ACL, so the ACL takes longer to process, introducing more latency into network communications.

- **Source and destination ports** - Properly controlling the traffic between two hosts requires symmetric access control elements for inbound and outbound ACLs. Address and port information for traffic generated by a replying host is the mirror image of address and port information for traffic generated by the initiating host.

- **Use of the established keyword** - The **established** keyword increases the security provided by an ACL. However, if the keyword is applied incorrectly, unexpected results may occur.

- **Uncommon protocols** - Misconfigured ACLs often cause problems for protocols other than TCP and UDP. Uncommon protocols that are gaining popularity are VPN and encryption protocols.

The **log** keyword is a useful command for viewing ACL operation on ACL entries. This keyword instructs the router to place an entry in the system log whenever that entry condition is matched. The logged event includes details of the packet that matched the ACL element. The **log** keyword is especially useful for troubleshooting and also provides information on intrusion attempts being blocked by the ACL.

Refer to **Online Course** for Illustration

8.2.3.5   Transport Layer Troubleshooting – NAT for IPv4

There are a number of problems with NAT such as not interacting with services like DHCP and tunneling. These can include misconfigured NAT inside, NAT outside, or ACL. Other issues include interoperability with other network technologies, especially those that contain or derive information from host network addressing in the packet. Some of these technologies include:

- **BOOTP and DHCP** - Both protocols manage the automatic assignment of IPv4 addresses to clients. Recall that the first packet that a new client sends is a DHCP-Request broadcast IPv4 packet. The DHCP-Request packet has a source IPv4 address of 0.0.0.0. Because NAT requires both a valid destination and source IPv4 address, BOOTP and DHCP can have difficulty operating over a router running either static or dynamic NAT. Configuring the IPv4 helper feature can help solve this problem.

- **DNS** - Because a router running dynamic NAT is changing the relationship between inside and outside addresses regularly as table entries expire and are recreated, a DNS server outside the NAT router does not have an accurate representation of the network inside the router. Configuring the IPv4 helper feature can help solve this problem.

- **SNMP** - Similar to DNS packets, NAT is unable to alter the addressing information stored in the data payload of the packet. Because of this, an SNMP management station on one side of a NAT router may not be able to contact SNMP agents on the other side of the NAT router. Configuring the IPv4 helper feature can help solve this problem.

- **Tunneling and encryption protocols** - Encryption and tunneling protocols often require that traffic be sourced from a specific UDP or TCP port, or use a protocol at the transport layer that cannot be processed by NAT. For example, IPsec tunneling protocols and generic routing encapsulation protocols used by VPN implementations cannot be processed by NAT.

Refer to
Online Course
for Illustration

8.2.3.6   Application Layer Troubleshooting

Most of the application layer protocols provide user services. Application layer protocols are typically used for network management, file transfer, distributed file services, terminal emulation, and email. New user services are often added, such as VPNs and VoIP.

The figure shows the most widely known and implemented TCP/IP application layer protocols include:

- **SSH/Telnet** - Enables users to establish terminal session connections with remote hosts.

- **HTTP** - Supports the exchanging of text, graphic images, sound, video, and other multimedia files on the web.

- **FTP** - Performs interactive file transfers between hosts.

- **TFTP** - Performs basic interactive file transfers typically between hosts and networking devices.

- **SMTP** - Supports basic message delivery services.

- **POP** - Connects to mail servers and downloads email.

- **Simple Network Management Protocol (SNMP)** - Collects management information from network devices.

- **DNS** - Maps IP addresses to the names assigned to network devices.

- **Network File System (NFS)** - Enables computers to mount drives on remote hosts and operate them as if they were local drives. Originally developed by Sun Microsystems, it combines with two other application layer protocols, external data representation (XDR) and remote-procedure call (RPC), to allow transparent access to remote network resources.

The types of symptoms and causes depend upon the actual application itself.

Application layer problems prevent services from being provided to application programs. A problem at the application layer can result in unreachable or unusable resources when the physical, data link, network, and transport layers are functional. It is possible to have full network connectivity, but the application simply cannot provide data.

Another type of problem at the application layer occurs when the physical, data link, network, and transport layers are functional, but the data transfer and requests for network services from a single network service or application do not meet the normal expectations of a user.

A problem at the application layer may cause users to complain that the network or the particular application that they are working with is sluggish or slower than usual when transferring data or requesting network services.

Refer to
Interactive Graphic
in online course

8.2.3.7   Activity - Identify the OSI Layer Associated with a Network Issue

8.2.4   Troubleshooting IP Connectivity

Refer to
Online Course
for Illustration

8.2.4.1   Components of Troubleshooting End-to-End Connectivity

Diagnosing and solving problems is an essential skill for network administrators. There is no single recipe for troubleshooting, and a particular problem can be diagnosed in many different ways. However, by employing a structured approach to the troubleshooting process, an administrator can reduce the time it takes to diagnose and solve a problem.

Throughout this topic, the following scenario is used. The client host PC1 is unable to access applications on Server SRV1 or Server SRV2. The figure shows the topology of this network. PC1 uses SLAAC with EUI-64 to create its IPv6 global unicast address. EUI-64 creates the Interface ID using the Ethernet MAC address, inserting FFFE in the middle, and flipping the seventh bit.

When there is no end-to-end connectivity, and the administrator chooses to troubleshoot with a bottom-up approach, these are common steps the administrator can take:

Step 1. Check physical connectivity at the point where network communication stops. This includes cables and hardware. The problem might be with a faulty cable or interface, or involve misconfigured or faulty hardware.

Step 2. Check for duplex mismatches.

Step 3. Check data link and network layer addressing on the local network. This includes IPv4 ARP tables, IPv6 neighbor tables, MAC address tables, and VLAN assignments.

Step 4. Verify that the default gateway is correct.

Step 5. Ensure that devices are determining the correct path from the source to the destination. Manipulate the routing information if necessary.

Step 6. Verify the transport layer is functioning properly. Telnet can also be used to test transport layer connections from the command line.

Step 7. Verify that there are no ACLs blocking traffic.

Step 8. Ensure that DNS settings are correct. There should be a DNS server that is accessible.

The outcome of this process is operational, end-to-end connectivity. If all of the steps have been performed without any resolution, the network administrator may either want to repeat the previous steps or escalate the problem to a senior administrator.

Refer to
Interactive Graphic
in online course

8.2.4.2   End-to-End Connectivity Problem Initiates Troubleshooting

Usually what initiates a troubleshooting effort is the discovery that there is a problem with end-to-end connectivity. Two of the most common utilities used to verify a problem with end-to-end connectivity are **ping** and **traceroute**, as shown in Figure 1.

Ping is probably the most widely-known connectivity-testing utility in networking and has always been part of Cisco IOS Software. It sends out requests for responses from a specified host address. The **ping** command uses a Layer 3 protocol that is a part of the TCP/IP suite called ICMP. Ping uses the ICMP echo request and ICMP echo reply packets. If the host at the specified address receives the ICMP echo request, it responds with an ICMP echo reply packet. Ping can be used to verify end-to-end connectivity for both IPv4 and IPv6. Figure 2 shows a successful ping from PC1 to SRV1, at address 172.16.1.100.

The **traceroute** command in Figure 3 illustrates the path the IPv4 packets take to reach their destination. Similar to the **ping** command, the Cisco IOS **traceroute** command can be used for both IPv4 and IPv6. The **tracert** command is used with Windows operating system. The trace generates a list of hops, router IP addresses and the final destination IP address that are successfully reached along the path. This list provides important verification and troubleshooting information. If the data reaches the destination, the trace lists the interface on every router in the path. If the data fails at some hop along the way, the address of the last router that responded to the trace is known. This address is an indication of where the problem or security restrictions reside.

As stated, the ping and traceroute utilities can be used to test and diagnose end-to-end IPv6 connectivity by providing the IPv6 address as the destination address. When using these utilities, the Cisco IOS utility recognizes whether the address is an IPv4 or IPv6 address and uses the appropriate protocol to test connectivity. Figure 4 shows the **ping** and **traceroute** commands on router R1 used to test IPv6 connectivity.

Note   The **traceroute** command is commonly performed when the **ping** command fails. If the **ping** succeeds, the **traceroute** command is commonly not needed because the technician knows that connectivity exists.

> Refer to
> **Online Course**
> for Illustration

8.2.4.3   Step 1 - Verify the Physical Layer

All network devices are specialized computer systems. At a minimum, these devices consist of a CPU, RAM, and storage space, allowing the device to boot and run the operating system and interfaces. This allows for the reception and transmission of network traffic. When a network administrator determines that a problem exists on a given device, and that problem might be hardware-related, it is worthwhile to verify the operation of these generic components. The most commonly used Cisco IOS commands for this purpose are **show processes cpu**, **show memory**, and **show interfaces**. This topic discusses the **show interfaces** command.

When troubleshooting performance-related issues and hardware is suspected to be at fault, the **show interfaces** command can be used to verify the interfaces through which the traffic passes.

The output of the **show interfaces** command in the figure lists a number of important statistics that can be checked:

- **Input queue drops** - Input queue drops (and the related ignored and throttle counters) signify that at some point, more traffic was delivered to the router than it could process. This does not necessarily indicate a problem. That could be normal during traffic peaks. However, it could be an indication that the CPU cannot process packets in time, so if this number is consistently high, it is worth trying to spot at which moments these counters are increasing and how this relates to CPU usage.

- **Output queue drops** - Output queue drops indicate that packets were dropped due to congestion on the interface. Seeing output drops is normal for any point where the aggregate input traffic is higher than the output traffic. During traffic peaks, packets are dropped if traffic is delivered to the interface faster than it can be sent out. However, even if this is considered normal behavior, it leads to packet drops and queuing delays, so applications that are sensitive to those, such as VoIP, might suffer from performance issues. Consistently seeing output drops can be an indicator that you need to implement an advanced queuing mechanism to implement or modify QoS.

- **Input errors** - Input errors indicate errors that are experienced during the reception of the frame, such as CRC errors. High numbers of CRC errors could indicate cabling problems, interface hardware problems, or, in an Ethernet-based network, duplex mismatches.

- **Output errors** - Output errors indicate errors, such as collisions, during the transmission of a frame. In most Ethernet-based networks today, full-duplex transmission is the norm, and half-duplex transmission is the exception. In full-duplex transmission, operation collisions cannot occur; therefore, collisions and especially late collisions often indicate duplex mismatches.

Refer to **Interactive Graphic** in online course

8.2.4.4   Step 2 - Check for Duplex Mismatches

Another common cause for interface errors is a mismatched duplex mode between two ends of an Ethernet link. In many Ethernet-based networks, point-to-point connections are now the norm, and the use of hubs and the associated half-duplex operation is becoming less common. This means that most Ethernet links today operate in full-duplex mode, and while collisions were seen as normal for an Ethernet link, collisions today often indicate that duplex negotiation has failed, and the link is not operating in the correct duplex mode.

The IEEE 802.3ab Gigabit Ethernet standard mandates the use of autonegotiation for speed and duplex. In addition, although it is not strictly mandatory, practically all Fast Ethernet NICs also use autonegotiation by default. The use of autonegotiation for speed and duplex is the current recommended practice.

However, if duplex negotiation fails for some reason, it might be necessary to set the speed and duplex manually on both ends. Typically, this would mean setting the duplex mode to full-duplex on both ends of the connection. If this does not work, running half-duplex on both ends is preferred over a duplex mismatch.

Duplex configuration guidelines include:

- Autonegotiation of speed and duplex is recommended.

- If autonegotiation fails, manually set the speed and duplex on interconnecting ends.

- Point-to-point Ethernet links should always run in full-duplex mode.

- Half-duplex is uncommon and typically encountered only when legacy hubs are used.

Troubleshooting Example

In the previous scenario, the network administrator needed to add additional users to the network. To incorporate these new users, the network administrator installed a second switch and connected it to the first. Soon after S2 was added to the network, users on both switches began experiencing significant performance problems connecting with devices on the other switch, as shown in Figure 1.

The network administrator notices a console message on switch S2:

```
*Mar 1 00:45:08.756: %CDP-4-DUPLEX_MISMATCH: duplex mismatch discovered
on FastEthernet0/20 (not half duplex), with Switch FastEthernet0/20
(half duplex).
```

Using the **show interfaces fa 0/20** command, the network administrator examines the interface on S1 used to connect to S2 and notices it is set to full-duplex, as shown in Figure 2. The network administrator now examines the other side of the connection, the port on S2. Figure 3 shows that this side of the connection has been configured for half-duplex. The network administrator corrects the setting to **duplex auto** to automatically negotiate the duplex. Because the port on S1 is set to full-duplex, S2 also uses full-duplex.

The users report that there are no longer any performance problems.

Refer to
Interactive Graphic
in online course

8.2.4.5   Step 3 - Verify Layer 2 and Layer 3 Addressing on the Local Network

When troubleshooting end-to-end connectivity, it is useful to verify mappings between destination IP addresses and Layer 2 Ethernet addresses on individual segments. In IPv4, this functionality is provided by ARP. In IPv6, the ARP functionality is replaced by the neighbor discovery process and ICMPv6. The neighbor table caches IPv6 addresses and their resolved Ethernet physical (MAC) addresses.

IPv4 ARP Table

The **arp** Windows command displays and modifies entries in the ARP cache that are used to store IPv4 addresses and their resolved Ethernet physical (MAC) addresses. As shown in Figure 1, the **arp** Windows command lists all devices that are currently in the ARP cache. The information that is displayed for each device includes the IPv4 address, physical (MAC) address, and the type of addressing (static or dynamic).

The cache can be cleared by using the **arp -d** Windows command if the network administrator wants to repopulate the cache with updated information.

Note   The **arp** commands in Linux and MAC OS X have a similar syntax.

IPv6 Neighbor Table

As shown in Figure 2, the **netsh interface ipv6 show neighbor** Windows command lists all devices that are currently in the neighbor table. The information that is displayed for each device includes the IPv6 address, physical (MAC) address, and the type of addressing. By examining the neighbor table, the network administrator can verify that destination IPv6 addresses map to correct Ethernet addresses. The IPv6 link-local addresses on all of R1's interfaces have been manually configured to FE80::1. Similarly, R2 has been configured with the link-local address of FE80::2 on its interfaces and R3 has been configured with the link-local address of FE80::3 on its interfaces. Remember, link-local addresses only have to be unique on the link or network.

Note   The neighbor table for Linux and MAC OS X can be displayed using **ip neigh show** command.

Figure 3 shows an example of the neighbor table on the Cisco IOS router, using the **show ipv6 neighbors** command.

Note   The neighbor states for IPv6 are more complex than the ARP table states in IPv4. Additional information is contained in RFC 4861.

Switch MAC Address Table

When a destination MAC address is found in the switch MAC address table, the switch forwards the frame only to the port that has the device that has that particular MAC address. To do this, the switch consults its MAC address table. The MAC address table lists the MAC address connected to each port. Use the **show mac address-table** command to display the MAC address table on the switch. An example of a switch MAC address table is shown in Figure 4. Notice how the MAC address for PC1, a device in VLAN 10, has been discovered along with the S1 switch port to which PC1 attaches. Remember, a switch's MAC address table only contains Layer 2 information, including the Ethernet MAC address and the port number. IP address information is not included.

VLAN Assignment

Another issue to consider when troubleshooting end-to-end connectivity is VLAN assignment. In the switched network, each port in a switch belongs to a VLAN. Each VLAN is considered a separate logical network, and packets destined for stations that do not belong to the VLAN must be forwarded through a device that supports routing. If a host in one VLAN sends a broadcast Ethernet frame, such as an ARP request, all hosts in the same VLAN receive the frame; hosts in other VLANs do not. Even if two hosts are in the same IP network, they will not be able to communicate if they are connected to ports assigned to two separate VLANs. Additionally, if the VLAN to which the port belongs is deleted, the port becomes inactive. All hosts attached to ports belonging to the VLAN that was deleted are unable to communicate with the rest of the network. Commands such as **show vlan** can be used to validate vlan assignments on a switch.

Troubleshooting Example

Refer to the topology in Figure 5. To improve the wire management in the wiring closet, the cables connecting to S1 were reorganized. Almost immediately afterward, users started calling the support desk stating that they could no longer reach devices outside their own network. An examination of PC1's ARP table using the **arp** Windows command shows that the ARP table no longer contains an entry for the default gateway 10.1.10.1, as shown in Figure 6. There were no configuration changes on the router, so S1 is the focus of the troubleshooting.

The MAC address table for S1, as shown in Figure 7, shows that the MAC address for R1 is on a different VLAN than the rest of the 10.1.10.0/24 devices including PC1. During the re-cabling, R1's patch cable was moved from Fa 0/4 on VLAN 10 to Fa 0/1 on VLAN 1. After the network administrator configured S1's Fa 0/1 port to be on VLAN 10, as shown in Figure 8, the problem was resolved. As shown in Figure 9, the MAC address table now shows VLAN 10 for the MAC address of R1 on port Fa 0/1.

Refer to
Interactive Graphic
in online course

8.2.4.6   Step 4 - Verify Default Gateway

If there is no detailed route on the router or if the host is configured with the wrong default gateway, then communication between two endpoints in different networks does not work. Figure 1 illustrates that PC1 uses R1 as its default gateway. Similarly, R1 uses R2 as its default gateway or gateway of last resort.

If a host needs access to resources beyond the local network, the default gateway must be configured. The default gateway is the first router on the path to destinations beyond the local network.

Troubleshooting Example 1

Figure 2 shows the **show ip route** Cisco IOS command and the **route print** Windows command to verify the presence of the IPv4 default gateway.

In this example, the R1 router has the correct default gateway, which is the IPv4 address of the R2 router. However, PC1 has the wrong default gateway. PC1 should have the default gateway of R1 router 10.1.10.1. This must be configured manually if the IPv4 addressing information was manually configured on PC1. If the IPv4 addressing information was obtained automatically from a DHCPv4 server, then the configuration on the DHCP server must be examined. A configuration problem on a DHCP server usually affects multiple clients.

Troubleshooting Example 2

In IPv6, the default gateway can be configured manually, using stateless autoconfiguration (SLAAC), or by using DHCPv6. With SLAAC, the default gateway is advertised by the router to hosts using ICMPv6 Router Advertisement (RA) messages. The default gateway in the RA message is the link-local IPv6 address of a router interface. If the default gateway is configured manually on the host, which is very unlikely, the default gateway can be set either to the global IPv6 address or to the link-local IPv6 address.

As shown in Figure 3, use the **show ipv6 route** Cisco IOS command to check for the IPv6 default route on R1 and use the **ipconfig** Windows command to verify if a PC has an IPv6 default gateway.

R1 has a default route via router R2, but notice the **ipconfig** command reveals the absence of an IPv6 global unicast address and an IPv6 default gateway. PC1 is enabled for IPv6 because it has an IPv6 link-local address. The link-local address is automatically created by the device. Checking the network documentation, the network administrator confirms that hosts on this LAN should be receiving their IPv6 address information from the router using SLAAC.

Note   In this example, other devices on the same LAN using SLAAC would also experience the same problem receiving IPv6 address information.

Using the **show ipv6 interface GigabitEthernet 0/0** command in Figure 4, it can be seen that although the interface has an IPv6 address, it is not a member of the All-IPv6-Routers multicast group FF02::2. This means the router is not enabled as an IPv6 router. Therefore, it is not sending out ICMPv6 RAs on this interface. In Figure 5, R1 is enabled as an IPv6 router using the **ipv6 unicast-routing** command. The **show ipv6 interface Gigabit-Ethernet 0/0** command now reveals that R1 is a member of FF02::2, the All-IPv6-Routers multicast group.

To verify that PC1 has the default gateway set, use the **ipconfig** command on the Microsoft Windows PC or the **ifconfig** command on Linux and Mac OS X. In Figure 6, PC1 has an IPv6 global unicast address and an IPv6 default gateway. The default gateway is set to the link-local address of router R1, FE80::1.

Refer to
Interactive Graphic
in online course

8.2.4.7   Step 5 - Verify Correct Path

Troubleshooting the Network Layer

When troubleshooting, it is often necessary to verify the path to the destination network. Figure 1 shows the reference topology indicating the intended path for packets from PC1 to SRV1.

In Figure 2, the **show ip route** command is used to examine the IPv4 routing table.

The IPv4 and IPv6 routing tables can be populated by the following methods:

- Directly connected networks

- Local host or local routes

- Static routes

- Dynamic routes

- Default routes

The process of forwarding IPv4 and IPv6 packets is based on the longest bit match or longest prefix match. The routing table process will attempt to forward the packet using an entry in the routing table with the greatest number of far left matching bits. The number of matching bits is indicated by the route's prefix length.

Figure 3 shows a similar scenario with IPv6. To verify that the current IPv6 path matches the desired path to reach destinations, use the **show ipv6 route** command on a router to examine the routing table. After examining the IPv6 routing table, R1 does have a path to 2001:DB8:ACAD:4::/64 via R2 at FE80::2.

The following list, along with Figure 4, describes the process for both the IPv4 and IPv6 routing tables. If the destination address in a packet:

- Does not match an entry in the routing table, then the default route is used. If there is not a default route that is configured, the packet is discarded.

- Matches a single entry in the routing table, then the packet is forwarded through the interface that is defined in this route.

- Matches more than one entry in the routing table and the routing entries have the same prefix length, then the packets for this destination can be distributed among the routes that are defined in the routing table.

- Matches more than one entry in the routing table and the routing entries have different prefix lengths, then the packets for this destination are forwarded out of the interface that is associated with the route that has the longer prefix match.

Troubleshooting Example

Devices are unable to connect to the server SRV1 at 172.16.1.100. Using the **show ip route** command, the administrator should check to see if a routing entry exists to network 172.16.1.0/24. If the routing table does not have a specific route to SRV1's network, the network administrator must then check for the existence of a default or summary route entry in the direction of the 172.16.1.0/24 network. If none exists, then the problem may be with routing and the administrator must verify that the network is included within the dynamic routing protocol configuration, or add a static route.

Refer to
Interactive Graphic
in online course

8.2.4.8   Step 6 - Verify the Transport Layer

Troubleshooting the Transport Layer

If the network layer appears to be functioning as expected, but users are still unable to access resources, then the network administrator must begin troubleshooting the upper layers. Two of the most common issues that affect transport layer connectivity include ACL configurations and NAT configurations. A common tool for testing transport layer functionality is the Telnet utility.

Caution: While Telnet can be used to test the transport layer, for security reasons, SSH should be used to remotely manage and configure devices.

A network administrator is troubleshooting a problem where someone cannot send email through a particular SMTP server. The administrator pings the server, and it responds. This means that the network layer, and all layers below the network layer, between the user and the server is operational. The administrator knows the issue is with Layer 4 or up and must start troubleshooting those layers.

Although the Telnet server application runs on its own well-known port number 23 and Telnet clients connect to this port by default, a different port number can be specified on the client to connect to any TCP port that must be tested. This indicates whether the connection is accepted (as indicated by the word "Open" in the output), refused, or times out. From any of those responses, further conclusions can be made concerning the connectivity. Certain applications, if they use an ASCII-based session protocol, might even display an application banner, it may be possible to trigger some responses from the server by typing in certain keywords, such as with SMTP, FTP, and HTTP.

Given the previous scenario, the administrator Telnets from PC1 to the server HQ, using IPv6, and the Telnet session is successful, as shown in Figure 1. In Figure 2 the administrator attempts to Telnet to the same server, using port 80. The output verifies that the transport layer is connecting successfully from PC1 to HQ. However, the server is not accepting connections on port 80.

The example in Figure 3 shows a successful Telnet connection from R1 to R3, over IPv6. Figure 4 is a similar Telnet attempt using port 80. Again, the output verifies a success transport layer connection, but R3 is refusing the connection using port 80.

Refer to
Interactive Graphic
in online course

8.2.4.9   Step 7 - Verify ACLs

On routers, there may be ACLs configured that prohibit protocols from passing through the interface in the inbound or outbound direction.

Use the **show ip access-lists** command to display the contents of all IPv4 ACLs and the **show ipv6 access-list** command to show the contents of all IPv6 ACLs configured on a router. The specific ACL can be displayed by entering the ACL name or number as an option for this command; you can display a specific ACL. The **show ip interfaces** and **show ipv6 interfaces** commands display IPv4 and IPv6 interface information that indicates whether any IP ACLs are set on the interface.

Troubleshooting Example

To prevent spoofing attacks, the network administrator decided to implement an ACL preventing devices with a source network address of 172.16.1.0/24 from entering the inbound S0/0/1 interface on R3, as shown in Figure 1. All other IP traffic should be allowed.

However, shortly after implementing the ACL, users on the 10.1.10.0/24 network were unable to connect to devices on the 172.16.1.0/24 network, including SRV1. The **show ip access-lists** command shows that the ACL is configured correctly, as shown in Figure 2. The **show ip interfaces serial 0/0/1** command reveals that the ACL was never applied to the inbound interface on Serial 0/0/1. Further investigation reveals that the ACL was accidentally applied to the G0/0 interface, blocking all outbound traffic from the 172.16.1.0/24 network.

After correctly placing the IPv4 ACL on the Serial 0/0/1 inbound interface, as shown in Figure 3, devices are able to successfully connect to the server.

Refer to
Interactive Graphic
in online course

8.2.4.10   Step 8 - Verify DNS

The DNS protocol controls the DNS, a distributed database with which you can map hostnames to IP addresses. When you configure DNS on the device, you can substitute the hostname for the IP address with all IP commands, such as **ping** or **telnet**.

To display the DNS configuration information on the switch or router, use the **show running-config** command. When there is no DNS server installed, it is possible to enter names to IP mappings directly into the switch or router configuration. Use the **ip host** command to enter name to IPv4 mapping to the switch or router. The **ipv6 host** command is used for the same mappings using IPv6. These commands are demonstrated in Figure 1. Because IPv6 network numbers are long and difficult to remember, DNS is even more important for IPv6 than for IPv4.

To display the name-to-IP-address mapping information on the Windows-based PC, use the **nslookup** command.

Troubleshooting Example

The output in Figure 2 indicates that either the client was unable to reach the DNS server or the DNS service on the 10.1.1.1 device was not running. At this point, the troubleshooting needs to focus on communications with the DNS server, or to verify the DNS server is running properly.

To display the DNS configuration information on a Microsoft Windows PC, use the **nslookup** command. There should be DNS configured for IPv4, IPv6, or both. DNS can provide IPv4 and IPv6 addresses at the same time, regardless of the protocol that is used to access the DNS server.

Because domain names and DNS are a vital component of accessing servers on the network, many times the user thinks the "network is down" when the problem is actually with the DNS server.

Refer to
Interactive Graphic
in online course

8.2.4.11   Activity - Identify Commands to Troubleshoot a Network Issue

Refer to **Packet Tracer Activity** for this chapter

8.2.4.12   Packet Tracer - Troubleshooting Enterprise Networks 1
Background/Scenario

This activity uses a variety of technologies you have encountered during your CCNA studies including VLANs, STP, routing, inter-VLAN routing, DHCP, NAT, PPP, and Frame Relay. Your task is to review the requirements, isolate and resolve any issues, and then document the steps you took to verify the requirements.

Refer to **Packet Tracer Activity** for this chapter

8.2.4.13   Packet Tracer - Troubleshooting Enterprise Networks 2

Background/Scenario

This activity uses IPv6 configurations including DHCPv6, EIGRPv6, and IPv6 default routing. Your task is to review the requirements, isolate and resolve any issues, and then document the steps you took to verify the requirements.

Refer to **Packet Tracer Activity** for this chapter

8.2.4.14   Packet Tracer - Troubleshooting Enterprise Networks 3

Background/Scenario

This activity uses a variety of technologies you have encountered during your CCNA studies including routing, port security, EtherChannel, DHCP, NAT, PPP, and Frame Relay. Your task is to review the requirements, isolate and resolve any issues, and then document the steps you took to verify the requirements.

Refer to **Packet Tracer Activity** for this chapter

8.2.4.15   Packet Tracer - Troubleshooting Challenge - Using Documentation to Solve Issues

Background/Scenario

This is Part II of a two-part activity. Part I is Packet Tracer - Troubleshooting Challenge - Documenting the Network, which you should have completed earlier in the chapter.
In Part II, you will use your troubleshooting skills and documentation from Part I to solve connectivity issues between PCs.

8.3   Summary

Refer to **Online Course** for Illustration

8.3.1.1   Class Activity - Documentation Development

Documentation Development

As the network administrator for a small business, you want to implement a documentation system to use with troubleshooting network-based problems.

After much thought, you decide to compile simple network documentation information into a file to be used when network problems arise. You also know that if the company gets larger in the future, this file can be used to export the information to a computerized, network software system.

To start the network documentation process, you include:

- A physical diagram of your small business network.

- A logical diagram of your small business network.

- Network configuration information for major devices, including routers and switches.

Refer to **Packet Tracer Activity** for this chapter

8.3.1.2   Packet Tracer - CCNA Skills Integration Challenge

In this comprehensive CCNA skills activity, the XYZ Corporation uses a combination of eBGP and PPP for WAN connections. Other technologies include NAT, DHCP, static and default routing, EIGRP for IPv4, inter-VLAN routing, and VLAN configurations. Security configurations include SSH, port security, switch security, and ACLs.

Refer to
Online Course
for Illustration

8.3.1.3 Summary

For network administrators to be able to monitor and troubleshoot a network, they must have a complete set of accurate and current network documentation, including configuration files, physical and logical topology diagrams, and a baseline performance level.

The three major stages to troubleshooting problems are gather symptoms, isolate the problem, then correct the problem. It is sometimes necessary to temporarily implement a workaround to the problem. If the intended corrective action does not fix the problem, the change should be removed. In all process steps, the network administrator should document the process. A troubleshooting policy, including change control procedures, should be established for each stage. After the problem is resolved, it is important to communicate this to the users, anyone involved in the troubleshooting process, and to other IT team members.

The OSI model or the TCP/IP model can be applied to a network problem. A network administrator can use the bottom-up method, the top-down method, or the divide-and-conquer method. Less structured methods include shoot-from-the-hip, spot-the-differences, and move-the-problem.

Common software tools that can help with troubleshooting include network management system tools, knowledge bases, baselining tools, host-based protocol analyzers, and Cisco IOS EPC. Hardware troubleshooting tools include a NAM, digital multimeters, cable testers, cable analyzers, and portable network analyzers. Cisco IOS log information can also be used to identify potential problems.

There are characteristic physical layer, data link layer, network layer, transport layer, and application layer symptoms and problems of which the network administrator should be aware. The administrator may need to pay particular attention to physical connectivity, default gateways, MAC address tables, NAT, and routing information.

Go to the online course to take the quiz and exam.

Chapter 8 Quiz

This quiz is designed to provide an additional opportunity to practice the skills and knowledge presented in the chapter and to prepare for the chapter exam. You will be allowed multiple attempts and the grade does not appear in the gradebook.

Chapter 8 Exam

The chapter exam assesses your knowledge of the chapter content.

Your Chapter Notes

Index